A331·31

740578

Child L

# Child Labor and Education in Latin America

## An Economic Perspective

*Edited by*
*Peter F. Orazem, Guilherme Sedlacek, and*
*Zafiris Tzannatos*

palgrave
macmillan

CHILD LABOR AND EDUCATION IN LATIN AMERICA: AN ECONOMIC PERSPECTIVE

First published in 2009 by
PALGRAVE MACMILLAN®
in the United States—a division of St. Martin's Press LLC,
175 Fifth Avenue, New York, NY 10010.

Where this book is distributed in the UK, Europe and the rest of the world,
this is by Palgrave Macmillan, a division of Macmillan Publishers Limited,
registered in England, company number 785998, of Houndmills,
Basingstoke, Hampshire RG21 6XS.

Palgrave Macmillan is the global academic imprint of the above companies
and has companies and representatives throughout the world.

Palgrave® and Macmillan® are registered trademarks in the United States,
the United Kingdom, Europe and other countries.

ISBN-13: 978–0–230–61459–8
ISBN-10: 0–230–61459–0

Library of Congress Cataloging-in-Publication Data

Child labor and education in Latin America : an economic perspective /
[edited by] Peter F. Orazem, Guilherme Sedlacek, Zafiris Tzannatos.
p. cm.
Includes bibliographical references.
ISBN 0–230–61459–0
1. Child labor—Latin America. 2. Education—Latin America. 3. School
enrollment—Latin America. I. Orazem, Peter F. II. Sedlacek, Guilherme Luís,
1949– III. Tzannatos, Zafiris, 1953–

HD6250.L292C45 2009
331.3'1098—dc22                                        2008034379

A catalogue record of the book is available from the British Library.

Design by Newgen Imaging Systems (P) Ltd., Chennai, India.

First edition: April 2009

10 9 8 7 6 5 4 3 2 1

Printed in the United States of America.

To our parents who taught us the importance of hard work,
a good education, and a supportive family

Frank and Slava Orazem, in memoriam

Guilherme and Ilka Sedlacek

Evangelinos and Maria Tzannatos

And to Matthew, Katie, Savitri, Gino, Antonia, and Mariam:
may you live in a world free from the abusive forms of child labor,
Your Dads

# Contents

List of Figures ix

List of Tables xi

Abstract xv

Preface xvii

Acronyms xix

## Part I: Introduction

Introduction: Child Labor and Education in Latin America 3
*Peter F. Orazem, Guilherme Sedlacek, and Zafiris Tzannatos*

## Part II: Background

1. Changing Patterns of Child Labor around the World
   since 1950: The Roles of Income Growth, Parental Literacy,
   and Agriculture 21
   *Victoria Gunnarsson, Peter F. Orazem, and Guilherme Sedlacek*

2. Child Labor, Schooling, and Poverty in Latin America 33
   *Guilherme Sedlacek, Suzanne Duryea,*
   *Nadeem Ilahi, and Masaru Sasaki*

## Part III: Behavioral Inferences

3. The Responses of Child Labor, School Enrollment, and Grade
   Repetition to the Loss of Parental Earnings in Brazil, 1982–1999 55
   *Marcelo Côrtes Neri, Emily Gustafsson-Wright,*
   *Guilherme Sedlacek, and Peter F. Orazem*

4. Dynamics of Child Labor: Labor-Force Entry and
   Exit in Urban Brazil 69
   *Jasper Hoek, Suzanne Duryea, David Lam, and*
   *Deborah Levison*

5. How Does Working as a Child Affect Wages, Income, and
   Poverty as an Adult? 87
   *Nadeem Ilahi, Peter F. Orazem, and Guilherme Sedlacek*

6. The Intergenerational Persistence of Child Labor          103
   *Patrick M. Emerson and André Portela F. de Souza*

7. The Impact of Child Labor Intensity on Mathematics and
   Language Skills in Latin America                          117
   *Mario A. Sánchez, Peter F. Orazem, and Victoria Gunnarsson*

## Part IV: Policy Evaluations

8. The Impact of Cash Transfers on Child Labor and
   School Enrollment in Brazil                               133
   *Eliana Cardoso and André Portela F. de Souza*

9. Limiting Child Labor through Behavior-based
   Income Transfers: An Experimental Evaluation of
   the PETI Program in Rural Brazil                          147
   *Yoon-Tien Yap, Guilherme Sedlacek, and Peter F. Orazem*

10. The Impact of PROGRESA on Child Labor and
    Schooling                                                167
    *Emmanuel Skoufias and Susan W. Parker*

11. Education and Child Labor: Experimental Evidence from
    a Nicaraguan Conditional Cash Transfer Program           187
    *John A. Maluccio*

## Part V: Conclusions

12. Policy Options to Eradicate Child Labor and
    Promote Education in Latin America                        207
    *Zafiris Tzannatos, Peter F. Orazem, and Guilherme Sedlacek*

*Bibliography*                                                219

*List of Contributors*                                       227

# Figures

| | | |
|---|---|---|
| 1.1a | Real Per Capita GDP and Child Labor, 1960 | 22 |
| 1.1b | Real Per Capita GDP and Child Labor, 2000 | 23 |
| 2.1 | Employment and Attendance Rates for Children Ages 10–14 | 34 |
| 2.2 | Average Enrollment Rates in 18 Latin American Countries, by Household Income Level and Age, 1999 | 36 |
| 2.3 | Average Years of Completed Schooling for 16- to 18-Year-Olds in Latin America, by Country | 48 |
| 3.1 | Stages of Investment in School | 57 |
| 3.2 | The Impact of Adverse Income Shocks or Child Wage Increases on Investment in School | 58 |
| 4.1 | Proportion of 14-Year-Old and 16-Year-Old Males and Females Employed, 6 Metropolitan Areas, 1982–99, Brazil, Three-Month Moving Averages | 74 |
| 4.2 | Proportion of 14-Year-Olds Employed, by Education of Mother, 6 Metropolitan Areas, 1982–99, Three-Month Moving Averages, Brazil PME | 76 |
| 4.3 | Rates of Entry into and Exit from Employment, 14-Year-Old Boys and Girls, 6 Metropolitan Areas, 1982–99, Three-Month Moving Averages, Brazil PME | 78 |
| 4.4 | Rates of Entry into and Exit from Employment, 14-Year-Old Boys, by Mother's Education, 6 Metropolitan Areas, 1982–99, Three-Month Moving Averages, Brazil PME | 79 |
| 4.5 | Rates of Entry into and Exit from Employment in Salvador, São Paulo, and Porto Alegre, 14-Year-Old Boys, 1982–99, Yearly Averages, Brazil PME | 81 |
| 5.1 | Cumulative Distribution of Age at Workforce Entry in Brazil, by 1996 Age Cohort | 89 |
| 5.2 | Educational Attainment by Age-at-Entry in the Workforce in Brazil, by Cohorts | 89 |
| 6.1 | Child Human Capital as a Function of Parental Human Capital | 105 |
| 6.2 | The Increased Probability that a 12-Year-Old Child Works Attributed to His/Her Parents Having Been Child Laborers | 110 |

9.1     Partitioning the Sample into Eligible Treated, Eligible
        Untreated, and Controls                                          153
10.1    The Effect of Conditional Cash Transfers on Children's
        School Attendance and Work                                       170
11.1a   RPS Average Impact on Enrollment for 7- to 13-Year-Olds
        Who Have Not Completed Fourth Grade, by Age                      194
11.1b   RPS Average Impact on Enrollment for 7- to 13-Year-Olds
        Who Have Not Completed Fourth Grade, by Expenditure
        Group and by Gender                                              195
11.2a   RPS Average Impact on Attendance for 7- to 13-Year-Olds
        Who Have Not Completed Fourth Grade, by Age                      196
11.2b   RPS Average Impact on Attendance for 7- to 13-Year-Olds
        Who Have Not Completed Fourth Grade, by Expenditure
        Group and by Gender                                              196
11.3a   RPS Average Impact on Work for 7- to 13-Year-Olds
        Who Have Not Completed Fourth Grade, by Age                      197
11.3b   RPS Average Impact on Work for 7- to 13-Year-Olds
        Who Have Not Completed Fourth Grade, by Expenditure
        Group and Gender                                                 197
11.4a   Schooling and Work for 7- to 13-Year-Olds, RPS Baseline
        Intervention Areas Only                                          202
11.4b   Schooling and Work for 7- to 13-Year-Olds, RPS Follow-up
        Intervention Areas Only                                          202

# Tables

1.1 Percent Child Labor Participation by Continent, 1950–2000    25

1.2 Population Weighted Per Capita GDP, Agricultural Share of GDP, and Illiteracy, by Year and Continent    26

1.3 Regression Analysis of Child Labor-Force Participation Rates by Country, 1950–2000    28

2.1 Employment Rates for Children Aged 10 to 14 by Country, Urban or Rural Residence, and Gender    38

2.2 Employment and Enrollment Rates for Children Aged 10 to 14 by Country and Labor-Market Status    38

2.3 Distribution of Daily Hours Worked by Children Aged 10 to 14 by Country and Gender    39

2.4 Percentage of Children Aged 10 to 14 Lagging Behind Expected Grade Level by Country, Gender, and Labor-Market Status    39

2.5 Econometric Determinants of Child Labor, by Country    42

2.6 Econometric Determinants of Current Enrollment, by Country    44

2.7 Econometric Determinants of Falling Behind in School, by Country    46

2.8 Effect of Child Work on School Outcomes for Children Aged 10–16 from 17 Countries in Latin America    49

3.1 Static Indicators of School Performance and Child Labor (Children between 10 and 15 Years of Age)    62

3.2 Dynamic Indicators of School Performance and Child Labor (Children between 10 and 15 Years of Age)    62

3.3 Logistic Estimation of the Probability a Child Leaves School    63

3.4 Logistic Estimation of the Probability a Child Enters the Labor Market    65

3.5 Logistic Estimation of the Probability a Child Fails to Advance to the Next Grade    67

4.1 Employment Rates and Employment Transition Rates for 10–12-, 13–14-, and 15–16-Year-Old Boys and Girls, 6 Metropolitan Areas, 1982–84 and 1996–98, Brazil PME    72

4.2     Hours Worked among Employed 10–12-, 13–14-, and
        15–16-Year-Old Boys and Girls, 6 Metropolitan Areas,
        1982–84 and 1996–98, Brazil PME                                      75
5.1     Proportion of Population over 18 in the Lowest Income
        Quintiles, 1996, by Age of Labor-Force Entry and Education           90
5.2     Distribution of Wage (R$/Hr.) for Population over 18, by
        Age of Workforce Entry and Education, 1996                           91
5.3     Retrospective and Contemporaneous Measures of
        the Incidence of Child Labor in Brazil, Ages 10 to 14               92
5.4     Summary Statistics for Sample of All Adults over 18                 95
5.5     The Effects of Child Labor on Lifetime Wages and Poverty,
        Using Full Sample of Adults                                         96
6.1a    Unconditional Probabilities of a Child Working Strictly
        Positive Hours, Given a Parent's Work Status at
        Age 14 or Younger                                                   107
6.1b    Unconditional Probabilities of a Child Working at Least
        20 Hours per Week, Given a Parent's Work Status at
        Age 14 or Younger                                                   107
6.2     Child Labor Persistence. Probit on Child Labor
        Indicator Variable                                                  108
6.3     Child Labor Persistence. Probit on Child Labor Indicator
        Variable Including Family Income as Explanatory Variable            110
6.4     Effect of Child Labor on Log of Adult Earnings of
        Fathers and Mothers. OLS and Heckman Model Estimates               112
7.1     Child Labor, Test Scores, and Representative Characteristics
        by Country                                                          121
7.2     Average Language and Mathematics Test Scores by
        Country and Level of Child Labor                                    122
7.3     Definitions and Summary Statistics for Variables Used
        to Explain Test Scores                                              125
7.4     Pooled Educational Production Function Estimation                   126
7.5     Ordinary and Two-Stage Least Squares Estimates of
        the Impact of Child Labor on Test Scores                            128
8.1     Changes in Child Labor Participation and School
        Enrollment for Children Aged 10 to 17 in Brazil,
        1992–2001, by Gender, Age, and Household Attributes                 137
8.2     Child Labor Incidence for Children Aged 10–15 in
        Brazil, 2000                                                        138
8.3     Percent Child Labor Participation (CLP) by Gender and
        Urban and Rural Areas for Brazil and for the Five Highest
        States, 2000                                                        140
8.4     The Effects of Transfers on Child Time Use                          143
8.5     Summary of Logit Coefficients Indicating the Effect of
        Income Transfers on Child Labor Participation and School
        Enrollment for Children Aged 10 to 15 in Brazil, 2000              144

9.1   Sample Means for Children and Households in Pernambuco, Bahia, and Sergipe                                         151
9.2   Occupational Distribution and Weekly Hours of Working Children in Pernambuco, Bahia, and Sergipe.                  152
9.3   Probability of PETI Participation among Eligible Households   155
9.4   Tobit Estimates of PETI Impact on Weekly School Hours        157
9.5   Probit Estimates of PETI Impact on the Probability of Child Labor                                                 159
9.6   Probit Estimates of PETI Impact on the Probability of a Child Working at Least 10 Hours per Week                  159
9.7   Ordinary Least Squares Estimates of PETI Impact on Grade-for-Age                                                  161
9.8   Ordered Probit Estimates of PETI Impact on Hazardous Child Labor                                                  163
10.1  Monthly Amount of Educational Grant (Pesos), Second Semester 2000                                                 169
10.2  The Impact of PROGRESA on the Probability of Working: Boys and Girls                                              176
10.3  The Impact of PROGRESA on the Probability of Being Enrolled in School: Boys and Girls                            177
10.4  The Impact of PROGRESA on Leisure: Boys and Girls           180
10.5  The Impact of PROGRESA on Time Use—Work and School—of Boys and Girls                                              181
11.1  RPS Eligibility, Benefits, and Co-responsibilities          190
11.2  RPS Average Impact on Enrollment for 7- to 13-Year-Olds Who Have Not Completed Fourth Grade                       198
11.3  RPS Average Impact on Percentage of Students Aged 7 to 13 Continuing in School, by Grade                          199
11.4  RPS Average Impact on Percentage of Students Aged 7 to 13 Continuing in School, by Expenditure Group             199
11.5  RPS Average Impact on Percent Working of 10- to 13-Year-Olds Who Have Not Completed Fourth Grade                  201
12.1  Decision Matrix for Government Intervention in Child Labor   211

# Abstract

In a series of integrated chapters written by leading scholars in the field of child labor, this book examines the stylized facts concerning child labor in Latin America—how it varies over time; across countries; and in comparison to other areas of the world. Within countries, it shows how the incidence of child labor varies by gender; by age of child; and by household income level. It also shows that the incidence of child labor varies dramatically over the year in response to variation in labor demand and to household income shocks. Child labor is shown to have long-term effects on the well being of the child, lowering years of schooling, reducing performance on test scores, and increasing the persistence of poverty across generations in "dynastic poverty traps". The book then examines the evidence regarding the successes and failures in the policy battle against child labor in Latin America during the last decade. The relative success of conditional transfer programs aimed at lessening child labor in Mexico, Brazil and Nicaragua are investigated using experimental designs. The rich evidence presented in the book supports the view that the root causes of child labor can be identified, that child labor has identifiable costs that can last across generations, and that there are policy alternatives that can succeed in its eradication.

# Preface

The research underlying this book started as a project at the World Bank, as part of its Global Child Labor Program, and evolved into a cooperative effort with the Inter American Development Bank. Its objective was to analyze and summarize key facts to improve the understanding of the two organizations and regional and country policy makers of the root causes and consequences of persistent child labor and to evaluate policies to address it. The authors and editors of the book are thankful for the support and encouragement they received throughout the course of this project. We are especially indebted to Gobind Nankani who, while Country Director of Brazil, recognized the importance of the topic and its relevance to the country department work program. The project began with the financial and logistical support of the Latin America and Caribbean Human Development Department, and was completed with the financial support from the Department of Evaluation and Oversight of the IADB for the editing and preparation of the manuscript.

Peter Orazem thanks Mary Anne and Bob Martins and Pat White for their hospitality during his trips to Washington, DC, to meet Guilherme and Zafiris. He also is grateful to the University of Kansas School of Business and their Center for Applied Economics where he spent a year as Koch Visiting Professor of Business Economics while working on this book.

We received outstanding advice, guidance, and encouragement from Emma Hamilton and Laurie Harting at Palgrave-Macmillan. We also very much appreciate the help of Mark Lansky at the *International Labour Review* (chapter 4); Ines ter Horst at the University of Chicago Press and *Economic Development and Cultural Change* (chapter 6); and Catherine Canuto at *Economía* and Robin L. Becht at Brookings Institution Press (chapter 10) in securing the rights to present material they had previously published in their journals. We thank Tracy S. Petersen for her assistance in editing the chapters. Patricia Cotter helped compile the bibliography.

Finally, we are in debt to the fine authors and researchers who were willing to write integrated chapters in order to tell a more coherent story about child labor in Latin America. To do so, the authors had to read the others chapters as well as to work on their own. We believe the result is a book that reads more as if it had a single author than the twenty who lent their time and expertise to this project. Even more, we are grateful for their patience as this book worked its way from initial conception to publication.

# Acronyms

| | |
|---|---|
| 2DIF | Difference-in differences (or double difference) estimator |
| CCT | Conditional Cash Transfer |
| ENCASEH (Mexico) | Encuesta de Características Socioeconómicas de los Hogares (Survey of Household Socioeconomic Characteristics) |
| ENCEL (Mexico) | Encuesta de Evaluación de Hogares (Evaluation Survey of PROGRESA) |
| FISE (Nicaragua) | Fondo de Inversión Social de Emergencia (Emergency Social Investment Fund) |
| GDP | Gross Domestic Product |
| IBGE (Brazil) | Instituto Brasileiro de Geografia e Estatística (Geography and Statistical Institute) |
| IFPRI | International Food Policy Research Institute |
| ILO | International Labour Organization |
| IMF | International Monetary Fund |
| IMSS (Mexico) | Instituto Mexicano del Seguro Social (Social Security Institute) |
| LLECE (Chile) | Laboratorio Latinoamericano de Evaluación de la Calidad de la Educación (Latin American Laboratory of Quality of Education) |
| NGO | Non-Governmental Organization |
| PACES (Colombia) | Programa de Ampliación de Cobertura de la Educación Secundaria (Secondary Education Expansion Voucher Program) |
| PAI (Costa Rica) | Programa de Atención Inmediata (Immediate Attention Program) |
| PATH (Jamaica) | Program for the Advancement through Health and Education |
| PETI (Brazil) | Programa de Erradicação do Trabalho Infantil (Child Labor Eradication Program) |
| PME (Brazil) | Pesquisa Mensal de Emprego (Monthly Labor Survey) |

| | |
|---|---|
| PNAD (Brazil) | Pesquisa Nacional por Amostra de Domicílios (National Household Survey) |
| PRAF (Honduras) | Programa de Asignación Familiar (Family Allowance Voucher Program) |
| PROGRESA (Mexico) | Programa de Educación, Salud y Alimentación (Education, Health, and Nutrition Voucher Program) |
| RPS (Nicaragua) | Red de Protecion Social (Social Safety Net) |
| SES | Socio-Economic Status |
| UNESCO | United Nations Educational, Scientific and Cultural Organization |
| UNICEF | United Nations Children's Fund |

I

# Introduction

# Introduction

# Child Labor and Education in Latin America

*Peter F. Orazem, Guilherme Sedlacek, and Zafiris Tzannatos*

This book is the result of a collaborative project between the Inter-American Development Bank, the World Bank, and country and institutional partners working in the field of child labor in Latin America. It aims to improve our understanding of the root causes and consequences of persistent child labor and to contribute to the policy debate with the goal of enhancing the current and future welfare of all children in Latin America. The evidence presented demonstrates that understanding the behavior of households, markets, institutions, and the local political economy is critical for reducing and eliminating child labor in the region. The research supports the view that working as a child creates a lifetime of costs in the form of lower earnings and increased probability of living in poverty as an adult. It has intergenerational consequences by creating "dynastic poverty traps" whereby the children of child laborers are also likely to be poor, as are their children. It also explores promising policy alternatives for breaking free of these traps.

The chapters in this book are written by different authors, each of which makes a compelling and consistent case for the many and different challenges faced in combating child labor, the likely rewards from that effort, and the likely strategies for successfully mitigating and ultimately eradicating it. At the risk of oversimplifying, we lay out a thumbnail sketch of the main findings in order of the chapters. We then elaborate on how each chapter derives its conclusions. Finally, we invite the reader to examine each chapter in turn for details on how these results are substantiated.

## Findings

*Conclusion I: Eradicating child labor requires more than income growth. To be successful government interventions need to raise the value of child time in school relative to work.*

Chapter 1: The incidence of child labor is strongly inversely related to the level of per capita income in a country, particularly so for countries at the lowest incomes. As per capita incomes have increased over time, child labor has declined, but the rate of decline in child labor has slowed. As a result, it may take a long time for a country to eliminate child labor through per capita income growth alone. In Latin America, child labor remains high despite the fact that many countries have reached middle-income levels.

Chapter 2: Child labor persists, even in households at the top of the income distribution. Therefore, unconditional income transfers alone are unlikely to eliminate child labor. Factors that lower child labor also increase enrolment and years of schooling. Consequently, there is a prima facie case that one can combat child labor through policies that encourage children to spend more time in school.

Chapter 2: The pattern of enrollments by age indicates that the largest gains in school enrollment through targeted transfers could be attained at the youngest ages (preschool through age 7) and after age 12. It is those ages that demonstrate the largest enrollment gaps between the poorest and richest households. Almost all children are enrolled in school between ages 8 and 11, suggesting only small gains from transfers conditioned on enrollment at those ages.

Chapters 2 and 7: On the margin, government regulation in the form of truancy laws and age of school entry can affect time in school. In particular, children who enter school early are less likely to enter the labor market at an early age, other things equal. Therefore, making preschool mandatory or lowering the age of school entry can lower the incidence of child labor.

*Conclusion II: Household income is volatile. A household that is observed above the poverty threshold in one month may fall below the poverty threshold in the next. Programs that target households on the basis of current income will miss many observationally equivalent households that are equally disadvantaged on average but cannot be detected at the time of the survey.*

Chapter 3: Income shocks (such as those from job loss, lower farm yields, bankruptcy, or catastrophic health events) matter, but not to all households. Wealthier households that experience adverse income shocks do not change their children's schooling or employment patterns. However, households at the bottom of the income distribution may respond to income shocks by taking their children out of school and sending them to work. Even transitory spells of child labor can have permanent adverse effects by limiting school attainment.[1]

*Conclusion III: The child labor force is characterized by short employment spells with frequent entry and exit from the child labor market. Therefore, the annual incidence of spells of household child labor is greater than would be apparent from survey data eliciting information on current (monthly or weekly) labor supply behavior.*

Chapter 4: Child labor spells tend to be short and are experienced by many households over the course of a year. The proportion of households with child laborers at some point in the year can be two to three times larger than the proportion with working children in a given week.

*Conclusion IV: There are potentially large future welfare gains from current public expenditures aimed at eradicating child labor.*

Chapter 5: Child labor lowers the wage these children will earn as adults. It also increases the likelihood that the children will live in poverty as adults. The estimated effects are large, so that males who entered work before age 12 earn 20% less per hour and are 8% more likely to be in the lowest income quintile than are comparable males who entered the labor force after age 12. Delaying age of labor-market entry lessens the need for future poverty alleviation programs and raises the future tax base.

Chapter 6: Child labor persists across generations. If a parent worked as a child, his or her own children are more likely to work at young ages. Delaying the age of labor-force entry for current children delays labor-market entry for the next generation, as well.

Chapter 7: Even if a child remains enrolled while working, he or she learns less per year in school. The estimated effects are large, suggesting that children who work often have 16% lower scores on language exams and 14% lower scores on mathematics exams than do comparable children who do not work outside the home. These effects are of comparable size to the estimated effect of child labor on adult earnings reported in chapter 5. This makes a strong circumstantial case that the mechanism by which early labor-market entry lowers adult wages is the associated loss of human capital attributable to child labor. Delaying age of labor-market entry raises cognitive achievement in schools.

*Conclusion V: Conditional cash transfers (CCT) to the poor can reduce child labor. The magnitude of the effect depends on the pre-transfer level of child labor and on the conditions placed on the transfer. It also depends on the amount of the transfer.*

Chapters 8 through 11: Transferring income to poor households in exchange for an agreement that the children will attend school can lower the incidence of child labor.

Chapters 8 and 9: The effect is larger if the school day is lengthened, thus constraining the amount of time that the child can work.

Chapter 8: With half-day school schedules, small transfers can induce working children to attend school, but the children may not stop working.

Chapters 8 through 11: CCTs appear to have more impact when they are aimed at all the poor or near-poor in an area, and not just a subset of the poor. This suggests a role for mutual reinforcement of the desired behavior, whether it is increased school attendance, lower child labor, improved nutrition, or increased utilization of health clinics.[2]

Chapters 10 and 11: CCTs have a bigger impact when they teach parents about the value of school and when they incorporate nutrition and/or health components along with the educational component.

Chapters 8 and 11: CCTs have a bigger impact when they are placed in areas that have high levels of child labor or low enrollment rates. In those areas, a high proportion of the program's expenditures will go toward altering parents' choices. In areas that already have low child labor participation and high enrollment rates, the transfer will serve mainly to reward households that were already engaged in the desired behaviors.

The early experiences from several Latin American experiments in child labor eradication, including others we do not formally evaluate in this book,[3] indicate some important successes in the use of income transfer programs that are conditional on children being in school and that target poor households. Having said that, many of these evaluations are of short duration, and we do not yet know if the long-term record will corroborate some of the shorter-term successes we report in this volume. Nevertheless, the other chapters that lay out the empirical regularities regarding the interrelationships between child labor, time in school, school performance, lifetime incomes, and intergenerational transmission of poverty can aid in the future design of targeted transfer programs to combat child labor.

## Child Labor around the World

Globally, child labor has declined steadily since the 1950s. It has been virtually eliminated in the wealthiest economies of Europe and North America, but these regions already had low levels of child labor in 1950. The biggest improvement was in Asia, where the proportion of children working declined 20 percentage points, mainly in the high-performing economies of East Asia. The incidence of child labor declined only 10 percentage points in Africa from a high base, and that continent (especially sub-Saharan Africa) retains the world's highest rates of child labor. Child labor declined by 8 percentage points from a relatively low base in Latin America, allowing it to maintain its forty-year standing as having the lowest incidence of child labor outside the developed world. Today Latin America not only has countries with negligible child labor, including Argentina, Chile, and Uruguay, but also has countries with some of the highest incidence: Bolivia, 25%, Peru, 28%, and Ecuador, 34%.

Despite the past progress on child labor, working children are still found in high numbers in many developing countries. Child labor surfaced as a major target of international policy initiatives in the 1980s. These culminated in a series of international conventions addressing child welfare, including the 1989 United Nations Convention on the Rights of the Child, the 1999 International Labour Organization Convention 182 on the Worst Forms of Child Labor, and the 2000 United Nations Millennium Declaration that set specific objectives such as universal enrollment in basic education, gender parity in schooling, and reduction in infant mortality. The documents from these three conventions share the common and rare characteristic of having been signed by practically all of the world's countries.

The increased interest in child labor has arisen for a variety of reasons. First, there has been increased international concern related to the process of globalization and its impact on child labor. It is less clear whether this concern arises from the adverse impacts of globalization on children in developing countries or the impacts of globalization on the competitive position of producers in developed countries. Child labor is a means by which some countries can lower production costs, but it may harm the children in the process. The call for minimum labor standards in developing countries also may be motivated by protectionist motives in the already industrialized countries. Regardless of the driving motive, attempts to install core labor standards into multilateral or bilateral trade agreements attest to the fact that child labor is gaining importance in the development agenda.

Second, the "win-win" pattern of more or less continuous economic growth since World War II experienced a series of setbacks in the last two decades. Economists had held some combination of two stylized development views: that growth can be continuous as long as the correct combination of fiscal and monetary policies are pursued, or that laissez-faire policies favoring expansion of the private sector will broadly disseminate the benefits of growth throughout the population, including the poorest households. Either paradigm would lead to rising incomes and a decline in the need for child labor. However, as economic growth in many developing countries slowed from its early postwar rates, income inequality rose and faith in governmental ability to foment change in the economy weakened, so the presumption that child labor would wither away on its own lost credibility.

Third, only recently have household surveys begun measuring the extent and conditions of child labor.[4] Even the best current data sets fail to measure the worst forms of child labor, such as prostitution or drug trafficking.[5] In addition, because most child labor is unpaid and not-for-market work that is done within the household, child labor often goes undetected in official statistics, particularly for girls doing work inside the home.

A much-quoted figure in the early 1990s referred to 90 million child laborers. However, according to the latest and most reliable estimates, there are 211 million "economically active" children between the ages of 5 and 14 and 186 million "child laborers" in the same age group.[6] More than 9% of children are engaged in work considered hazardous by International Labor Organization (ILO) standards. Even these best estimates are subject to considerable error. On the one hand, defining a child laborer as one who works as little as one hour per week would tend to overstate the problem. On the other hand, child labor spells often are seasonal or of short duration, so estimates based on an observation during a particular week will miss work performed outside the survey week.[7] Child labor in household businesses is difficult to distinguish from household chores, causing further measurement errors. This last problem is particularly severe in measuring the labor participation of girls.

Latin America presents abundant opportunities for the study of child labor. Levels of child labor are unusually high relative to countries of comparable development. The pace of reduction in child labor slowed over the past twenty years, even though per capita incomes continued to increase. At the same time, the region has developed some of the best household-level data sets for the purpose of analyzing the determinants of child labor. Finally, some of the most innovative public policies targeting child labor have been installed in the region.

Several of our chapters deal with Brazil. This emphasis reflects the fact that Brazil was an early innovator in efforts to combat child labor, and so Brazil is a natural focus for studies evaluating the impact of CCTs. In addition, Brazil's Household Labor Surveys covering a period of more than two decades have been made easily accessible to researchers. Occasionally, these surveys have added questions that are uniquely relevant for our purposes, particularly those that allow us to identify households with working children or adults who started working as children. Because Brazil offers such diversity along ethnic, geographic and socioeconomic lines, we expect that the Brazilian experience will still offer relevant lessons for the other countries in the region. At least, the strength of the studies presented in this book may convince other Latin American countries to add similar questions to their own labor-market surveys in the future.

We believe this collection of studies takes great advantage of the wealth of information from various sources available for the study of child labor in Latin America. The focus and findings of each study are summarized below.

## Chapter Summaries

*Chapter 1: Gunnarsson, Orazem, and Sedlacek* use country-level data to lay out the broad stylized facts regarding the relationship between child labor and per capita GDP, adult literacy, and the share of agriculture in the economy. The relationship between child labor-force participation and per capita income is convex and stable over time. The implication is that as a country develops, child labor will decrease, but at a slowing rate of decline. At some point, further reductions in child labor may require more than just increasing per capita income.

In Latin America, all three of these factors have contributed to decreases in child labor since 1950. Real per capita incomes in Latin America more than doubled between 1950 and 1990, but only served to lower child labor by 2.9 percentage points. Many of the countries of Latin America are in income ranges where further increases in income would be expected to have only modest effects on child labor. Consistent with that presumption, the 28% increase in real per capita income since 1970 has had no measurable effect on child labor in the region.

Other factors have had a measurable impact on child labor since 1970. Adult illiteracy fell by 12 percentage points since 1970 (earlier data was not available), contributing to a 4.2 percentage point reduction in child labor participation since 1970. Agriculture's share of production fell 5.6 percentage points since 1970, lowering child labor by an additional 1.2 percentage points.

*Chapter 2: Sedlacek, Duryea, Ilahi, and Sasaki* probe further into how household attributes affect the probability that children will work, enroll, or progress in school. They frame their analysis using four similar household surveys in Brazil, Ecuador, Nicaragua, and Peru. Their findings are similar to the macro evidence reported in chapter 1: child labor is more common in rural areas and in households with less-educated parents. Income affects child labor more in the poorer countries than in Brazil.

The chapter demonstrates that enrollment rates understate the true extent of the differences in human capital investment between poor children and their more well-off counterparts. Even if they are enrolled in school, working children do not perform as well as their nonworking classmates, suggesting that work can have an adverse effect on learning even if it does not have a significant effect on enrollment. The distribution of hours worked per day by children suggests that a high proportion of child laborers work too many hours to be successful in school. More than half the working children in Nicaragua work more than five hours per day, as do just under half of the working children in Brazil. The proportions in Ecuador (34%) and Peru (15%) are modest in comparison, but still high enough to suggest a problem.

The chapter then uses variation in truancy laws across countries to disentangle the causal effects of child labor on school attendance. A 10% reduction in the probability of child labor raises school attendance by 7% and lowers the probability of lagging behind grade level by 12%. This is strong evidence that one mechanism for improving human capital production in schools lies in combating child labor.

*Chapter 3: Neri, Gustafsson-Wright, Sedlacek, and Orazem* examine how the loss of the household head's income in Brazil affects the likelihood that children will drop out of school, enter the labor market, or fail to advance to the next grade level. For the poorest households, adverse income shocks increase the probability that their children will start working, fail their grade level, or leave school. Children in higher-income households are not adversely affected by income loss of the household head. It appears that wealthier households can self-insure against adverse income shocks, but that poor households must use other means, including child labor, to replace lost earnings of the household head. Furthermore, once a child begins to lag behind in school, there is an increased likelihood that the child will drop out and/or start working at a younger age, so even short-term increased probability of nonpromotion can lead to permanent lifetime consequences.

*Chapter 4: Hoek, Duryea, Lam, and Levison* discover that child labor is characterized by short employment spells and large transition rates into and out of employment. This "intermittent employment" is consistent with the findings of the previous chapter that poor children often enter the labor market to meet short-term income needs for the household. The implication for measures of child labor-force participation rates are striking. Measured child labor participation rates based on point-in-time surveys can be half to one-third the participation rate based on children who worked at least part of the year. Furthermore, there is little difference between households whose children are working and households with children who are in school; children observed in school one period could easily be in the labor market the next.

The intermittent patterns of children's work and schooling have important implications for the design of programs intended to encourage families to keep children in school and out of the labor force. Income transfer policies should target households broadly rather than on current child labor-market status. It may be as important to shore up income in poor households whose children are currently enrolled, as it is to direct income transfers to households with children currently out of school. The high levels of intermittency also suggest that the cash transfers intended to replace the income earned in the labor market may be set too high, since many children do not receive a consistent stream of income. This would imply that the extra cost associated with the underestimate of child workers might be offset by a lower subsidy per child.

*Chapter 5: Ilahi, Orazem, and Sedlacek* use a retrospective data set that identified when current adults first started working to study how child labor affects adult earnings. Adding up the positive and negative effects of child labor on earnings through its impacts on work experience, years of schooling, and returns per year of schooling completed, they find that adults who entered the labor market before age 13 earn 20% less per hour, have 26% lower incomes, and are 14% more likely to be in the lowest two income quintiles. These magnitudes are sufficiently large to suggest that current government investments to combat child labor can be at least partially repaid by higher lifetime earnings or tax returns and lower need for poverty alleviation programs when the children mature.

*Chapter 6: Emerson and Souza* answer two related questions. First, are parents who worked as children more likely to have their own children work? Evidence indicates the answer is yes. Second, is this link only a function of permanent family income or is there a direct link between the child-labor status of the parents and their children? They find evidence that such a direct link exists. The perpetuation of child labor across generations represents a likely mechanism for the perpetuation of intergenerational poverty traps. While the underlying cause for the child labor link is unclear, whether through social norms (Basu, 1999; Lopez-Calva, 2002) or unmeasured household-specific human capital, the link appears strong enough to suggest that delaying the age of labor-market entry for one generation will delay the age of entry for the next generation, as well.

*Chapter 7: Sánchez, Orazem, and Gunnarsson* use a unique data set on language and mathematics test scores for third- and fourth-graders in eleven different Latin American countries to determine whether child labor raises or lowers school achievement. Their findings are amazingly consistent across countries. In every country, child labor lowers performance on tests of language and mathematics proficiency, even when controlling for school and household attributes. The magnitude of the effect is similar to the percentage reduction in adult wages from child labor reported by Ilahi, Sedlacek, and Orazem in chapter 5. The adverse impact of child labor on test performance is larger when children work regularly rather than occasionally. Even modest levels of child labor at early ages cause adverse consequences for the development of cognitive abilities. These findings are not altered when controlling for joint causality between school achievement and child labor.

*Chapter 8: Cardoso and Souza* examine evidence of the impact of the Bolsa Escola using national data from the 2000 Brazilian Census. Because Bolsa Escola was first adopted at the local level without central coordination, there was tremendous variation in the design, implementation, and funding level of the programs. Evidence across all of these various programs suggests that targeted income transfers raised school enrollment by 3% to 4% for both boys and girls.

However, the programs had no net effect on child labor. While the proportion of children who only work fell, the proportion combining work with schooling rose. There is convincing evidence that children learn less in school when they work. Consequently, some of the potential gains from increased enrollment are lost because the increased time in school does not come from reduced time in the labor market.

Two hypotheses are advanced to explain the lack of an impact on child labor. One is that the amount transferred is too small to compensate for the child's value of time in the labor market. The second is that the school day is too short, so the child can attend and still spend time at work. The latter possibility is explored in more detail in the next chapter.

*Chapter 9: Yap, Sedlacek, and Orazem* examined the impact of a conditional transfer program known as PETI that targeted poor households in rural areas of Brazil. They measure the impact on school enrollment, labor participation, hours worked, academic progress, and dangerous work in recipient households compared to poor households in other municipalities that were not included in the program. They found that participating children spent more time in school, less time at work, and less time in risky work, and progressed in school at a faster rate. Although the program may have had some adverse effects on children from nonparticipating households, those were swamped by the positive effects on participating children. The positive effects appear to be largest in programs that have been implemented the longest.

The innovative feature of the PETI is the use of an after-school program (Jornada Ampliada) that participating children were required to attend. The program effectively doubled the length of the school day, virtually eliminating the chance that parents could both meet the school attendance requirement and have the child work. The program also was installed in areas with high incidence of child labor and included all the poor in the community, increasing the program's scope for affecting child time use.

Whereas the targeted income transfer may be necessary to obtain the dramatic increases in voluntary time in school, the use of Jornada Ampliada also makes it feasible to monitor a truancy law that requires children to spend the day in school. The PETI experience suggests that by increasing time in school, whether voluntarily or through government mandate, child labor can be reduced.

*Chapter 10: Skoufias and Parker* evaluate the impact of Mexico's PROGRESA program on child time use. PROGRESA transferred income to poor households in exchange for household participation in education, nutrition, and health programs. To qualify for all three benefits, children must attend school and the family must make scheduled health clinic visits. Skoufias and Parker design their evaluation around three questions:

1. Does the program increase school attendance? Yes for both boys and girls. Because most younger children were already in school, the biggest attendance effect was for older children. Because more regular attendance increases the pace at which children progress through school, the program raised years of school completed by an average of 10% with an implied improvement in life-time earnings of about 8%. The gain in enrollments from PROGRESA occur at one-tenth the cost of building and staffing more middle schools.
2. Does the program reduce child labor? The program lowers market work significantly for boys and it lowers household work marginally for girls.
3. Does the added time in school come at the expense of child leisure time of children? The answer is no for boys—the added time of boys in school comes from less time at work. For girls, the added school participation comes from a modest reduction in leisure time, with the balance coming from a combination of reduced time at home or in market production.

PROGRESA offers an additional insight into the factors that lead to successful interventions. While it shares the features of tying transfers to enrollment and targeting poor communities rather than just a subset of the poor, it also embeds the enrollment program in a more comprehensive program that reinforces the value of education, health, and nutrition to poorly educated parents. As a result, the program can break down some of the cultural factors that lead to intergenerational transmission of child labor. The various human capital interventions can reinforce each other by influencing the desired household behaviors regarding education, nutrition, and health.

*Chapter 11: Maluccio* presents the results of a randomized community-based trial that evaluated the Red de Protecion Social in Nicaragua. As with PROGRESA, recipients received income transfers conditional on child enrollment, but also conditional on household participation in complementary human capital development programs aimed at improving child nutrition and health. Parents also were required to attend training programs. Compared to the Mexican program, the Nicaraguan communities were even poorer, with higher baseline levels of child labor and lower enrollment rates, so a high proportion of treated households would have to alter their behavior to get the transfer. Because virtually all households in the community were poor, virtually all households were part of the program. In such a fertile environment, the program's effects are found to be large: significant and substantial improvements in schooling matriculation and enrollment and significant decreases in child labor during the first year of operation. His findings suggest that PROGRESA-type interventions may hold promise for the poorest countries with the worst educational outcomes.

## Targeted Conditional Cash Transfers (CCT)

Over the past decade, Latin American countries have taken the lead in designing and implementing novel programs to address child labor and education demand constraints faced by poor households. The common mechanism is the use of targeted conditional grants. Ongoing projects can be found throughout Latin America. These programs target poor households with the goal of removing income constraints that may hinder school enrollment, attendance, and grade progression, and adequate nutrition or health.[8]

CCT programs have similar contractual forms: cash grants are given to households in exchange for agreement to engage in behavior that improves their children's human capital. The "good" behavior varies from program to program. For example, the Recife Bolsa Escola program in Brazil requires that families keep their 7- to 14-year-olds in school. The Costa Rican program provides a food coupon provided that all children in the family aged 6 to 18 attend school. In countries with a higher educational attainment, such as Mexico, Colombia, and Jamaica, this component also benefits secondary school–age adolescents. PETI requires children to regularly attend an after-school program. The Mexican and Nicaraguan programs also require that the households participate in nutrition and health components.

These programs have five main objectives:

1. They hope to increase educational attainment and/or improve health outcomes for children so that when they mature, they will be more productive and less likely to be poor.
2. By restricting grants to the poor and by improving their health, they aim to reduce current poverty.
3. By requiring children in beneficiary households to maintain minimum attendance in school, the programs hope to lower the time available for child labor.
4. By providing income support to poor families, they implicitly act as a partial safety net; that is, they provide a regular source of income that may smooth household consumption in the event of an adverse income shock.
5. By providing supply-side financial support to schools and health facilities, some programs aim to improve the quality of service provision.

The evidence we present in this volume shows that Latin America fits the type of environment in which such programs could succeed. Households face irregular income streams and intermittent child labor patterns. Many more households are exposed to these conditions than is apparent from current income or employment states. Households move fluidly from poverty to near poverty conditions and back again. Children move easily into and out of the child labor market. Children exposed to such environments are more likely to drop out of school or work while in school. Evidence from this book demonstrates that working while in school leads to nonpromotion, reductions in cognitive development, decreased lifetime earnings, and increased probability of living in poverty as an adult. Evidence also shows that working as a child increases the probability that one's own children will work, leading to a cycle of poverty.

Our findings lay out some lessons that have been learned from the CCT programs to date:

*The program must have sound criteria for selection and targeting to be cost-effective.* The federally administered programs use geographical targeting at the national level. Geographic targeting is appropriate when the population is predominantly poor or near poor and many households face uncertain income and employment streams, as we have found in Latin America. In Mexico, PROGRESA chose the poorest localities in the country first. In Brazil, PETI was installed in the localities with the highest incidence of worst forms of child labor.

Targeting also involves identifying the right behavior and age on which to focus. It is important to set conditions that actually bite, meaning they actually force behavior away from what the households would do in the absence of the transfer.[9] For example, most CCT programs do not address child labor explicitly. Instead, they concentrate on providing incentives for children to remain in school. If the targeted age is set too young, virtually all children will already be in school and the program will have no impact. In the PETI case that sought to directly mitigate the incidence and impact of the worst forms of child labor, program effectiveness required that area be selected which already had large numbers of children engaged in dangerous work. Selecting areas or age ranges where few children work would mean that the transfer would have little effect. Another requirement is that the parents actually want what is best for their children. CCT programs may not be effective against some the worst forms of child labor such as street children, children involved in traffic of drugs and commercial sexual exploitation, in that the parents of these children have revealed themselves to be indifferent to the health and well being of their offspring (see Tabatabai, 2007).

Some interventions were too financially constrained to benefit all deserving households, which limits the effectiveness of the CCT. This was particularly true in the Bolsa Escola programs in Brazil where beneficiaries represented as few as 2% of the households that would potentially qualify (Levinas and Barbosa, 2001). There are some significant advantages to covering all deserving households. There is the obvious ethical problem of helping some poor households and not others. However, there are also returns to scale in addressing the needs of many households at once: the costs of administering the program can be spread over many more households.

Furthermore, concentrating benefits on only a subset of the poor children in a neighborhood may create the illusion of success without any change in average time use in the neighborhood as a whole. Children excluded from the program are near perfect substitutes in production activities for children that are in the program. It is possible that any reductions in child labor or increases in school attendance among program children will be counteracted by increased child labor and reduced attendance for the excluded children. This substitution possibility is greatest when only a small fraction of the potentially qualified children are included in the program, leaving a large residual group of potential substitutes. In such circumstances, the program could create the illusion of success in that program children raise attendance and decrease child labor compared to nonprogram children in the same neighborhood, when in fact, the program is responsible for both the gains to the treated children and the harm to the excluded children.[10]

Finally, if it is important to change a culture of child labor and illiteracy, it would seem important to transform the entire community rather than affecting just a subset of the households. In our evaluations, the interventions with more complete coverage appeared to be more successful. A necessary area of future research is to assess whether that assessment is in fact true—that is, whether poor households in neighborhoods in which only some of the poor were allowed into the program altered their behavior less than did households in neighborhoods with complete coverage.

*There is strong evidence that these programs can reduce current poverty.* Bolsa Escola, PETI, PROGRESA, and RED reached intended beneficiaries and raised household incomes sufficiently to reduce the degree of income vulnerability of participating families. One issue not yet resolved is the proper amount of the transfer. The answer may depend on whether the aim is to reduce child labor or to raise household income sufficiently to escape poverty. The answer is not a matter of academic debate—with limited budgets, the more one transfers per household, the fewer households one can help. Our assessment is that relatively small transfers may be sufficient to reduce the incidence of child labor and raise academic performance.[11]

*The programs have improved educational indicators and outcomes.* Three of the four programs evaluated in this volume (PETI in Brazil, PROGRESA in Mexico, and RED in Nicaragua) had significant impacts on time in school. It is likely that with longer-term evaluations, the educational enhancement would be more apparent because it is likely that recipient households will send their children to school longer. Limited evidence supporting that conjecture already has been found in the first few years of the PETI and PROGRESA programs. To date, there are only limited and inconclusive results relating the CCTs to improved test scores. That should also be a priority for future research because improved cognitive achievement is a necessary condition if CCTs are to raise future earnings and lower the incidence of poverty among recipients.

*There is evidence of reduction of child labor.* Three of the four programs we evaluate showed evidence of reduced child labor. The magnitude of the decrease varied from 2 to 3 percentage points in Mexico, to 9% for 10- to 13-year-olds in Nicaragua, to 4 to 26 percentage points in rural Brazil, depending on the state. The reduction in child labor was largest in rural areas, where child labor participation rates were highest before the programs were implemented. There was no change in child labor in urban Brazil where child labor participation rates were smallest before the program was implemented.

*There is evidence that more comprehensive programs have larger impacts on child labor.* The PROGRESA and RED programs covered health and nutrition as well as education. There may be economies of scope in delivering these programs simultaneously in that the administrative costs may be spread over multiple programs. Furthermore, the programs may reinforce each other by changing parental attitudes about investing in their children's human capital. This assessment is speculative, given the lack of a formal evaluation of whether child labor falls more rapidly in single-sector versus multisector approaches, but the issue merits investigation. The Honduras PRAF program represents just such an evaluation. There, the government is seeking to explicitly evaluate the impact of different combinations of supply and demand interventions.

*The research agenda that remains outstanding.* Although the success of these programs has generated a high degree of support and much optimism that the proposed objectives can be achieved, many challenges remain. Among them, the need:

1. to quantify the impact of these programs on the incidence of the worst forms of child labor;
2. to better understand the replicability of the Brazil PETI program, and in this context to understand why more governments have not adopted similar programs considering that a decade of evidence has accumulated demonstrating its significant impact;
3. to establish the optimal transfer level that maximizes impact subject to governmental budget constraints;
4. to understand the long-run impacts of these programs on behavior;
5. to identify the factors that ensure programs are financially sustainable in the long run;
6. to adapt the program design to the variety of country conditions in the region;
7. to overcome the institutional barriers that have constrained the ownership and adoption of these programs by the ministries of health and education; and
8. to better understand the complementary relationship between the supply and demand side interventions.

## Moving Forward

The accepted challenge confronting Latin American governments is ensuring that child labor is eradicated over time, and during the transition period, that it does not significantly impair the development and welfare of their children. Children often work because of economic needs, but that is also often due to social norms. It follows that the trade-off between possible gains derived from early entry into the labor force and future welfare costs be quantified and analytically understood. While the current volume contributes to this policy debate, it cannot be debated that many child-labor activities are fundamentally harmful to the development and health of children, regardless of their potential current economic reward. Programs such as PETI in Brazil help bring clarity to the debate by defining the worst forms of child labor as a priority policy issue, and providing support in the organization of a robust safety net system that prioritizes the needs of the most vulnerable children.

This volume also highlights some of the successful and promising policy efforts by Latin American governments to combat child labor through CCT programs. Among their desirable attributes, CCT programs differ from most other social programs in their demonstrable effort to learn from evaluations of past and current policy experiences. These programs are also remarkable for their evident broad political support and the social consensus that enables their installation and continuation. The evaluations have demonstrated some early successes in affecting behavior: more children are in school, use of health clinics and services has increased, and child labor has decreased. However, we do not yet have evidence that these programs lead to more permanent outcomes: improved learning, healthier children, and higher labor-market earnings.

The editors recognize the many outstanding issues were left out or only partially addressed in this effort to analyze the determinants and consequences of child labor. Among these we can highlight: (1) the need to better understand hidden child labor groups, from those working as domestic servants to child prostitution; (2) the health impact of the worst forms of child labor and its interaction with poverty-related vulnerabilities; (3) the organization of the secondary schools in which poor working students may attend low-quality night classes; and (4) the determinants of the transition between school and work and their impact on future poverty incidence.

# Notes

1. Similar findings are reported by Guarcello et al. (2003) for Guatemala.
2. Zelizer (1985)' and Lopez-Calva (2004) argue that social norms can raise or lower the perceived stigma associated with child labor. Broad-based efforts to combat child labor may be able to take advantage of mutual reinforcement among households to a greater extent than can more limited interventions that concentrate on only a small subset of households in a neighborhood or village.
3. Examples of other conditional transfer programs not formally evaluated in this book include Colombia (Familias en Accion); Costa Rica (Supremonos); Honduras (PRAF); and Jamaica (PATH).
4. Several recent surveys covering the theoretical and empirical research on child labor have been published in recent years. Among the published papers, Grootaert and

Kanbur (1995) set out the issues and covered much of the early work on child labor. Grootaert and Patrinos (1999) provide findings of comparable research studies on Cote d'Ivoire, Colombia, Bolivia, and the Philippines. Basu (1999), Basu and Tzannatos (2003), Edmonds and Pavcnik (2005a), and Edmonds (2008) provide excellent reviews of concepts, theory, and policy, and also cover various aspects of the empirical evidence from around the globe.

5.  Edmonds (2008) presents a discussion of these worst forms including references to some of his recent work on the topic.

6.  ILO defines "child laborers" and "economically active children" in the same way for children in the 5 to 11 age group (i.e., those who did one hour or more work in the reference week). This "one hour" requirement renders a child economically active in the 12 to 14 age group, but to be considered a laborer a child should spend this hour (or more) in hazardous work, or else do fourteen hours or more of non-hazardous work per week.

7.  Using Brazilian data chapter 4 shows that child labor participation in one week understates annual participation rates by one-third to two-thirds. If the worldwide estimates provided in the chapter are subject to similar measurement errors, then the true number of economically active children would be between 274 million and 352 million.

8.  Rawlings and Rubio (2003) and Brière and Rawlings (2006) present a comprehensive review of the features of the conditional transfer programs installed in Latin America since 1997, both those covered in this book and others. They also review some of the early evaluations of those programs.

9.  Chapter 10 presents a summary of the theoretical issues regarding household responses to CCTs.

10.  Chapter 10 includes a rare demonstration of how conclusions regarding the success of a program can be sensitive to whether the change in child labor supply following the program's introduction into a community only includes the participating children or all children in the community.

11.  Nevertheless, the transfer must be large enough to compensate for the child's opportunity cost of schooling. In Honduras the transfer averaged 4% of household income, although a child's labor often contributed more than 20% of household income for the poorest households. As a consequence, while the program had a small positive impact on enrollment and promotion rates, it had no effect on child labor (Glewwe et al., 2004).

# II

# Background

# 1

# Changing Patterns of Child Labor around the World since 1950: The Roles of Income Growth, Parental Literacy, and Agriculture

*Victoria Gunnarsson, Peter F. Orazem, and Guilherme Sedlacek*

Child labor has long been considered a social problem that must be minimized, if not eliminated. The 1989 Convention on the Rights of the Child, which required that children be protected from work that harms their health, educational opportunities, and mental, physical, social, or moral development, was signed by 191 countries. Despite this widespread condemnation, about one in every eight children aged 10 to 14 worldwide works.

Nevertheless, there has been progress in lowering the incidence of child labor over the past half century. To formulate policy to maintain that progress, it is important to take stock of why child labor has decreased in the past. This study explores the roles of rising per capita income, improving adult literacy, and economic transformation from a rural agrarian economy to an urban industrialized base. All prove to be important in explaining why child labor has declined over time, why child labor persists, and how it may be combated in the future.

## Factors Affecting Child Labor

Throughout history, children have worked to contribute to family income. In turn-of-the-century households in the United States, income derived from child labor was used primarily for immediate household consumption needs (Parsons and Goldin, 1989). Some child labor involved parents who wanted to maximize their own consumption at the expense of their children's future. For example, Galbi (1997) found that child labor substituted for adult labor in the early years of the industrial revolution. Horrell and Humphries (1995) argued that industrialization also caused children to initiate work at younger ages as their older siblings gained independence and therefore left the household. However, the increase in child labor during the early period of the industrial revolution was driven most by falling income opportunities for parents. Adults without factory experience proved to be poor factory workers. As the first generation of working children aged and became parents, their children were less likely to work. Therefore, the time path of child labor participation during the industrial revolution appears to be consistent with most contemporary studies that find the incidence of child labor declines as adult income rises.

The preponderance of evidence across many different countries finds that child labor is primarily a result of material needs and not parental indifference to their children's welfare. That conclusion is immediately apparent in figures 1.1a and 1.1b. The figures show scatter plots for the proportion of children aged 14 and under who work in a country against that country's per capita income in 1960 and 2000. Several conclusions can be derived from the plots. First, there has been a clear reduction in the incidence of child labor. While nearly 25% of children were working in 1960, the average by 2000 had fallen to 11%. Worldwide, the decrease in child labor over time corresponds to a decline in the number of countries with very low income. Countries such as Burkina Faso, Mali, Niger, and Thailand experienced large reductions in child labor-force participation rates as their real incomes rose from absolute poverty levels. Countries that did not experience rising real per capita incomes (Laos, Nicaragua) maintained their high levels of child labor.

A second implication of the scatter plots is a clear negative cross-sectional relationship between a county's income level and its use of child labor. Low-income countries use child labor heavily while high-income countries use child labor little if at all. The cross-sectional relationship is convex, so at first, child labor declines rapidly as per capita income rises. However, as

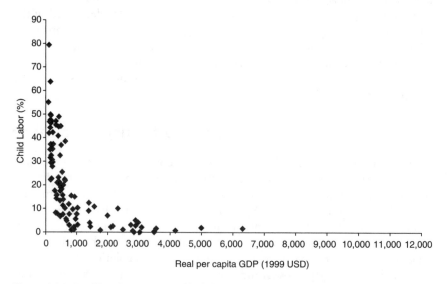

Figure 1.1a   Real Per Capita GDP and Child Labor, 1960

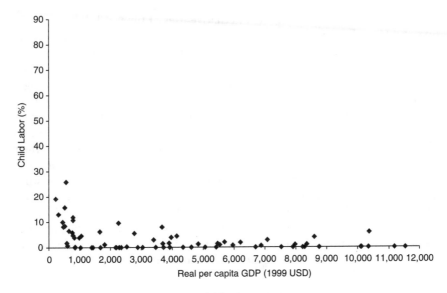

**Figure 1.1b**    Real Per Capita GDP and Child Labor, 2000

per capita income continues to increase beyond $2,000 (in 1999 dollars), additional decreases in child labor participation rates become more modest. In addition, while some countries have eliminated child labor with per capita incomes as low as $1,800, there are other countries with per capita income levels above $7,000 that still have above-average child-labor rates.

The general pattern of declining child labor-force participation rates with rising per capita incomes, both across time periods and across countries, has led some observers to suggest that income growth will correct the child labor problem by itself. However, while changes in income are negatively correlated with changes in child labor participation rates, the correlation is only −0.26. Moreover, the persistence of child labor in some of the countries well beyond the $2,000 income threshold also suggests that raising income alone may not be enough to eradicate child labor. Child labor may still persist if there are other factors that raise the value of child time in the labor market, or if there are low perceived returns to alternative uses of child time, particularly in school.

Several studies have shown that child time allocation responds to the strength of the local labor market for children. Levy (1985), Rosenzweig and Evenson (1977), and King et al. (1999b) found that as local market wages or demand conditions for children rise, the probability of child labor rises. By far the heaviest user of child labor is agriculture. Ashagrie (1997) estimates that 70% of working children are engaged in agricultural activities. The next heaviest users of child labor have much smaller shares, including manufacturing (8.3%), trade (8.3%) and personal services (6.5%). This suggests that the importance of agriculture in the economy can be used as a proxy for the relative strength of child labor demand in the country.

Child labor and education are alternative uses of time. While most working children also are enrolled in school, evidence presented in the following chapters suggests that working children have less academic success and complete fewer years of school. Consequently, factors that make schooling more productive may cause child labor to decline. Most empirical investigations of the factors influencing whether parents send their children to school find that, other things equal, parental education has a strong positive impact on their children's schooling (Rosenzweig and Wolpin, 1994; Grootaert and Patrinos, 1999). More educated parents can increase the productivity of their child's time in school, whether by reinforcing what is learned in school, helping with homework, or valuing their children's efforts in school. Many studies have found that mothers' education is particularly important for their children's schooling success (World Bank, 2001), but often fathers' education has proven important as well. Regardless of the specific mechanism, it is anticipated that improvements in adult literacy would increase child time in school and thus lower the incidence and intensity of child labor.

## Stylized Facts regarding Child Labor

The previous discussion suggests that the incidence of child labor in a country should be explained by the country's income level, its industry mix, and its adult literacy rate. While past analysis has concentrated on household-level data sets, similar arguments can justify an attempt to explain the variation in child labor participation rates across countries.

### Data

The International Labour Organization (ILO) has generated estimates of the employment rates for children aged 10 to 14 by country since 1950. The data, reported by the ILO's Bureau of Statistics (2004), are based on survey questionnaires, ILO internal data, and data computed from ILO estimates and projections.[1] Information is available for up to 202 countries per decade from 1950 through 2000.[2] Summary information on child labor participation rates by year and region is reported in table 1.1.

The worldwide incidence of child labor has declined steadily in the last half century, from 28% in 1950 to 11% in 2000. It has been virtually eliminated in the wealthiest economies of Europe and North America, but these countries already had low levels of child labor in 1950. The biggest improvement was in Asia, where the proportion of working children has declined by 26 percentage points to reach 10% in 2000. The incidence of child labor declined by about 14 percentage points in Africa, which nevertheless retains the world's highest current rates of child labor at 25%. Child labor has declined by 11 percentage points in Latin America, but still persists for 8% of the children in that region.

The incidence of child labor by region appears to be inversely related to the level of economic development. The simple correlation between

**Table 1.1**  Percent child labor participation by continent, 1950–2000

| Continent | 1950 | 1960 | 1970 | 1980 | 1990 | 2000 |
|---|---|---|---|---|---|---|
| World | 27.5 | 24.7 | 22.3 | 19.9 | 14.7 | 11.2 |
| Africa | 38.6 | 36.0 | 33.1 | 30.9 | 27.9 | 25.0 |
| Asia | 36.1 | 32.2 | 28.4 | 23.4 | 15.1 | 10.2 |
| Latin America & Caribbean | 19.4 | 16.5 | 14.6 | 12.7 | 11.3 | 8.2 |
| North America, Western Europe, and Australia | 3.0 | 2.7 | 1.7 | 0.0 | 0.0 | 0.0 |

*Source:* ILO LABORSTA, Economically Active Populations Estimates and Projections: 1950–2010 (2004).

per capita income level and child labor across countries is −0.82, suggesting a strong inverse relationship between a country's income level and its incidence of working children. Population weighted indices by region are reported in table 1.2. World per capita real income rose very slowly between 1950 and 1980 before making some rapid gains in the 1980s. However, those gains were limited to the countries of Asia and the industrialized West. Latin America experienced some rapid gains in per capita real income before 1980, stagnated in the 1980s, and then rose again in the 1990s. Africa experienced the slowest income gains before 1980, and it has stagnated since then. Africa's slow progress on child labor corresponds to its slow income growth.

Statistics on child labor by industry imply that countries relying most heavily on agriculture should have the highest demand for child labor. The World Bank's estimates of agriculture's share of total gross domestic product (GDP) by country is used to index this source of potential demand for child labor. While agriculture's importance in the economy varies considerably across regions, it has fallen most in Asia, which also experienced the greatest reduction in child labor. Modest reductions in agriculture's share in Latin America and Africa match the slower progress on child labor in those regions. The simple correlation between agriculture's share of GDP and child labor is 0.78, so there is strong evidence that agrarian countries use children's labor services more intensively.

Over the same period, the World Bank reports the share of the adult population (aged 25 years or older) that is considered functionally illiterate. We use this as a measure of parental education. More educated parents are believed to have a stronger taste for schooling and to make child time in school more productive. Between 1970 and 2000, the proportion of the world's adult population that was illiterate fell by nearly 27 percentage points. The adult illiteracy rate fell by 45% in Africa and Asia, and it fell by over 50% in Latin America. Improving parental education levels would be expected to positively influence their children's schooling. Children who spend more time in school would be expected to spend less time at work. Consistent with that conjecture, the simple

**Table 1.2** Population weighted per capita GDP, agricultural share of GDP, and illiteracy, by year and continent

| Continent | 1950 | 1960 | 1970 | 1980 | 1990 | 2000 |
|---|---|---|---|---|---|---|
| World | | | | | | |
| Per capita GDP[a] | 2559 | 2242 | 2974 | 2968 | 4046 | 5455 |
| Agriculture Share[b] | — | 29.0 | 18.6 | 13.6 | 12.5 | 10.9 |
| Illiteracy[c] | — | — | 50.6 | 41.1 | 31.3 | 23.7 |
| Africa | | | | | | |
| Per capita GDP[a] | — | 824 | 1050 | 1416 | 1449 | 1282 |
| Agriculture Share[b] | — | — | 25.8 | 19.8 | 20.9 | 20.8 |
| Illiteracy[c] | — | — | 71.6 | 60.7 | 48.1 | 40.5 |
| Asia | | | | | | |
| Per capita GDP[a] | — | 728 | 1287 | 1698 | 2192 | 3169 |
| Agriculture Share[b] | — | — | 26.9 | 20.4 | 18.0 | 15.2 |
| Illiteracy[c] | — | — | 51.2 | 41.4 | 32.8 | 27.8 |
| Latin America & Caribbean | | | | | | |
| Per capita GDP[a] | 1981 | 2340 | 3215 | 4541 | 4132 | 6679 |
| Agriculture Share[b] | — | 15.0 | 13.1 | 10.2 | 10.0 | 8.5 |
| Illiteracy[c] | — | — | 27.2 | 21.1 | 15.3 | 12.9 |
| North America, Western Europe and Australia | | | | | | |
| Per capita GDP[a] | 5574 | 7141 | 10132 | 10953 | 13756 | 16985 |
| Agriculture Share[b] | — | — | 1.3 | 2.7 | 1.4 | 1.1 |
| Illiteracy[c] | — | — | 1.3 | 1.7 | 0.7 | 0.5 |

*Notes:*
[a]Author's calculations based on GDP per capita in 1985 US dollars.
*Source:* Penn World Tables.
[b]Author's calculations based on Agricultural share of GDP.
*Source:* World Bank and Penn World Tables.
[c]Author's calculations based on Adult Illiteracy rates computed by the World Bank.

correlation between the level of adult illiteracy and the incidence of child labor is 0.78.

## Regression Analysis and Simulation Outcomes: World

Simple correlations support the conjecture that child labor is strongly influenced by a country's level of income, adult literacy, and reliance on agriculture. To evaluate the relative importance of these factors, the following regression model is formulated:

$$CL_{it} = \alpha + \beta_1 \ln (Y_{it}) + \beta_2 [\ln (Y_{it})]^2 + \beta_3 AGSHARE_{it} + \beta_4 ILLITERACY_{it} + \Sigma D_t + e_{it} \tag{1.1}$$

where $CL_{it}$ is the percentage of children aged 10 to 14 in country i and year t who are working; $\ln (Y_{it})$ is the natural logarithm of real per capita GDP; $AGSHARE_{it}$ is agriculture's share of GDP; $ILLITERACY_{it}$ is the adult illiteracy rate; $D_t$ is a vector of yearly dummy variables which control for worldwide time-specific changes in the demand for child labor which could be due to international efforts to combat child labor or to encourage child schooling; and $e_{it}$ is a random error term. The logarithmic form of per capita GDP proved to fit better than the linear form. The quadratic specification in $[\ln (Y_{it})]$ also proved most consistent with the data. The quadratic specification could not be rejected, but higher order terms proved unnecessary.

The regression results are reported in table 1.3.[3] The full period could only include the quadratic terms in $[\ln (Y_{it})]$ because the information on AGSHARE and ILLITERACY was not available. The full specification could be estimated only over the 1970–2000 period.

The estimates are remarkably stable over time. In fact, the null hypothesis that the coefficients on per capita income are the same for all years could be only weakly rejected over the 1950–2000 period and could not be rejected over the 1970–2000 period.[4] The implication is that as real per capita incomes have risen, countries have reduced child labor-force participation at a stable rate.[5] The convex shape of the relationship between income and child labor has another implication: that progressively larger increases in per capita income are necessary to lower child labor by another percentage point. As a consequence, the poorest countries can experience rapid reductions in child labor if they can raise their income levels. Using our table 1.3 estimates, a country at the lowest quartile per capita income level would expect a decrease of child labor of about 1.2 percentage points for every $100 increase in per capita income. In contrast, a country at the median level of per capita income worldwide will experience a 0.3 percentage point decrease in child labor for every $100 increase in per capita income. In other words, planners can concentrate on fostering economic development and income growth in the poorest countries and expect child labor to fall in response. However, the sensitivity of child labor to further increases in average income decreases, so planners cannot expect to eradicate child labor solely on the strength of further increases in income.

The regression analysis is repeated over the more recent time frame in which there is access to information on AGSHARE and ILLITERACY. The conclusions from the regression in the first column of table 1.3 stand out. The test of the null hypothesis that the impact of changes in per capita income on child labor is constant over time could not be rejected at standard significance levels. As before, the conclusion is that reductions in child labor follow the progress of the country's path of income growth, but that the relationship flattens out as the country's per capita income rises above the median. In addition, as a country's AGSHARE and ILLITERACY increases,[6] child labor increases significantly. A 10% increase in agriculture's share of GDP increases child labor by just over 20%. A 10% increase in adult illiteracy raises child labor by just under 20%. The implication is that increasing adult literacy and/or developing the nonagricultural sector

**Table 1.3**  Regression analysis of child labor-force participation rates by country, 1950–2000

| Variable | World Sample | | Latin America Sample | |
|---|---|---|---|---|
| | 1950–2000 | 1970–2000 | 1950–2000 | 1970–2000 |
| ln Y | −61.13** | −55.82** | −7.58** | 0.87 |
| | (−12.30) | (−9.60) | (−6.76) | (0.53) |
| (ln Y)$^2$ | 3.10** | 3.12** | | |
| | (9.81) | (8.84) | | |
| AGSHARE | | 0.21** | | 0.20** |
| | | (4.55) | | (2.35) |
| ILLITERACY | | 0.19** | | 0.38** |
| | | (7.84) | | (6.78) |
| D$_{50}$ | 0.76 | | 5.02* | |
| | (0.47) | | (1.95) | |
| D$_{60}$ | 2.99** | | 0.61 | |
| | (2.22) | | (0.25) | |
| D$_{70}$ | 4.11** | 1.79 | 1.50 | −0.22 |
| | (3.13) | (1.44) | (0.66) | (−0.14) |
| D$_{80}$ | 5.05** | 4.11* | 1.45 | 0.88 |
| | (3.95) | (1.15) | (0.67) | (0.59) |
| D$_{90}$ | 1.87 | 1.99 | −1.17 | 1.17 |
| | (1.39) | (1.78) | (−0.50) | (0.73) |
| Constant | 298.15** | 246.11** | 69.44** | −9.18 |
| | (15.60) | (10.17) | (7.23) | (−0.61) |
| R$^2$ | 0.68 | 0.80 | 0.38 | 0.58 |
| N | 652 | 376 | 144 | 85 |
| Observed Change in CLFP[a] | −11.15 | −12.46 | −6.94 | −4.26 |
| $\beta_i(dX_{it}/d_t)$[b] | | | | |
| ln Y | −14.39 | −12.18 | −4.17 | 0.29 |
| AGSHARE | | −1.61 | | −0.93 |
| ILLITERACY | | −5.11 | | −5.43 |
| $\sum_i \beta_i(dX_{it}/d_t)$[c] | −14.39 | −18.90 | −4.17 | −6.07 |

*Notes:*
  t-statistics in parentheses.
  *Significance at the 0.10 level.
  **Significance at the 0.05 level.
  [a]Change in population-weighted child labor force participation rate.
  [b]Change in population-weighted mean of the regressor times its respective coefficient.
  [c]Sum of all changes in child labor attributable to changes in weighted sample means of real per capita income, agriculture share and adult illiteracy rate.

of the economy will lower the incidence of child labor, even if child labor is no longer sensitive to income growth.

The pattern of coefficients on the year dummies suggests that until 1980, child labor was actually on an upward trend worldwide. Absent increases in per capita income, adult literacy, and the nonagricultural share of the world economy, pervasive trends in child labor would have led to increasing child labor-force participation for much of the period after 1950.

These simple models appear to do a reasonable job of capturing the time series and cross sectional variation in child labor. The quadratic relationship in per capita income explained 68% of the variation in child labor across countries from 1950 to 2000. After adding agricultural intensity and illiteracy, the model explained 80% of the variation in child labor across countries between 1970 and 2000. The parameter estimates allow measurement of how much of the change in child labor can be attributed to changes in the levels of per capita income, agriculture, and illiteracy over time, computed as $\beta_j \, dX_{jt}/dt$. This is directly estimable as the change in the sample mean of the $j^{th}$ variable over the sample period ($dX_{jt}/dt$) multiplied by its respective coefficient ($\beta_j$).[7] The estimates are reported at the bottom of table 1.3. They suggest that over the 1950–2000 period, increases in real per capita income alone would have generated more than the observed 11 percentage point reduction in child labor. The implication is that rising real per capita incomes also counteracted a slight tendency toward rising child labor participation rates over the period. When the fuller specification is employed over the shorter sample period, increases in per capita income still are shown to explain a reduction of roughly 12 percentage points in the incidence of child labor. Reductions in adult illiteracy lowered the incidence of child labor by an additional 5.1 percentage points, while reductions in AGSHARE explained 1.6 percentage point decrease in child labor-force participation. The reduction in child labor explained by these three factors more than explains the observed reduction in child labor, again implying that child labor would have trended upward over time had these factors not induced changes that counteracted those trends.

### Regression Analysis and Simulation Outcomes: Latin America

Using the worldwide regressions as a frame of reference, a similar regression methodology was employed over the sample of countries from South America, Central America, and the Caribbean. The implications of that analysis are similar to those based on the world sample, although the relative importance of the factors is different in Latin America. Over the full 1950–2000 time period, increases in real per capita income significantly reduced the child labor-force participation rate in Latin America. Evaluated at changes in sample means over the 1950–2000 period, increases in real per capita incomes lowered the child labor participation rate by 4.2 percentage points or roughly 60% of the total change. This is much smaller than the 14 percentage point drop in child labor that could be attributed to improvements in per capita income worldwide. This is because per capita incomes in Latin America already were at or above the median per capita income in the world, placing those countries in the range of flatter tradeoffs between child labor and income.

By 1970, per capita income in Latin America had further risen relative to world averages, and so child labor would be expected to be even less sensitive to further income growth. In fact, from 1970 to 2000, changes in real per capita income had no effect on average child labor participation in Latin America. However, reductions in adult illiteracy and agriculture's share of production had significant negative effects on child labor. The reduction in adult illiteracy is responsible for a 5.4 percentage point reduction in child labor participation, similar to the 5.1 percentage point decline attributable to falling illiteracy worldwide. Reductions in agriculture's share of production lowered child labor by an additional 0.9 percentage points compared to the 1.6 percentage point drop worldwide.

It is important to emphasize that the negligible impact of improvements in average per capita income on child labor in Latin America over the 1970–2000 period does not imply that income is unimportant. In fact, holding average income constant, higher levels of illiteracy and agricultural production suggest a more unequal income distribution. Consequently, the large effects of adult illiteracy and agricultural share on child labor may be due to a larger share of low-income households within a given country. It is possible that changes in average incomes would not affect child labor, but that raising income at the lower tail of the distribution would still have an effect. As the next chapter demonstrates, however, child labor is found at even the upper tail of the income distribution in these countries. Consequently, income transfer programs alone will not eliminate child labor in Latin America.

## Conclusions

The preponderance of evidence suggests that child labor is strongly tied to the level of household income. In fact, increases in per capita incomes can explain all of the reduction in worldwide child labor since 1950. However, child labor becomes less responsive to additional increases in per capita income as the level of per capita income rises. In Latin America, where average per capita income exceeds the world median level, it may take a very large increase in average income, and consequently, a very long time to eliminate child labor through income growth alone.

The sensitivity of child labor participation rates to adult literacy rates and the share of agriculture in total production suggest other avenues by which policy could reduce child labor. Policies that lower the value of child time at work, such as truancy laws or child labor prohibitions could be sufficient, except that they are nearly impossible to enforce in the informal labor markets in which child labor occurs most frequently. Alternatively, policies that raise the value of child time in school relative to work, such as tying income transfers to child attendance or schooling success could decrease incentives to send children to work. Adult literacy programs or other outreach programs that advertise the importance of education may lead parents to place greater value on their children's schooling. Much of this book will be devoted to reviewing evidence of factors that would affect the success of such policies and how they have worked in practice.

# Notes

1. See Ashagrie (1993) for details on these estimates.
2. Information on some countries is spotty, especially for 1950 and 1960. In addition, countries change over time through splits and mergers. To correct for possible random measurement error, we use the averaged data across countries within a region. Random measurement error should be less important in the averaged data as compared with the individual country estimates.
3. The sample of countries used in the regressions differs from those used in table 1.1, as only those for whom necessary information was available on per capita incomes, agricultural share, and adult literacy are included in the regression sample. This tends to exclude some of the poorer countries while including a higher share of countries with already low child-labor rates in 1950. Consequently, the implied decrease in child-labor incidence in the regression sample is smaller than the change reported in table 1.1, particularly for the comparisons going back to 1950.
4. The F-statistic is 3.42 for the full sample that exceeds the critical value, but the only individual coefficients that differed significantly from sample averages were in 1990. The test of stability over the specification including AGSHARE and ILLITERACY could only be conducted over the data since 1970. There, the F-test of the null hypothesis of stable coefficients over time could not be rejected at the .05 level of significance $(F(12,356) = 1.72)$.
5. Although developed countries have a very low incidence of child labor, this was not the case earlier in their histories, when their per capita incomes were more similar to those of developing countries today. For example, in 1910, the labor-force participation rate for boys aged 10–13 in the United States was 17%, and it was more than 40% in the states of the Deep South. Over 72% of the working children were employed in agriculture. Interestingly, per capita incomes at the time in the United States would be equivalent to that of countries at the twenty-fifth percentile of per capita incomes today, much higher than per capita incomes in most of the developing world.
6. The share of agriculture in the economy also may be a proxy for the distribution of income. As a rule, agricultural households lag behind urban households in average income, just as more agrarian countries lag behind industrialized countries in average income. Poverty rates in rural areas exceed those in urban areas. Consequently, holding per capita income constant, the variance of per capita income would be expected to increase as agriculture's share increases. Consistent with this presumption, measures of income inequality are typically larger in developing than developed countries.
7. For the estimated impact of changes in per capita income on child labor, the formula is $\beta_1\{\ln(Y_{it}) - \ln(Y_{it-1})\} + \beta_2\{[\ln(Y_{it})]^2 - [\ln(Y_{it-1})]^2\}$.

# 2

# Child Labor, Schooling, and Poverty in Latin America

*Guilherme Sedlacek, Suzanne Duryea,*
*Nadeem Ilahi, and Masaru Sasaki*

One of the challenges in designing policies to combat child labor is the puzzling finding from chapter 1 that as economic growth progresses, the pace of reductions in child labor appears to slow. Consequently, policies that raise per capita income may not, by themselves, lower the incidence of child labor. If they do lower child labor, the reductions may only occur over a period of decades. This appears to be the current challenge to reducing child labor in Latin America, where per capita income is now high enough that child labor has become relatively insensitive to further income gains.

Many countries restrict child labor with the belief that reducing child labor increases educational attainment. Two issues regarding the relationship between child labor and education warrant a policy maker's attention. First, research establishing the nature of the relationship between child labor and education is surprisingly limited. For instance, it is not clear whether child labor discourages school attendance or if it only lowers the quality of school attainment. This distinction is important because the policy tools aimed at increasing enrollment are different from those aimed at raising the productivity of time spent in school. This issue is particularly relevant in Latin America, where most working children are enrolled in school. Previous research has not established whether a child's time in work adversely affects the productivity of his or her time in school.

Second, child labor and its effect on education do not operate in a vacuum. Both are outcomes of complex household-level decisions. Both child labor and education are intimately related to other factors affecting households, such as the number of children in the household, the household's access to income, and the parents' interest in schooling.

Once further improvement in child labor has become insensitive to overall economic growth, policies must alter incentives to send children to work. It is therefore important that an analysis that explores the association between child labor and education incorporate these household-level factors.

This chapter shows that in Latin America, child labor has a negative and significant effect on educational enrollment. However, it has an even greater adverse effect on progression through school and the quality of attainment through attendance. These results are stronger for the poor. Thus, targeted conditional cash transfer programs for human development, such as PROGRESA (now Oportunidades) and Bolsa Familia, are correct to require beneficiary children to actually attend school rather than simply concentrate on enrollment.

## Stylized Facts on Child Labor and Schooling in Latin America

Employment rates for children aged 10 to 14 in eighteen Latin American countries are shown in figure 2.1. The data are taken from the most recently available surveys. Child employment rates range widely, from 1% in Chile to 36% in Ecuador. The average is 12.5% across all eighteen countries, roughly equal to the worldwide child labor participation rate. Whereas employment rates in Chile and Argentina are among the lowest of all developing countries, employment rates in Bolivia, Ecuador, and Peru are among the highest.

Figure 2.1 also shows that 90% of the children aged 10 to 14 in the eighteen countries are enrolled in school. There is an apparent inverse relationship between school enrollment and child labor. Of the nine countries

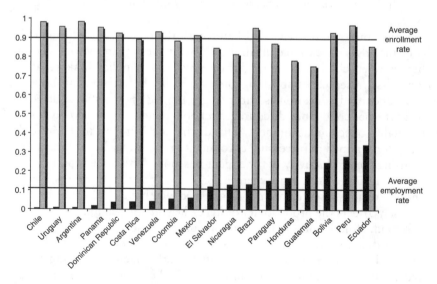

**Figure 2.1**  Employment and Attendance Rates for Children Ages 10–14

with above-average child employment rates, six have below-average enrollment rates. The simple cross-sectional correlation between enrollment and employment rates is −0.4. The relationship is hardly definitive. Brazil, Bolivia, and Peru have above-average enrollment rates despite having above-average child employment rates. In fact, across these countries, 63% of the children aged 10 to 14 reported as working also are reported as being enrolled in school.

While one of the potential consequences of early entry into the labor market is that the child's education will be cut short, past empirical evidence of child labor's impact on education is mixed. Child labor actually may enhance educational opportunities by raising household income and thus the ability to afford education. As Ravallion and Wodon (2001) argue, work and school are not mutually exclusive for children. Patrinos and Psacharopoulos (1997) found evidence suggesting that child labor and enrollment were complementary activities. While in all eighteen countries enrollment rates for working children are lower than for children who are not working, it is clear that working and schooling are not mutually exclusive. This leads to the question: if child labor does not remove children from school, does it actually lower the human capital production of poor children? If it does not, then policies that limit opportunities for child labor are almost certainly counterproductive.

Not only is there a wide distribution of child employment rates across these countries, but there also is a wide variety of time paths of employment rates. In Honduras and Venezuela, labor-force participation rates for 10- to 14-year-olds during the decade of the 1990s. In Mexico, child labor initially rose from 6% to 9% but has fallen since 1998. Child labor in Uruguay has varied narrowly between 1% to 2% from 1981 to 2000. Meanwhile, child labor participation has been falling in Brazil, Colombia, and Costa Rica. The various experiences provide another challenge for researchers to explain the uneven success in combating child labor. The timing of improvements in child labor rates in Brazil and Mexico corresponds roughly to the installation of government policies to combat child labor, suggesting that government intervention may provide an effective avenue for addressing the problem.[1]

Figure 2.2 shows one source of variation in schooling investments across Latin American countries. Enrollment rates are traced for different ages and income groups. Enrollment rates peak at 10 years of age, then begin to drop off. The pattern occurs even in the wealthier households, but is particularly pronounced among poor children. Those in the poorest income groups in Latin America are slow to enter school and quick to exit. Enrollment rates in the wealthiest families are more than 90% for children aged 6 to 15. For the poorest children, enrollment rates do not rise above 90% until age 8, and fall below 90% again by age 12. While the enrollment gap across income groups is only a few percentage points for children aged 8 to 11, about 15% of the poorest children already have spent one or two fewer years in school by age 8 than children in the wealthiest

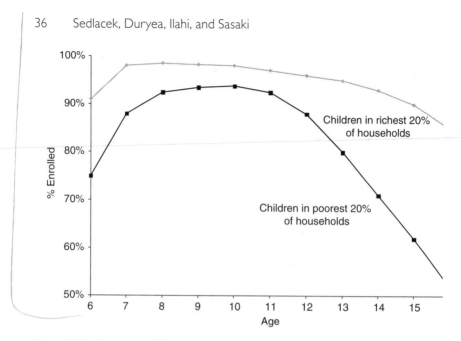

**Figure 2.2** Average Enrollment Rates in 18 Latin American Countries, by Household Income Level and Age, 1999

households. In addition, those poorest children begin to drop out of school in large numbers after age 11. For children aged 14 to 16, the difference in enrollment rates between rich and poor grows from 20 to 34 percentage points. Consequently, the small differences in enrollment rates across income groups for 8- to 11-year-olds masks large differences in past and future acquisitions of human capital between income groups. This suggests that enrollment rates may mislead researchers about the extent to which the poor and wealthy invest in the human capital of their children.

Across Latin America, the simple correlation between levels of per capita income and child labor is −0.44. Worldwide, this is roughly half the correlation between the two factors, which indicates that Latin American countries are positioned in the flat region of the tradeoff between income and child labor described in chapter 1. It also is comparable to the correlation between child labor and school enrollment in Latin America. Consequently, policies to combat child labor in Latin America may not be very effective if they rely on raising income or school enrollment alone. The chance of success is enhanced if the policies address both.

## Detailed Descriptive Data on Child Labor and Schooling

Four Latin American countries have conducted recent household surveys that allow a much more detailed investigation of child labor and schooling. The data sets include the Living Standards Measurement Surveys (LSMS) of

Ecuador, Nicaragua, and Peru, as well as the Brazilian national household survey (PNAD). These four countries are broadly representative of the region. Brazil is in the upper-middle income category. There, child labor has been declining but it remains high for an upper-middle income country.[2] Peru and Ecuador represent the majority of the countries in the region, that is, those in the lower-middle income category. Both of these countries have relatively high levels of child labor. Nicaragua represents the low-income countries, but has a child employment rate at the median of the countries in the region.

The incidence of child labor-force participation for children aged 10 to 14 by country, urban-rural residence, and gender is reported in table 2.1.[3] The patterns are similar across all four countries. Child labor is more common in rural than in urban areas. Rural child labor participation rates are four times higher than urban rates in Brazil and Peru, 2.7 times higher in Nicaragua, and 1.6 times higher in Ecuador. Boys are more likely than girls to work in all four countries. While some of this difference may be because girls may be more likely to perform household chores without pay, perhaps the more important point is that girls' employment rates are high in their own right. Consequently, child labor is not just an issue for young boys, but for young girls, as well.

Table 2.2 shows how child labor interacts with school enrollment rates. Child labor rates range from 11% in Nicaragua to 36% in Ecuador; however, the two countries have identical enrollment rates. Peru has the highest enrollment rates, even though 29% of Peruvian children work. Although working children in these countries are 5 to 29 percentage points less likely to be in school than their nonworking counterparts, clearly, child labor and education often coexist in Latin America.

However, working children may not perform as well in school. The more children have to work, the more tired they will be when in school and the less time they will have for study. Consequently, work may have an adverse effect on learning while in school, even if it does not have a large effect on enrollment.[4] The distribution of hours worked per day for children aged 10 to 14, shown in table 2.3, suggests that a high proportion of working children work too many hours to succeed in school. More than half the working children in Nicaragua work more than five hours per day, as do just under half of the working children in Brazil. The proportions in Ecuador (34%) and Peru (15%) are modest in comparison, but still high enough to suggest a problem.

The impact of child labor on student learning is quantified in chapter 7 by examining achievement test results. This chapter uses a less direct indicator—whether the child's years of completed education is at the level expected for the child's age. If labor limits the amount of time a child can devote to study, working children would be expected to fail in greater proportions than would students whose attention is not divided between work and school.

As shown in table 2.4, it is common for children in Latin America to lag behind in school. The percentages vary from 31% in Peru to 56% in

**Table 2.1**  Employment rates for children aged 10 to 14 by country, urban or rural residence, and gender

| | Urban | | | | Rural | | | | Total | | | |
|---|---|---|---|---|---|---|---|---|---|---|---|---|
| | *Brazil* | *Ecuador* | *Nicaragua* | *Peru* | *Brazil* | *Ecuador* | *Nicaragua* | *Peru* | *Brazil* | *Ecuador* | *Nicaragua* | *Peru* |
| Total | 8% | 22% | 6% | 13% | 32% | 36% | 16% | 51% | 14% | 36% | 11% | 29% |
| Boys | 11% | 25% | 8% | 14% | 44% | 44% | 27% | 59% | 19% | 44% | 17% | 33% |
| Girls | 5% | 18% | 5% | 12% | 20% | 28% | 6% | 44% | 9% | 28% | 5% | 26% |

**Table 2.2**  Employment and enrollment rates for children aged 10 to 14 by country and labor-market status

| | *Brazil* | *Ecuador* | *Nicaragua* | *Peru* |
|---|---|---|---|---|
| Employment Rate | 14% | 36% | 11% | 29% |
| Enrollment Rate | 91% | 81% | 81% | 95% |
| Not Employed | 93% | 93% | 85% | 97% |
| Employed | 79% | 75% | 56% | 92% |

Table 2.3  Distribution of daily hours worked by children aged 10 to 14 by country and gender

| | Brazil | | | Ecuador | | | Nicaragua | | | Peru | | |
|---|---|---|---|---|---|---|---|---|---|---|---|---|
| | Boys | Girls | Total | Boys | Girls | Total | Boys | Girls | Total | Boys | Girls | Total |
| Under 5 Hours | 51% | 51% | 51% | 63% | 70% | 66% | 39% | 62% | 44% | 83% | 87% | 85% |
| 5–10 Hours | 43% | 43% | 43% | 36% | 25% | 31% | 50% | 28% | 45% | 15% | 11% | 13% |
| Over 10 Hours | 6% | 6% | 6% | 1% | 5% | 3% | 11% | 10% | 11% | 2% | 2% | 2% |

Table 2.4  Percentage of children aged 10 to 14 lagging behind expected grade level by country, gender, and labor-market status

| | Total | | | | Boys | | | | Girls | | | |
|---|---|---|---|---|---|---|---|---|---|---|---|---|
| | Brazil | Ecuador[a] | Nicaragua | Peru | Brazil | Ecuador[a] | Nicaragua | Peru | Brazil | Ecuador[a] | Nicaragua | Peru |
| School Only | 42% | 47% | 35% | 28% | 45% | 49% | 38% | 28% | 40% | 45% | 32% | 29% |
| School & Work | 54% | 55% | 45% | 36% | 54% | 55% | 48% | 38% | 49% | 55% | 38% | 34% |
| Work Only | 69% | 54% | 79% | 43% | 73% | 50% | 81% | 42% | 61% | 62% | 64% | 45% |
| Total | 46% | 56% | 42% | 31% | 50% | 59% | 46% | 31% | 43% | 54% | 38% | 30% |

*Note:*
[a]Note that Ecuadorian children aged 13 to 14 years are excluded due to a lack of data on the highest grade for those children.

Ecuador.[5] Girls are more likely to be promoted than boys, but even so, 30% or more of the girls are behind their age-appropriate grade level.

A high proportion of children who are not working are behind grade level; children who are working while attending school are even further behind. With the exception of Ecuador, children who are only working are even further behind, so it appears that enrolled children who work are still making academic progress. However, that progress is markedly slower than that of children who do not work. This suggests that working children will complete fewer years of schooling than will children who do not work.[6] Estimates of returns per year of schooling suggest that there is a significant loss of lifetime earnings for each year of schooling lost. Psacharopoulos (1985) estimated that the private returns to a year of primary schooling in Latin America averaged 61%, so even a few years of schooling sacrificed to gain current child earnings could significantly lower lifetime earnings.

Tables 2.1 through 2.4 suggest that while the majority of working children are enrolled in school, child labor hinders academic achievement per year spent in school. Consequently, each year that a child avoids entering the labor market will result in some increased earnings as an adult, either because the child will make more rapid progress through school or because the child will complete more years of schooling. This hypothesis will be tested rigorously in later chapters and found to be consistent with the data.

## Statistical Analysis

The four household surveys for Brazil, Ecuador, Nicaragua, and Peru support regression analyses of household decisions and child schooling outcomes. The dependent variables in this analysis are measures of child labor, schooling, and educational attainment. Child labor is defined as child time spent on income-generating activities, whether in a family enterprise or in wage work for others. Work that does not generate income, such as household chores, is not considered work by this definition. Therefore, some forms of child labor, particularly forms that are most important for girls, are likely to be underreported.

Child schooling is measured whether or not the child is currently enrolled in school. This does not capture intensity of schooling, as would a measure of school attendance. However, attained schooling, which is an outcome measure that should capture variation in the intensity of schooling, is reported in all data sets. The measure of schooling attainment is based on the number of years a child lags behind the level that would represent normal progress for the child's age. This inverse estimate of grade-for-age is computed by:

$$IGFA = 100\left[1 - \left(\frac{Grade}{Age - 6}\right)\right]; \text{ Age} > 6 \tag{2.1}$$

An *IGFA* of zero implies the child's attained years of schooling equal the expected level for the child's age. An *IGFA* score of 100 implies the child has never completed a year of schooling.

The household-level variables, which will be used to explain the variation in the dependent variables, include the child's age and gender, number of members in the household, and number of children less than 5 years of age. Parent information includes the age, gender, and educational attainment of the household head. The remaining measures include a series of dummy variables indicating progressively higher income quintiles and a dummy variable indicating rural residence.

### Econometric Determinants of Child Labor

Probit regressions indicating how various factors affect the probability of child labor are reported in table 2.5. For ease of interpretation, coefficients have been converted into derivatives of the probability of child labor with respect to the exogenous variables. Two specifications, including and excluding the income quintiles, are reported for each country. Except for Brazil, the income quintiles add significantly to the explanatory power of the regressions, so discussion will concentrate on the fuller specifications. The estimated effects are consistent across all four countries in both sign and magnitude. Therefore, it appears that similar forces in all four countries drive the decision to send children to work.

Child labor appears to respond to market opportunities. As a child ages, the probability of working increases, consistent with the presumption of rising child wages with age. With the exception of the improbably large marginal effect at age 11 in Ecuador, the probability of child labor rises monotonically with age. As children age from 10 to 14, the probability of working rises 14 to 24 percentage points, depending on the country. Child labor is significantly more prevalent in rural areas where demand is greatest. The rural-urban differential is only 6 percentage points in Nicaragua, but it is larger elsewhere. Rural children are about 20% more likely to work than urban children in Brazil and Ecuador and 34% in Peru.

Girls have a significantly lower probability of working for income than do boys; the effect varies from −8% in Peru to −16% in Ecuador. Child labor is not particularly sensitive to the composition of the household or the attributes of the household head. Only in Peru does the presence of young children in the household affect the probability of work for the older children; there, child-labor probability rises 4 percentage points for every young child in the household. The impact of overall household size is small in all countries and has consistent signs. If one reason for child labor is that some children need to work to raise income sufficiently to allow their siblings to go to school, these results suggest that the impact is very small in all of these countries.

The age and gender of the household head have no appreciable impact on the probability that children will work. However, parental education has a strong negative effect on the probability that the children will work.

**Table 2.5** Econometric determinants of child labor, by country

| | Brazil | | Ecuador | | Nicaragua | | Peru | |
|---|---|---|---|---|---|---|---|---|
| Age = 11[a] | 0.041** | 0.041** | 0.616** | 0.586* | 0.084** | 0.082** | 0.022 | 0.018 |
| Age = 12[a] | 0.091** | 0.091** | 0.124** | 0.118** | 0.076** | 0.077** | 0.039 | 0.039 |
| Age = 13[a] | 0.139** | 0.139** | 0.254** | 0.246** | 0.135** | 0.134** | 0.131** | 0.127** |
| Age = 14[a] | 0.209** | 0.208** | 0.238** | 0.228** | 0.154** | 0.154** | 0.143** | 0.139** |
| Female | −0.089** | −0.089** | −0.164** | −0.161** | −0.103** | −0.102** | −0.081** | −0.079** |
| Rural | 0.191** | 0.192** | 0.206** | 0.266** | 0.060** | 0.064** | 0.342** | 0.344** |
| Number of Children Under 5 | 0.002 | 0.002 | −0.021 | −0.013 | 0.002 | 0.003 | 0.038** | 0.045** |
| Household Size | 0.005** | 0.005** | 0.011** | 0.022** | 0.001 | 0.001 | −0.021** | −0.015** |
| Household Head's Age | −0.001** | −0.001** | −0.002** | −0.002** | −0.001** | −0.001** | −0.003** | −0.003** |
| Household Head is Female | 0.002 | 0.003 | −0.016 | −0.003 | −0.002 | −0.002 | 0.023 | 0.023 |
| Household Head's Highest | −0.008** | −0.009** | −0.003 | −0.006 | −0.007** | −0.007** | −0.007** | −0.011** |
| Education | | | | | | | | |
| Quintile 2[b] | | −0.004 | −0.062** | | 0.013 | | −0.061** | |
| Quintile 3[b] | | 0.002 | −0.127** | | −0.015 | | −0.069** | |
| Quintile 4[b] | | −0.006 | −0.138** | | −0.022 | | −0.147** | |
| Quintile 5[b] | | −0.002 | −0.211** | | 0.007 | | −0.115** | |
| Observations | 37,343 | 37,343 | 2,831 | 2,831 | 3,114 | 3,114 | 2,341 | 2,341 |
| LR Chi2(15): | 5283 | 5281 | 467 | 418 | 274 | 267 | 516 | 488 |
| Predicted Probability | 0.096 | 0.096 | 0.324 | 0.326 | 0.081 | 0.082 | 0.253 | 0.256 |

*Notes:*

[a] Age = 10 is the reference dummy.

[b] Bottom quintile is the reference dummy.

All coefficients have been transformed into marginal probabilities associated with the variable.

*Significant at the .10 level.

**Significant at the .05 level.

Parental education consistently lowers the probability of child labor in all countries. For every year of parental schooling attainment, the probability of child labor falls 0.3 to 0.8 percentage points.

The effect of poverty on the decision to work is explored through the use of income quintiles.[7] For each country, two regressions were run: one that includes quintile dummies and one that does not. This is because income quintiles can be endogenous, in that they can be affected by the behavior being measured in the dependent variable (i.e., whether or not the household sends children to work). If household income is endogenous, then the regression coefficients on the other regressors will be biased. The use of quintiles rather than income levels mitigates the problem somewhat in that child labor may alter income insufficiently to cause quintiles to change. A comparison of the estimated coefficients between regressions with and without quintiles reveals that if simultaneity bias exists, it is small.

A positive relationship between child labor and poverty is confirmed in only Ecuador and Peru. There, children in each progressively higher quintile have a lower probability of working. The data for Brazil and Nicaragua reveal no particular pattern between household income level and child labor. The implication from table 2.5 is that income transfers that raise household income may not alter child labor, although they may have the desired effect in Peru and Ecuador. In all countries, however, income-earning opportunities for children corresponding to age, rural residence, and gender appear to have a significant impact on child labor-force participation. Altering returns to child labor may have a larger effect.

### Economic Determinants of School Enrollment

Table 2.6 lists the results of enrollment regressions, with and without income quintiles. The null hypothesis that income quintiles do not affect enrollment probability is rejected in every country. Coefficients are robust to the inclusion or exclusion of the income quintiles, so the discussion is concentrated on the specifications including income quintiles.

The results show that despite high enrollment rates in all four countries, there are clear associations between some of the explanatory variables and enrollment. First, there is a monotonic decline in the propensity for enrollment with age. For instance, 14-year-olds exhibit significantly lower enrollment in school compared to 10-year-olds. Second, rural children show significantly lower enrollment than their urban counterparts by about 3% to 11%. Third, girls exhibit higher enrollment rates, but the estimated coefficients are statistically significant only in Brazil and Nicaragua.

All of these effects are opposite their marginal effects on child labor: factors that tend to raise enrollment also tend to lower child labor. Comparing coefficients in table 2.5 with their counterparts in table 2.6, opposite signs are found in fourteen of fifteen cases in all four countries. The cases in

**Table 2.6** Econometric determinants of current enrollment, by country

| | Brazil | | Ecuador | | Nicaragua | | Peru | |
|---|---|---|---|---|---|---|---|---|
| Age = 11[a] | −0.011** | −0.011** | −0.039* | −0.040 | −0.010** | −0.012 | −0.007 | −0.005 |
| Age = 12[a] | −0.021** | −0.021** | −0.118** | −0.124** | −0.061** | −0.056** | −0.009 | −0.009 |
| Age = 13[a] | −0.050** | −0.050** | −0.279** | −0.278** | −0.021 | −0.015 | −0.052** | −0.052** |
| Age = 14[a] | −0.109** | −0.108** | −0.362** | −0.359** | −0.110** | −0.105** | −0.085** | −0.083** |
| Female | 0.011** | 0.012** | 0.0005 | 0.002 | 0.034** | 0.040** | −0.005 | −0.005 |
| Rural | −0.048** | −0.057** | −0.063** | −0.113** | −0.025** | −0.060** | −0.032** | −0.034** |
| Number of Children Under 5 | −0.013* | −0.015* | 0.001 | −0.002 | −0.017** | −0.025** | −0.003 | −0.004 |
| Household Size | −0.001** | −0.002** | −0.002 | −0.010** | 0.008** | 0.003 | 0.001 | −0.0002 |
| Household Head's Age | 0.0003** | 0.0005** | 0.001* | 0.001* | 0.0004 | 0.001** | −0.0004 | −0.0003 |
| Household Head is Female | −0.026** | −0.031** | −0.001 | −0.010 | 0.034** | 0.032** | −0.011 | −0.011 |
| Household Head's Highest Education | 0.009** | 0.011** | 0.005* | 0.007** | 0.016** | 0.022** | 0.002* | 0.003** |
| Quintile 2[b] | | 0.014** | | 0.031** | | 0.064** | | 0.014** |
| Quintile 3[b] | | 0.023** | | 0.053** | | 0.091** | | 0.018** |
| Quintile 4[b] | | 0.035** | | 0.082** | | 0.105** | | 0.027** |
| Quintile 5[b] | | 0.042** | | 0.080** | | 0.119** | | 0.018 |
| Observations | 37,334 | 37,344 | 2,831 | 2,831 | 3,107 | 3,107 | 2,341 | 2,341 |
| LR Chi2(15): | 2833 | 2716 | 494 | 411 | 432 | 335 | 105 | 95 |
| Predicted Probability | 0.938 | 0.936 | 0.937 | 0.927 | 0.901 | 0.890 | 0.969 | 0.967 |

*Notes:*

[a] Age = 10 is the reference dummy.

[b] Bottom quintile is the reference dummy.

All coefficients have been transformed into marginal probabilities associated with the variable.

*Significant at the .10 level.

**Significant at the .05 level.

which signs were the same across the tables were those in which one or both coefficients were insignificantly different from zero. It is apparent that school enrollment and child labor have opposite responses to household attributes and measures of child market opportunities.

Household size has small effects of mixed signs. Where significant, the presence of children under the age of 5 lowers enrollment probability by 1 to 2 percentage points, which suggests that older children are withheld from school to help raise their younger siblings. However, there is no strong evidence that larger families are less likely to send children to school, or alternatively, that some children are withheld so others can attend school.

The age and gender of the household head have small, mixed effects. However, the education of the head has a consistently positive effect on child enrollment; that probability rises 0.2 to 1.6 percentage points per year of schooling attained. Each year of parental education lowers child labor by roughly the same amount as it raises school enrollment.

Measures of household income have much stronger effects on school enrollment than on child labor, although the effects may seem surprisingly small. In Brazil, children in the highest income quintile are only 4% more likely to enroll than are children in the lowest income quintile. The comparable estimates are 8% and 12% in Ecuador and Nicaragua respectively. In Peru, the effect is less than 2%.

### Economic Determinants of Lagging School Attainment

Although child labor may not significantly lower enrollment, it may affect grade attainment through its effect on attendance. Table 2.7 provides the results of a regression for lagging behind in school, defined here as the difference between actual and optimal grade-for-age. The specifications mimic those above except that age is excluded because it is already incorporated into the dependent variable. A general finding from a comparison of the signs and significance of the coefficients in tables 2.5 and 2.7 is that factors that raise the probability of child labor also cause a child to lag behind in school.[8] Therefore, the inverse relationship between allocating child time to work and a child's educational attainment is confirmed.

The role of income is strong and consistent. Children in the lowest quintiles lag 5% to 22% behind those in the highest quintile, depending on the country. As children's positions in the income distribution improves, their probability of lagging in schooling attainment falls. The impact of household income on the probability of lagging in school is stronger than the income effect on either child labor or enrollment.

To the extent that it is school attainment rather than enrollment that is important, the finding that child labor and attainment are inversely related further strengthens the notion that one can fight child labor through investing in schooling. This explains how countries with relatively high child

**Table 2.7** Econometric determinants of falling behind in school, by country

| | Brazil | | Ecuador | | Nicaragua | | Peru | |
|---|---|---|---|---|---|---|---|---|
| Female | −6.811** | −6.822** | −2.290 | −2.348 | −6.955** | −7.460** | −0.823 | −0.784 |
| Rural | 7.102** | 10.902** | 0.311 | 3.647** | 7.344** | 10.929** | 5.951** | 6.171** |
| Number of Children under 5 | 2.042** | 2.993** | 1.823* | 0.773* | 1.715** | 2.670** | 1.643** | 1.948** |
| Household Size | 1.570** | 2.167** | 0.124 | 2.294** | 0.733** | 1.316** | 0.843** | 1.098** |
| Household Head's Age | −0.055** | −0.119** | 0.099 | 0.089 | −0.272** | −0.330** | −0.127** | −0.152** |
| Household Head is Female | 4.278** | 6.051** | −2.500 | −1.781 | −2.607** | −2.297* | 0.245 | 0.331 |
| Household Head's Highest | −1.623** | −2.383** | −0.112 | −0.346 | −2.442** | −3.024** | −1.216** | −1.378** |
| Education | | | | | | | | |
| Quintile 2 | −10.760** | | −4.286** | | −13.225** | | −2.950** | |
| Quintile 3 | −16.125** | | −8.090** | | −16.014** | | −4.650** | |
| Quintile 4 | −18.813** | | −10.378** | | −17.735** | | −6.183** | |
| Quintile 5 | −18.877** | | −11.572** | | −21.988** | | −5.235** | |
| Observations | 37,315 | 37,315 | 1,602 | 1,602 | 3,105 | 3,105 | 2,316 | 2,316 |
| F | 1745 | 2209 | 6 | 6 | 108 | 146 | 40 | 59 |
| Root MSE | 23.5 | 24.3 | 28.6 | 28.7 | 30.1 | 30.7 | 20.7 | 20.8 |

*Notes:*

Age = 10 is the reference dummy.

Bottom quintile is the reference dummy.

Ecuadorian children aged 13 to 14 years are excluded due to a lack of data on the highest grade for those children.

All coefficients have been transformed into marginal probabilities associated with the variable.

*Significant at the .10 level.

**Significant at the .05 level.

labor rates still can exhibit high enrollment rates (figure 2.2) but with lower quality of actual attainment.

### Direct Effect of Child Labor on Schooling Outcomes

Although the results above are consistent with the presumption that child labor and schooling outcomes are inversely related, they do not prove that presumption. Duryea and Arends-Kuenning (2003) and Rosati and Rossi (2003) have shown that in Brazil, Pakistan, and Nicaragua, the school enrollment and work decisions for children are made simultaneously and are influenced by unobserved factors. When modeled as a bivariate probit, the error terms of the schooling and employment equations are negatively correlated, suggesting that there is a trade-off between the activities.

However, the correlation of unobservables from the two equations cautions one from measuring the direct effect of child employment on schooling outcomes since some portion of the relationship may be driven by outside factors. After purging the "contaminated" correlation from a regression, the effect of child labor on schooling outcomes can be explored. In other words, the children's employment will be predicted using the exogenous variables in the schooling equation and instrumental variables that are correlated with employment but not with schooling, rather than by their actual employment status.

In their seminal paper, Angrist and Krueger (1991) recognized that individuals with late birthdays have an exogenous reason to remain in school, according to U.S. compulsory schooling laws. Here the identification comes from cross-country variation in education policy, as reported by UNESCO (2002). Countries differ in the official ages children begin first grade and legally leave school. These differences in compulsory schooling laws are exogenous to the household's decision-making process. The official ages for beginning first grade vary from age 5 in Colombia; age 6 in Bolivia, Costa Rica, Chile, Dominican Republic, Peru, Ecuador, Mexico, Paraguay, Uruguay, Venezuela; and age 7 in Brazil, El Salvador, Guatemala, Honduras, and Nicaragua. The corresponding ages for terminating compulsory schooling are age 12 in Nicaragua and Honduras; age 13 in Bolivia, Chile, Dominican Republic, and Paraguay; age 14 in Brazil, Colombia, Ecuador, Mexico, and Uruguay; age 15 in Costa Rica, El Salvador, Guatemala, and Venezuela; and age 16 in Peru.

These legislative restrictions on truancy are indeed correlated with child time use. Figure 2.3 plots the average years of schooling attainment for youth aged 16 to 18 in the countries examined above. The countries that have late official ages of entering first grade are clustered at the lowest end of performance, whereas countries which officially start first grade at earlier ages have better average attainments for 16- to 18-year-olds. For example, schooling attainment for children in Brazil is under seven years, whereas children in Ecuador, Mexico, Bolivia and Peru attain more than eight years of schooling. A similar patterns exists

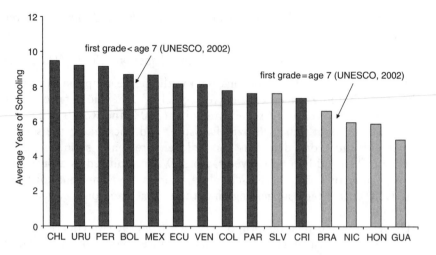

**Figure 2.3**    Average Years of Completed Schooling for 16- to 18-Year-Olds in Latin America, by Country

among older generations of adults, implying that education policies permitting or promoting late entry to school have costly and non-reversible long-term effects.

The information on legal school starting and leaving ages and household survey data is combined for all sixteen countries for children ages 10 to 16. Table 2.8 shows the results from a two-stage least squares regression model. The first two columns show the model for school attendance in which the exogenous variables include the child's age, sex, region of residence (urban or rural), number of children in the household younger than age 6, total household size, age and schooling of the household head, and whether the household is headed by a female.

The instruments for child work include both schooling policy variables—the age at which first grade begins and the modal age at which compulsory schooling is designed to end. The child's age also interacts with the policy variables. Because the individual-level observations do not vary across the policy-level variables, heteroskedasticity has been controlled for by estimating Huber-White standard errors.

After controlling for other family characteristics as well as country dummies, children who work are significantly less likely to attend school than their peers. Reducing the probability of working by 10% results in an increase in the probability of attending school by 7%. Child labor also has a cost in terms of lost attained schooling. The fourth and fifth columns of table 2.8 present a two-stage least squares regression in which the dependent variable is at least two years behind the appropriate grade for age in school. Controlling for endogeneity, children who work are significantly more likely to lag in school than their peers. Reducing the probability of working by 10% reduces the probability of lagging behind in school by

**Table 2.8**  Effect of child work on school outcomes for children aged 10–16 from 17 countries in Latin America

| | School Attendance | | Lagging in School | |
|---|---|---|---|---|
| | Coef. | Std. Err. | Coef. | Std. Err. |
| Constant | 1.291* | 0.051 | 0.704* | 0.06 |
| Child Work (instrumented)[a] | −0.733** | 0.351 | 1.231* | 0.21 |
| Child's Age | −0.017** | 0.008 | 0.008 | 0.007 |
| Female Child | −0.061*** | 0.032 | 0.061** | 0.028 |
| Rural | 0.014 | 0.017 | −0.024 | 0.048 |
| Children < age 6 | −0.023* | 0.007 | 0.017* | 0.005 |
| Household Size | 0.002 | 0.002 | 0.011* | 0.002 |
| Household Head Age | 0.001 | 0 | −0.001** | 0 |
| Household Head Female | −0.01** | 0.005 | 0.025*** | 0.014 |
| Household Head Schooling | 0.006* | 0.002 | −0.012* | 0.002 |
| 15 Country Dummies | included (not shown) | | included (not shown) | |
| No. Observations | 186,735 | | 186,753 | |
| No. Countries | 16 | | 16 | |
| Adj R-sq.[b] | 0.169 | | 0.188 | |

*Notes:*

[a]Instruments include: the schooling policy variables (age at which first grade begins and model age at which compulsory schooling ends); the child's age, sex, region of residence (urban or rural); and the age, sex, and schooling of the household head. The child's age is also interacted with the policy variables.

[b]Does not include share explained by country dummies.

*Significant at .01 level.

**Significant at .05 level.

***Significant at .10 level.

12%. Therefore, it appears that child labor is not only a symptom of unobserved stresses on the family but a direct negative influence on schooling outcomes.

## Policy Implications

In some Latin American countries, household income does not have a strong effect on child labor because as incomes rise, child labor becomes less sensitive to further increases in income. Thus, it is doubtful that child labor can be eliminated solely by increases in income. Policies may need to address other factors that influence the incidence of child labor, particularly the strength of demand for child workers.

Two findings from the empirical work merit additional emphasis. Past research has not been able to answer whether child labor just discourages enrollment or if child labor discourages both enrollment and school attainment. This distinction is important because the policy tools needed for increasing enrollment (say, by increasing access to schools) are different from those that improve school attainment (say, by increasing enforcement of truancy laws or improving school quality). The findings clearly indicate that child labor reduces both school enrollment and educational attainment in Latin America. Factors that raise the probability of child labor consistently lower school enrollment and grade-for-age. Furthermore, exogenous increases in child labor lower school attendance and increase the probability of lagging behind grade level. Thus, policy efforts geared toward increasing enrollment are not enough. Policy makers in Latin America need to explore how children can be induced to attend school more regularly, as well.

The findings demonstrate that choices regarding child labor and education are intimately related with each other and with household attributes. These choices are particularly sensitive to factors affecting the child's market opportunities and the household's income level. Policies that do not affect both household income and the value of a child's time in school relative to work may fail to address the problem.

Interventions that address child labor and low educational attainment such as the new breed of targeted conditional transfer programs for human development (such as Oportunidades in Mexico and Bolsa Familia in Brazil) may offer the right solution. First, these programs target poor families with children. Second, they make cash transfers to the beneficiaries on the condition that their children regularly attend school, raising the returns of child time in school relative to the values of child time in the labor force. Although these programs do not explicitly require or monitor a reduction in child labor, their critical design feature (i.e., children attend school a minimum number of days) is likely to be effective in both lowering child labor and increasing school attendance. These conjectures are tested formally in chapters 8 through 11 of this book.

## Notes

We thank Masaru Sasaki for assistance in compiling the data and conducting the analysis.

1. The timing of the decline in child-labor rates corresponds to implementation of PROGRESA, a targeted transfer program designed to combat child labor. See chapter 10 for a detailed evaluation of the PROGRESA program. Similarly, decreases in child-labor rates after 1994 in Brazil correspond to the initiation of the Bolsa Escola and PETI programs evaluated in chapters 8 and 9.
2. The classification of countries into low, lower-middle, and upper-middle categories is based on 1997 GNP per capita figures reported in the *World Development Report 1998–99*.
3. In table 2.1, the incidence of child labor is higher than the ILO estimates used in chapter 1. The difference is that the ILO only reports full-time work, while the survey data reports full- and part-time work.
4. Evidence supporting that conjecture has been found by Akabayashi and Psacharopoulos (1999).
5. The actual rate for Ecuador is higher than that reported in table 2.4 because lag rates could not be estimated for Ecuadorian children over age 12.
6. Psacharopoulos' (1997) analysis of data from Chile and Peru found that early entry into the labor market led to two fewer years of schooling completed.

7. The inclusion of the head's highest educational attainment in the regression is an excellent proxy for the permanent income of the household; thus, the income decile can be regarded as capturing more transitory spells or unpredicted income deviations.

8. The one exception is that in Peru, household size has a negative and significant effect on child labor but a positive and significant effect on falling behind in school.

# III

# Behavioral Inferences

# The Responses of Child Labor, School Enrollment, and Grade Repetition to the Loss of Parental Earnings in Brazil, 1982–1999

*Marcelo Côrtes Neri, Emily Gustafsson-Wright,*
*Guilherme Sedlacek, and Peter F. Orazem*

Results in chapter 2 suggest that in Latin America, poverty and child labor are positively linked at least in some countries, and that poverty and educational attainment are more consistently negatively linked across all countries.[1] Most of the research that has documented these links has concentrated on the impact of persistent poverty on child labor and time in school. Less understood is whether transitory shocks to household income also affect decisions regarding child time allocations. If poor households can absorb income shocks by borrowing against future income, then short-term income loss from unemployment, illness, or injury to adults in the household should not affect the schooling or work decisions of the children in the home. However, if poor households face constraints on borrowing because they lack collateral or other means of demonstrating ability to repay, then child work time may be used to substitute for lost adult work time. Even temporary exits from school can lead to permanent loss of human capital if school success is predicated on continuous participation.

Jacoby and Skoufias (1997; 1998) link incompleteness in financial markets to lower human capital accumulation in a study examining the response of children's school attendance to seasonal fluctuations in the income of agrarian households in rural India. They find that children's time is used as a buffer or a form of self-insurance for unforeseen income losses. Flug et al. (1998) found that areas without financial markets had lower secondary enrollment rates. Duryea (1998) found that in Brazil, when the father in a household becomes unemployed, his children are 4% less likely to advance in grade. Parker and Skoufias (2006) found that increased unemployment rates significantly increased the probability of child dropout.

Beegle et al. (2006) and Edmonds et al. (2005) find consistent results that income shocks are negatively correlated with child labor in Tanzania and South Africa, respectively.

This study examines how the loss of earnings by the head of a household in Brazil affects how his children spend their time in school and work. The study opens with a simple theoretical explanation of how income shocks may lead to socially inefficient school dropout and labor market entry by children in credit-constrained households. The theory is used to motivate an analysis of one-year transition rates from school to work and from school to no school. An analysis of non-promotion rates also is motivated by the theory.

The empirical model allows the impact of the earnings shock to differ by household income status before the earnings loss occurred. Children's time allocation in higher-income households was largely unaffected by the loss of earnings by the head. However, children in the poorest households were more likely to drop out, enter the labor force, and repeat the same grade in school. Because children who lag behind age-appropriate grade level are more likely to drop out or enter the labor market in the future, even those children whose education plans are not immediately altered may be permanently affected by the adverse consequences of the income shock on their chance for grade promotion.

These results are consistent with the presumption that the poorest households are credit-constrained, so children in those households will be more vulnerable to short-term fluctuations in household income due to parental job loss. Consequently, social insurance that provides a safety net against adverse income shocks to the poorest households may help to prevent premature and socially inefficient labor market entry or school dropout by children in the poorest households.

## Theory

The possible impact of household income shocks on child time in school or at work can be illustrated with a simple three-period variant of the Ben-Porath (1967) model. In the first stage, the child attends school full time, so attendance, $A = 1$. In stage 2, $0 < A < 1$, meaning the child divides time between school and work. In the third stage, the child specializes in working, setting $A = 0$.

To show how the length of stage 1 or stage 2 varies with shocks for income, it is assumed that there are positive but diminishing returns to school attendance so the amount of additional marketable skill developed per year of schooling decreases as years of schooling increase. Total marketable skill at any point in time is given by the wage the child can claim, $W(H_t)$.

Between any two periods, $t = 0$ and $t = 1$, the decision of whether to attend school will reflect the relative returns to schooling versus working. Let $r =$ the interest rate. If the child attends school so $A > 0$, he will earn $(1-A)\ W(H_0)$ in the current period and his value of time will be $W(H_1) = W(H(H_0, A))$, where human capital production depends positively on past human capital accumulation and attendance. If the child does not attend school, $A = 0$ and the child's value of time in both periods is $W(H_0)$.

The child will attend school if

$$(1 - A)W(H_0) + \frac{W(H_1)}{1 + r} \geqq W(H_0) + \frac{W(H_0)}{1 + r}$$

or

$$-AW(H_0) + \frac{W(H_1) - W(H_0)}{1 + r} \geqq 0 \tag{3.1}$$

Condition (3.1) says the child should attend if the present value of the wage increase attributable to schooling exceeds the cost of child time in school. If condition (3.1) holds with inequality, $A$ will be set equal to 1 and the child will spend the period in stage 1. If the condition holds with equality, optimal attendance will be in stage 2, where $0 < A < 1$. If the condition is violated, then the child will be in stage 3, where $A = 0$.

Because returns to human capital are positive but diminishing as the level of human capital increases, the first term on the left-hand side of (3.1) grows progressively larger in magnitude and the second term on the left-hand side becomes progressively smaller as the child ages. Consequently, the child's schooling pattern will go from full-time to part-time to leaving school, as illustrated in figure 3.1.

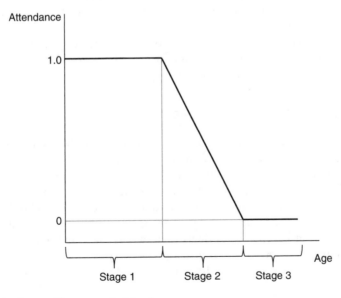

**Figure 3.1**   Stages of Investment in School

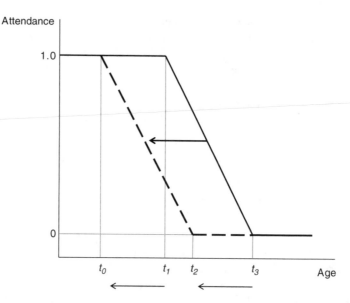

**Figure 3.2**   The Impact of Adverse Income Shocks or Child Wage Increases on Investment in School

Income shocks will alter condition (3.1) for two reasons. First, income may make schooling more productive so that $W(H_1)-W(H_0)$ rises with income. Second, the interest rate is a decreasing function of income if the poor are credit-constrained. As a consequence, the second term on the left-hand side of (3.1) decreases if the household suffers an adverse income shock, as illustrated in figure 3.2. A negative income shock shifts the attendance schedule to the left, causing children aged $t_0$ to $t_1$, who would otherwise attend school full-time, to enter the labor market. The shock also would induce children aged $t_2$ to $t_3$, who would otherwise attend part-time, to drop out of school. A large enough income shock could cause children in stage 1 to move all the way to stage 3.

## Data and Empirical Strategies

The data for this study are taken from the Pesquisa Mensal de Emprego (PME), a monthly employment survey conducted by the Brazilian census bureau. The survey concentrates on the six metropolitan areas of Brazil: Belo Horizonte, Porto Alegre, Recife, Rio de Janeiro, Salvador, and São Paulo. It elicits information from randomly selected households once a month for four consecutive months, drops them out of the sample for the next eight months, then interviews them again for four final months. The samples include about 5,000 households per city per month.

The PME is beneficial for this study because it tracks employment and income characteristics of parents and their children aged 10 or older, allowing us to follow an individual child's enrollment, educational progress, and labor supply behavior over sixteen months. It also allows us to measure the relationship between decisions regarding child time use and the parents' employment and earnings history.

This study uses data from February 1982 through February 1999. The sample is restricted to households with two parents and at least one child between 10 and 15 years of age. In the case of multiple children in that age range, the concentration is on the oldest child. The data set is further restricted to those households that completed all eight interviews. The concentration on two-parent households is to ensure that there are members of the household other than the child who could potentially alter labor supply behavior to smooth the household's income stream, were the head to lose labor earnings. To the extent that single-parent households would be even more vulnerable to income shocks because of the lack of other potential adult workers, the results understate the use of child labor as an income-smoothing mechanism.

### Endogenous Variables

This study uses three transition indicators. Conditional on a child being in stage 1 at the end of the fourth month, the first indicator evaluates whether or not the child has dropped out of school twelve months later. In effect, this represents a transition from stage 1 to stage 3. The second measure, also conditional on stage 1 status in the fourth month, indicates whether the child has started working twelve months later. This represents a transition from stage 1 to either stage 2 or stage 3. The final measure is conditional upon status in stage 2, meaning that the child is both in school and working in the fourth month. The indicator is whether or not the child has been promoted to the next grade.

In figure 3.2, an adverse income shock could induce the child to attend less while still enrolled. Although the PME does not include an attendance measure, an increased probability of failure to advance to the next grade should correspond to a decline in intensity of investment in school.

### Empirical Strategies

The theory suggests that unforeseen income shocks will increase the probability that a child will move out of schooling and into child labor. This suggests conditioning a sample of children on status in schooling-stage 1 or schooling-stage 2 and then examining how an income shock to the household affects the transition probability into another stage.

Formally, let $S_{1t}$ indicate that a child's schooling stage is 1 in period t, meaning that the child is in school and does not work; $U_{t+1}^H$ is a dummy variable that takes the value of 1 if the household head loses his job in period $t + 1$. The child's schooling stage at a later date is observed and denoted $S_{i, t+2}$, where $I = 1, 2, 3$. Guided by condition (3.1), the probability that a child leaves stage 1 is given by

$$P(S_{i \neq 1, t+2}/S_{1t}) = F(\alpha + \beta_U U_{t+1}^H + \gamma_C^W W^C(H_t)$$
$$+ \gamma_C^{dW} dW^C(H_t) + \gamma_A^W W_t^A + \delta Z_t) \qquad (3.2)$$

where F is the cumulative logistic distribution, $\alpha$, $\beta_U$, $\gamma_C^W$, $\gamma_C^{dW}$, $\gamma_A^W$ and $\delta$ are estimable parameters, $W^C(H_t)$ is an indicator of the market value of child time, given human capital accumulated to time t, $W_t^A$ is a vector of indicators of the market value of adult time, $dW^C(H_t)$ is the expected change in wage from another year of schooling, and $Z_t$ is a vector of time and region dummy variables. The prediction from the theory is that an income shock to the household will hasten the child's exit from stage 1 so that $\beta_U > 0$. Factors that raise the market opportunities for the child would also hasten the exit from school so that $\gamma_C^W > 0$, while factors that increase returns to schooling would slow exits. Increases in adult income would lower the probability of exiting stage 1, because the productivity of child time in school is enhanced and/or the parents face a lower discount rate on future earnings.

The ability of the household to self-insure against income shocks should be related to the household's income status before the shock occurred. This suggests that the impact of an income shock would be the most severe in the poorest households. That hypothesis can be tested by interacting $U_{t+1}^H$ with indicators of prior household income. Letting $Y_{jt}$ be a dummy variable indicating household income is in the $j^{th}$ quintile in the period before the shock, the interaction terms $\sum_{j=1}^{4} \beta_{Uj} Y_{jt} U_{t+1}^H$ are inserted into (3.2). If prior household income helps to absorb income shocks, then $\beta_{Uj}$ should fall in magnitude as prior income quintile rises.

### Market Opportunities for Children

The child's opportunity cost of spending time in school will be the value of a child's time in production activities inside or outside the home. While some children work for pay, the vast majority of child laborers work for no pay. Consequently, the value of child time is approximated by inserting proxy measures for the elements of $H_t$. In particular, it is assumed that

$$W^C(H_t) = \sum_{i=10}^{14} W_i^A AGE_{it} + W^M MALE$$

where $AGE_{it}$ is a series of dummy variables and will take the value of 1 if the child is age i and time t and zero otherwise, and MALE is a dummy variable indicating the child is a boy. The child's opportunity cost of schooling is expected to rise with age and boys are expected to claim a wage premium over girls. Children who are lagging behind in school face a slower increase in human capital per year in school, implying a smaller value of $dW^C(H_t)$.

## Market Opportunities for Parents

A parent may provide a potential source of substitute labor for an unemployed spouse, whether or not the parent currently works. Consequently, the relevant measure of adult income should reflect the human capital that the adults could supply to the market. For that reason, the adult earnings potential is represented by a sequence of dummy variables indicating education levels for the mother and father.

A measure of the relative income status of the household also is included. There is a concern that household income measures are subject to measurement error and endogeneity with respect to labor supply choices (Deaton, 1997). The measurement error problem is limited by using quintile income groupings, so modest errors will not move households into another quintile. In addition, the sample is restricted to households in which the head had positive labor earnings in the fourth month (for reasons that will become apparent) and the quintile placement is based solely on earnings of the head. Consequently, the potentially endogenous variation in labor supply behavior of the head is restricted.

The sample is conditional on positive labor earnings by the head because of the need to define an income shock to the household. The strategy is to define the shock by the absence of labor earnings of the head in the last month observed. Consequently, at some time in the previous twelve months, the household head lost his source of labor earnings, and that situation persisted through the last period of observation.[2] Note that this should give the household plenty of time to absorb the income shock, either by substituting other adult household member labor earnings to replace the lost earnings of the head, by sale of assets, or by other income-smoothing measures. Therefore, we may understate the adverse consequences of the income shock for child work or schooling if those responses have all occurred within the previous eight-month period when we do not observe how the child's time is allocated. On the other hand, if the adverse consequences of the income shock persist after this time, we can presume that the effects are not fleeting but will have a permanent effect on the child's employment and schooling patterns.

The remaining measures control for systematic variation in labor demand across time and labor markets. A series of seasonal, municipal, and year dummy variables represent demand shifts that are common across workers. These dummies control for shifts in household income that are predictable due to known seasonal, local, or trend factors.

# Results

Table 3.1 presents sample statistics for various indicators of the use of child time for all children aged 10 to 15. In these urban areas, 6.7% of the children were not in school. The proportion out of school is modestly larger for boys than girls; however, boys are more than twice as likely to be in the labor force than girls. The majority of the boys who enter the labor market remain in school, but their academic progress may suffer. Boys are more likely than girls to lag behind grade level. Nevertheless, the proportions lagging behind are very high for both boys and girls at 65% and 55%, respectively.

Table 3.2 presents transition rates for children over the sample period. Although boys and girls are equally likely to leave school at 0.5% per year, boys are more than twice as likely to start working and to start working while staying in school. It is interesting that the transition into stage 3 out of school is only slightly less likely from stage 1 than stage 2.

## Transition out of School

Table 3.3 presents estimates of transition probabilities from stage 1 to stage 3. The model is estimated using a logistic model. The coefficients and

**Table 3.1** Static indicators of school performance and child labor (children between 10 and 15 years of age)

|  | Total | | Boys | | Girls | |
|---|---|---|---|---|---|---|
|  | Prob. % | Standard Error | Prob. % | Standard Error | Prob. % | Standard Error |
| Not in school | 6.69 | 0.020 | 6.98 | 0.03 | 6.380 | 0.03 |
| Working | 8.07 | 0.013 | 11.03 | 0.03 | 5.009 | 0.02 |
| Working and in school | 5.38 | 0.018 | 7.60 | 0.03 | 3.083 | 0.02 |
| Behind age-years of schooling schedule | 60.11 | 0.038 | 64.69 | 0.05 | 55.371 | 0.06 |
| Number of observations | 2,466,675 | | 1,240,354 | | 1,226,321 | |

*Source:* Authors summary of data from the *Pesquisa Mensal de Emprego* (PME) 1982/1999. Elaboration: CPS/FGV.

**Table 3.2** Dynamic indicators of school performance and child labor (children between 10 and 15 years of age)

|  | Total | | Boys | | Girls | |
|---|---|---|---|---|---|---|
|  | Prob. % | Standard Error | Prob. % | Standard Error | Prob. % | Standard Error |
| *Probability of:* |  |  |  |  |  |  |
| Start working (1→2 or 3)[a] | 2.66 | 0.01 | 3.66 | 0.02 | 1.70 | 0.01 |
| Leave school given that does not work (1→3) | 0.44 | 0.005 | 0.43 | 0.01 | 0.45 | 0.01 |
| Leave school (1 or 2→3) | 0.49 | 0.005 | 0.51 | 0.01 | 0.48 | 0.01 |
| Start working given that attends school (1→2) | 2.18 | 0.01 | 3.05 | 0.02 | 1.33 | 0.01 |
| Number of observations | 2,466,675 | | 1,240,354 | | 1,226,321 | |

*Note:*

[a]Numbers in parentheses reflect transition from and to education stages.

**Table 3.3** Logistic estimation of the probability a child leaves school
Condition: In month 4, child is in stage 1 (attending school and not working) and head has positive earnings.

| | Estimate | t-statistic | Odds Ratios |
|---|---|---|---|
| *Male* (reference = female) | 0.04 | 0.88 | 1.04 |
| *Child's Age* (reference = 15) | | | |
| 10 years | −2.30** | −15.96 | 0.10 |
| 11 years | −1.88** | −16.48 | 0.15 |
| 12 years | −1.26** | −14.93 | 0.28 |
| 13 years | −0.65** | −9.70 | 0.52 |
| 14 years | −0.28** | −4.72 | 0.76 |
| 15 years | 0.00 | — | 1.00 |
| *Child Lags* | 1.15** | 14.84 | 3.17 |
| *Father's Education* (reference = 4–7 years) | | | |
| 0 years | 0.38** | 5.36 | 1.46 |
| 1–3 years | 0.29** | 4.87 | 1.33 |
| 4–7 years | 0.00 | — | 1.00 |
| 8–11 years | −0.32** | −3.61 | 0.73 |
| 12–15 years | −1.06** | −3.48 | 0.35 |
| 16+ years | −1.00** | −2.36 | 0.37 |
| *Mother's Education* (reference = 4–7 years) | | | |
| 0 years | 0.58** | 8.72 | 1.78 |
| 1–3 years | 0.27** | 4.45 | 1.31 |
| 4–7 years | 0.00 | — | 1.00 |
| 8–11 years | −0.56** | −5.45 | 0.57 |
| 12–15 years | −1.58** | −3.42 | 0.21 |
| 16 or more years | −18.24 | −0.00 | 0.00 |
| *Father's Earnings Quintiles* (reference = Quintile V) | | | |
| Quintile I | 0.75** | 5.21 | 2.11 |
| Quintile II | 0.64** | 6.41 | 1.89 |
| Quintile III | 0.57** | 6.22 | 1.77 |
| Quintile IV | 0.31** | 3.43 | 1.37 |
| Quintile V | 0.00 | — | 1.00 |
| *Income Shock*[a] | | | |
| $U^H$ (reference = Quintile V and $U^H = 0$) | −0.01 | −0.05 | 0.99 |
| Interactions (reference = Quintile V, $U^H = 1$)[b] | | | |
| Quintiles I*$U^H$ | 0.38 | 1.02 | 1.46 [1.43] |
| Quintiles II*$U^H$ | 0.22 | 0.69 | 1.24 [1.22] |
| Quintiles III*$U^H$ | 0.27 | 0.87 | 1.31 [1.30] |
| Quintiles IV*$U^H$ | 0.17 | 0.50 | 1.19 [1.16] |

Number of Observations: 56,080
Log Likelihood: −7290

*Notes:*
*Significance at the .10 level.
**Significance at the .05 level.
Regression also includes dummy variables for month, year, and metropolitan area.
[a]Joint test of $U^H$ and its interaction terms with quintile dummies is significant at the .05 level.
[b]Odds ratios in brackets in the last column are relative to the same earnings quintile with $U^H = 0$.

associated t-statistics are reported, but the odds ratios are the most directly interpretable magnitudes. Odds ratios greater than 1.0 indicate a greater likelihood of the outcome relative to the stated reference group.

Boys are 4% more likely to drop out than girls, but the difference is not significant. As the child ages, the probability of dropout rises monotonically. A 15-year-old is ten times more likely to leave school than a 10-year-old. Children who lag behind their expected grade for age are three times more likely to leave school than are children who make normal progress.

For both mothers and fathers, increasing parental education lowers the probability of exit. Children of fathers who never attended school are four times more likely to drop out than are children of college-educated fathers. The differences in school exit probability are even more sensitive to mothers' education levels.

As the level of the household head's earnings prior to the shock rises, the probability that the child leaves school falls. Relative to households in the upper earnings quartile, children in the lowest quintile are 2.1 times more likely to drop out.

The adverse earnings shock adds to the negative effect of low income on child dropout. The average effect across income quintiles implies that households in which the head loses earnings potential, even for a short time, are 24% more likely to have children leave school relative to households with similar incomes but a stable earnings stream. The joint test of significance of the five terms including $U^H$ easily rejects the null hypothesis of no effect.

The negative effect of adverse income shocks on child schooling appears to be related to credit constraints. As prior income level rises, the adverse effect of the income shock decreases. The reported odds ratios are relative to the added adverse effect of the income shock on households in the top income quintile. Income shocks in the top quintile have virtually no effect on child schooling. In contrast, an income shock for households in the lowest income quintile has a 46% larger effect on the probability of child dropout.

It is more interesting to convert the estimates so that the odds ratios are relative to households in the same income group that did not experience an income shock. Those estimates are reported in the last column of table 3.3. The results are revealing. In the lowest income quintile, an adverse earnings shock raises the probability of dropout by 43%. At the next three higher income quintiles, the adverse shock also increases the probability of drop out, but by smaller proportions.

### Labor Market Entry

Table 3.4 replicates the exercise for the probability that the child enters the labor market. This represents a move from stage 1 to stage 2 or stage 3. The results are similar to those in table 3.3: probability of labor market entry is 64% higher for boys than girls, rises with child age monotonically, and is higher for children who are lagging behind. More educated parents

**Table 3.4**  Logistic estimation of the probability a child enters the labor market
Condition: In month 4, child is in stage 1 (attending school and not working) and head has
positive earnings.

| | Estimate | t-statistic | Odds Ratios |
|---|---|---|---|
| *Male* (reference = female) | 0.49** | 15.35 | 1.64 |
| *Child's Age* (reference = 15) | | | |
| 10 years | −2.90** | −29.09 | 0.05 |
| 11 years | −2.41** | −30.73 | 0.09 |
| 12 years | −1.78** | −29.85 | 0.17 |
| 13 years | −0.91** | −20.37 | 0.40 |
| 14 years | −0.41** | −10.47 | 0.66 |
| 15 years | 0.00 | — | 1.00 |
| *Child Lags* | 0.22** | 5.57 | 1.24 |
| *Father's Education* (reference = 4–7 years) | | | |
| 0 years | 0.31** | 5.85 | 1.37 |
| 1–3 years | 0.22** | 5.13 | 1.24 |
| 4–7 years | 0.00 | — | 1.00 |
| 8–11 years | −0.26** | −5.22 | 0.77 |
| 12–15 years | −0.70** | −5.88 | 0.49 |
| 16+ years | −1.23** | −5.99 | 0.32 |
| *Mother's Education* (reference = 4–7 years) | | | |
| 0 years | 0.35** | 6.99 | 1.42 |
| 1–3 years | 0.19** | 4.62 | 1.21 |
| 4–7 years | 0.00 | — | 1.00 |
| 8–11 years | −0.37** | −6.81 | 0.69 |
| 12–15 years | −1.13** | −6.77 | 0.32 |
| 16 or more years | −1.99** | −3.39 | 0.14 |
| *Father's Earnings Quintiles* (reference = Quintile V) | | | |
| Quintile I | 0.49** | 5.13 | 1.63 |
| Quintile II | 0.40** | 6.51 | 1.50 |
| Quintile III | 0.38** | 6.88 | 1.47 |
| Quintile IV | 0.24** | 4.46 | 1.27 |
| Quintile V | 0.00 | — | 1.00 |
| *Income Shock*[a] | | | |
| $U^H$ (reference = Quintile V and $U^H = 0$) | −0.29* | −1.66 | 0.75 |
| *Interactions* (reference = Quintile V, $U^H = 1$)[b] | | | |
| Quintiles I*$U^H$ | 0.50** | 2.02 | 1.65 [1.23] |
| Quintiles II*$U^H$ | 0.28 | 1.41 | 1.33 [1.00] |
| Quintiles III*$U^H$ | 0.42** | 2.06 | 1.52 [1.14] |
| Quintiles IV*$U^H$ | 0.25 | 1.15 | 1.28 [0.96] |

Number of Observations: 56,080
Log Likelihood: −14087

*Notes:*
   *Significance at the .10 level.
   **Significance at the .05 level.
   Regression also includes dummy variables for month, year, and metropolitan area.
   [a]Joint test of $U^H$ and its interaction terms with quintile dummies is significant at the .05 level.
   [b]Odds ratios in brackets in the last column are relative to the same earnings quintile with $U^H = 0$.

are less likely to have their children work, and the probability of child labor market entry also drops monotonically as earnings quintile rises. All of these results are similar to the effects of these factors on school dropouts.

The joint test of the significance of the interaction terms between the income shock and prior household income quintile indicated no significant effect. However, there is support for the presumption that income shocks matter at the lower end of the income distribution where individual coefficients were statistically significant. Loss of earnings of the head increases the odds of a child entering the labor market by 33% to 65% in the lowest of three earnings quintiles relative to households in the top earnings quintile that experienced a loss of earnings from the head. Compared to other households at the same income quintile, a household in the lowest quintile experiencing an adverse earnings shock is 23% more likely to have its children enter the labor market.

### Non-promotion

Table 3.5 concentrates on children who are already in stage 2, in which they work while attending school. Non-promotion is taken as an indication of relatively little investment of time in school. Results suggest that boys are more likely to fail, as are children who already lag behind in school. There is no apparent relationship between non-promotion and child age, parental education, or household income.

The joint test of the null hypothesis that the income shock had equal effects across income quintiles was strongly rejected. Children in the lowest income quintile had significantly greater probability of non-promotion when their household experienced income loss of the head. At higher income quintiles, the adverse effect of the income shock on promotion disappears.

## Conclusions and Policy Considerations

This study confirms a strong positive correlation between household income status and the probabilities of labor market entry and school dropout. The finding suggests that income support programs can improve schooling outcomes for poor children. However, the study goes further to examine whether adverse shocks to a father's earnings causes a further increase in these probabilities. The answer depends on the poverty status of the household. Wealthier households appear able to self-insure against temporary income shocks caused by unemployment of the head. In those households, there is no evidence of changes in child time use in response to changes in parental labor market status. In the poorest households, however, loss of earnings by the household head increases the probability of dropout and labor market entry, and also increases the likelihood of non-promotion. This is consistent with the presumption that the poorest households may

**Table 3.5** Logistic estimation of the probability a child fails to advance to the next grade
Condition: In month 4, child is in stage 2 (attending school and working) and head has positive earnings

|  | Estimate | t-statistic | Odds Ratios |
|---|---|---|---|
| *Male* (reference = female) | 0.30** | 3.60 | 1.35 |
| *Child's Age* (reference = 15) | | | |
| 10 years | −0.56* | −1.84 | 0.57 |
| 11 years | −0.13 | −0.59 | 0.88 |
| 12 years | 0.23 | 1.50 | 1.25 |
| 13 years | −0.07 | −0.60 | 0.93 |
| 14 years | −0.04 | −0.50 | 0.96 |
| 15 years | 0.00 | — | 1.00 |
| *Child Lags* | 0.39** | 4.15 | 1.47 |
| *Father's Education* (reference = 4–7 years) | | | |
| 0 years | 0.11 | 0.10 | 1.12 |
| 1–3 years | 0.13 | 1.31 | 1.13 |
| 4–7 years | 0.00 | — | 1.00 |
| 8–11 years | −0.08 | −0.64 | 0.93 |
| 12–15 years | 0.27 | 0.89 | 1.31 |
| 16+ years | 0.10 | 0.22 | 1.11 |
| *Mother's Education* (reference = 4–7 years) | | | |
| 0 years | 0.02 | 0.21 | 1.02 |
| 1–3 years | 0.06 | 0.65 | 1.06 |
| 4–7 years | 0.00 | — | 1.00 |
| 8–11 years | −0.09 | −0.69 | 0.91 |
| 12–15 years | −0.40 | −0.10 | 0.67 |
| 16 or more years | −20.67 | −0.00 | 0.00 |
| *Father's Earnings Quintiles* (reference = Quintile V) | | | |
| Quintile I | −0.01 | −0.03 | 0.99 |
| Quintile II | 0.11 | 0.76 | 1.11 |
| Quintile III | 0.23* | 1.85 | 1.26 |
| Quintile IV | 0.04 | 0.30 | 1.04 |
| Quintile V | 0.00 | — | 1.00 |
| *Income Shock*[a] | | | |
| $U^H$ (reference = Quintile V and $U^H = 0$) | −0.98** | −2.15 | 0.37 |
| Interactions (reference = Quintile V, $U^H = 1$)[b] | | | |
| Quintiles I*$U^H$ | 1.24** | 2.09 | 3.47 [1.30] |
| Quintiles II*$U^H$ | 0.93* | 1.80 | 2.53 [0.95] |
| Quintiles III*$U^H$ | 0.76 | 1.49 | 2.14 [0.80] |
| Quintiles IV*$U^H$ | 0.74 | 1.35 | 2.09 [0.78] |

Number of Observations: 3,557
Log Likelihood: −2253

Notes:
*Significance at the .10 level.
**Significance at the .05 level.
Regression also includes dummy variables for month, year, and metropolitan area.
[a]Joint test of $U^H$ and its interaction terms with quintile dummies is significant at the .05 level.
[b]Odds ratios in brackets in the last column are relative to the same earnings quintile with $U^H = 0$.

be credit-constrained and will use child labor to smooth adverse income shocks.

There is some evidence that the adverse consequences of transitory income shocks have permanent adverse consequences for child schooling. The probability of dropout and labor market entry increases once a child begins to lag behind in school. Consequently, to the extent that loss of earnings of the head leads to non-promotion among children in the poorest households, there is a longer-term increased probability that the child will exit school at a young age and start working.

To the extent that child labor and school dropout are viewed as mechanisms by which poverty is transmitted across generations, these findings suggest that poor households may need some form of safety net to help them weather adverse income shocks in other ways than sending their children to work. Unemployment insurance schemes are already in place in Brazil, but they do not cover individuals who are displaced from informal activities, a large share of the workers in Brazil.

The dropout rate and labor market entry rate were highest for boys and older children, that is, those with the highest market opportunities outside school. It is likely that the problem of child labor cannot be combated by policies that target the poor for income support without also addressing labor market opportunities for children. This could be done by tying access to minimum income maintenance programs to school attendance, measures of school progress, or verifiable reductions in child labor. Whether by raising perceived returns to time in school or by lowering perceived returns from early labor market entry, such programs would slow the transition out of school and into work.

## Notes

1. For other studies see Grootaert and Patrinos (1999), Jensen and Nielsen (1997), Psacharopoulos (1997), and Tzannatos (2003), who found that low parental income leads to greater child labor. Barros and Lam (1996), Gomes-Neto and Hanushek (1994), Lam and Schoeni (1993), and Mello e Souza and Silva (1996) have found positive relationships between various measures of schooling outcomes and parents' income levels.
2. The study by Duryea et al. (2007) defines the shock in terms of reported unemployment rather than zero labor earnings. They find similar but smaller responses to the shock measure.

# Dynamics of Child Labor:
# Labor-Force Entry and Exit in Urban Brazil

*Jasper Hoek, Suzanne Duryea, David Lam, and Deborah Levison*

Relatively little is known about the dynamics of children's labor-force work, although child labor has been a subject of research and policy discussion since the days of Europe's Industrial Revolution (Edmonds, 2008). Small case studies from Latin America and elsewhere suggest that children tend to move in and out of different jobs, and in and out of the labor force, to a much greater extent than do adults. Still, policy discussions of child labor often seem to have an underlying unstated assumption that most children work long hours in jobs that, like those of adults, continue steadily from day-to-day and from week-to-week. Even if the jobs change, children are imagined to find other jobs immediately, because of the pressing needs generated by poverty. In this chapter, we report the results of an analysis of nearly twenty years of panel data for metropolitan Brazil, showing that employed children frequently stop work, then start working again—a phenomenon we call "intermittent employment." Children's tendency to work intermittently is reflected by differential employment levels, depending on the time interval used, and by monthly employment entry and exit rates. We use estimates of entry and exit rates and how they change over time to better understand the downward trend in employment levels that we document.

The intermittent nature of urban children's work patterns has implications for the optimal design of Brazilian programs intended to encourage families to keep children in school and out of the labor force. The most important of such programs are known as Bolsa Escola (or School Scholarship Program) and PETI (from Programa de Erradicação do Trabalho Infantil, or Program to Eradicate Child Labor) that have more recently been integrated into the Bolsa Familia conditional cash transfer program.[1] Starting in 1996, the Bolsa Escola program provided school scholarships to poor children in urban areas under the condition that the children attend school regularly. PETI, with the explicit aim of reducing hazardous child labor, also provided scholarships conditioned on school attendance; it was originally implemented in rural municipalities of Brazil with high rates of specific types of hazardous child labor.[2] Unfortunately since the panel data only covers metropolitan areas it cannot reflect whether the early years of the PETI program were successful. However, the analysis of the levels and transitions in the panel data can be useful, because the Brazilian government has since expanded a modified program to both urban and rural areas nationwide.

An understanding of children's employment transitions—their labor-force entries and exits—is critical to the appropriate formulation of policies aimed at reducing and regulating children's work. We set the stage by describing the data and the trends in child employment revealed for the 1980s and 1990s. Next, evidence regarding how often children move in and out of employment and how these entries and exits have changed over time is provided in both figures and tables. We conclude the chapter with a discussion about the implications of this evidence for policies and programs on children's work and schooling.

## Data

In their comprehensive review of the literature on child labor, Edmonds and Pavcnik (2005a; 2005b) note the frustrating state of data available to analyze key issues related to child labor. According to their assessment, the standard data collected by household surveys or special ILO surveys are incomplete in many aspects and leaves many questions unanswered about working and so-called "idle" children. The analysis in this chapter makes use of the Pesquisa Mensal de Emprego (PME), Brazil's monthly employment survey. The PME has been administered by the Brazilian statistical agency (the Instituto Brasileiro de Geografia e Estatística, IBGE) in its current format since February 1982 in Brazil's six largest cities— São Paulo, Rio de Janeiro, Belo Horizonte, Salvador, Recife, and Porto Alegre.[3] This survey is an exceptional resource for the study of urban labor markets in developing countries, distinguished by its panel structure, very large sample sizes, and over two decades of continuous fielding with minimal changes to the questionnaire.[4] The PME is similar in design to the United States Current Population Survey: households are interviewed once per month for four consecutive months, dropped from the survey for eight months, and then re-interviewed for four more months.[5] In each month, information is collected on labor-force status, education (completed and in-progress), household structure, and a host of details about labor-force activity for every member of the household ages 10 and over. About 35,000 households are interviewed each month, making possible an examination of labor market trends for fairly narrowly defined demographic groups.

While the PME's detail on employment trends over two decades is extremely valuable, an even more intriguing feature of the data is the ability to follow labor-force transitions of all individuals aged 10 and over. In this chapter, we make extensive use of this feature to examine patterns of entry into and exit from employment among 14-year-old boys and girls, at times disaggregating these groups even further by mother's education, which we use as a measure of socioeconomic status (SES). Despite the large samples of the PME, slicing up the data by city, month, age, sex, and SES can very quickly leave us with only a small number of observations—there are simply not many 14-year-old girls in the metropolitan area of Salvador observed making the transition between employment and non-employment in any given month. Where small samples become a problem, we aggregate across one or more of these dimensions, usually across time or cities (weighting by each city's population).

In the figures below, we include in our sample all children observed in any two consecutive calendar months. Due to the structure of the rotating panel, this is necessary for providing a complete picture of employment transitions over time. In the tables, however, some of the statistics we present are directed at understanding child employment patterns over a four-month period. For this we restrict the sample in the tables to children with non-missing data for the first four months of interviews. To make sure that this more select sample does not differ systematically from the previous one, we replicated all the numbers in the tables that do not require a four-month observation period using the sample used in the figures, with little appreciable difference in the results. For the analysis of children by socioeconomic status, we limit the sample further to those children who are sons, daughters, or other relatives of the head of the household. This is necessary because our proxy for socioeconomic status, mother's education, is not available for children unrelated to the household head; we are unable to link them to their families of origin. Finally, we note that sample attrition is not a major concern. Attrition involving children in the PME is discussed in detail in Levison et al. (2007) and Duryea et al. (2007). About 80% of children scheduled to be re-interviewed in one month's time are actually observed the following month, and there are few observable differences between the ones that return and the ones that do not.

## Trends in Child Employment Levels

In this analysis, we refer to children's employment status, not to their labor-force status. We classify all individuals as being either working or not working during the reference week of the survey. We do not distinguish between being unemployed (looking for work but not working) and being out of the labor force. We also ignore the large amount of non-labor-force work done by children, due to lack of data.[6] Table 4.1 presents employment rates by age and socioeconomic status for boys and girls during two three-year

**Table 4.1** Employment rates and employment transition rates for 10–12-, 13–14-, and 15–16-year-old boys and girls, 6 metropolitan areas, 1982–84 and 1996–8, Brazil PME

| | Boys 1982–84 | | | Boys 1996–98 | | |
|---|---|---|---|---|---|---|
| | 10–12 | 13–14 | 15–16 | 10–12 | 13–14 | 15–16 |
| Average percent employed | 4.8 | 16.9 | 40.3 | 1.4 | 6.5 | 23.3 |
| Low SES* | 7.1 | 22.7 | 47.3 | 2.3 | 10.1 | 30.1 |
| High SES* | 2.8 | 11.3 | 33.1 | 1.2 | 5.5 | 21.0 |
| Percent employed at least one month | 9.5 | 27.5 | 54.1 | 3.1 | 12.0 | 34.4 |
| Low SES* | 13.7 | 36.4 | 63.8 | 4.7 | 18.0 | 45.0 |
| High SES* | 5.9 | 19.0 | 44.2 | 2.7 | 10.3 | 30.8 |
| Percent employed all 4 months | 1.5 | 8.1 | 26.5 | 0.4 | 2.5 | 13.7 |
| Low SES* | 2.2 | 11.2 | 30.7 | 0.7 | 4.1 | 17.2 |
| High SES* | 0.9 | 5.0 | 22.1 | 0.3 | 2.1 | 12.5 |
| Entry Rate | 2.1 | 6.1 | 11.9 | 0.7 | 2.6 | 6.7 |
| Low SES* | 3.2 | 8.4 | 16.2 | 0.9 | 3.9 | 10.0 |
| High SES* | 1.3 | 4.1 | 8.5 | 0.6 | 2.2 | 5.7 |
| Exit Rate | 39.3 | 26.6 | 15.3 | 47.7 | 35.7 | 20.6 |
| Low SES* | 37.4 | 26.1 | 16.0 | 42.9 | 34.8 | 22.0 |
| High SES* | 43.6 | 27.5 | 14.3 | 50.4 | 36.1 | 20.0 |
| Sample Size | 21,865 | 14,196 | 13,970 | 14,893 | 10,913 | 11,310 |
| Low SES* | 10,259 | 6,893 | 6,874 | 3,534 | 2,670 | 2,966 |
| High SES* | 11,556 | 7,260 | 7,030 | 11,339 | 8,228 | 8,311 |

| | Girls 1982–84 | | | Girls 1996–98 | | |
|---|---|---|---|---|---|---|
| | 10–12 | 13–14 | 15–16 | 10–12 | 13–14 | 15–16 |
| Average percent employed | 2.1 | 9.5 | 23.5 | 0.6 | 3.3 | 12.4 |
| Low SES* | 3.0 | 12.9 | 30.8 | 0.9 | 4.5 | 14.1 |
| High SES* | 1.1 | 5.3 | 14.6 | 0.5 | 2.8 | 11.2 |
| Percent employed at least one month | 4.3 | 15.9 | 33.5 | 1.5 | 6.4 | 19.6 |
| Low SES* | 6.2 | 21.6 | 44.0 | 2.2 | 8.8 | 22.6 |
| High SES* | 2.3 | 9.4 | 22.1 | 1.2 | 5.5 | 17.9 |
| Percent employed all 4 months | 0.6 | 4.6 | 14.6 | 0.1 | 1.3 | 6.5 |
| Low SES* | 0.9 | 6.0 | 19.1 | 0.2 | 1.8 | 6.9 |
| High SES* | 0.3 | 2.2 | 8.3 | 0.1 | 1.1 | 5.8 |
| Entry Rate | 1.0 | 3.3 | 6.3 | 0.3 | 1.2 | 3.7 |
| Low SES* | 1.4 | 4.7 | 9.1 | 0.5 | 1.8 | 4.6 |
| High SES* | 0.5 | 1.9 | 4.2 | 0.3 | 1.0 | 3.3 |
| Exit Rate | 40.4 | 27.1 | 17.5 | 50.8 | 35.4 | 24.2 |
| Low SES* | 41.3 | 28.3 | 17.8 | 48.3 | 35.5 | 25.4 |
| High SES* | 43.5 | 30.0 | 19.7 | 52.0 | 36.8 | 24.6 |
| Sample Size | 21,420 | 14,037 | 14,150 | 14,591 | 10,684 | 11,283 |
| Low SES* | 10,064 | 6,754 | 6,486 | 3,429 | 2,605 | 2,806 |
| High SES* | 11,196 | 7,058 | 7,004 | 11,126 | 8,019 | 8,237 |

*Note:*

*Low SES refers to children whose mothers have less than 4 years of education; high SES refers to children whose mothers have at least 4 years of education. Neither group includes children who are not sons, daughters, or relatives of the household head; however, totals include all children in the household.

periods spanned by our data: 1982–84 and 1996–98. Data for boys are presented in the top panel, for girls in the bottom panel; data for the early period are presented in the first three columns, and for the later period in the last three columns.

In 1982–84, the employment rates for 10–12-year-olds are relatively low, with 2.1% of girls and 4.8% of boys working. Employment rates rise rapidly as age increases, with the proportion of boys rising to 16.9% at age 13–14 and to 40.3% at ages 15–16. Employment rates for males are typically about twice as high as employment rates for females. For 13–14-year-olds, employment rates are 16.9% for males and 9.5% for females.

It is likely that the PME underreports work done by children who tend to work short daily or weekly hours, as Levison (1991) found using Brazil's 1985 annual household survey data. While remunerated work is not subject to the fifteen-hour minimum of non-remunerated work to be measured in the survey, it may be that children who work few hours per week doing babysitting or occasional odd jobs are not being reported as working. The employment levels we present should therefore be viewed as describing a substantial level of work effort.

Table 4.1 includes separate estimates of employment levels for children from high and low socioeconomic status households. We use mothers' education level as a proxy for household socioeconomic status, dividing the sample into "lower-SES" and "higher-SES" groups.[7] The lower-SES group includes children whose mothers have completed fewer than four years of schooling, while the higher-SES group includes children whose mothers have completed four or more years of schooling.[8] Employment rates are approximately twice as high in the lower socioeconomic group as in the higher socioeconomic group for all age and gender groups, with the exception of the oldest group of boys.[9] As seen in table 4.1, 22.7% of boys ages 13–14 in the low-SES group are employed in the 1982–84 period, in comparison to 11.3% in the high-SES group. For girls in 1982–84, 12.9% are working in the low-SES group versus 5.3% in the high-SES group.

In the 1996–98 period, employment rates for the same groups of boys have fallen to 1.4%, 6.5% and 23.3% respectively. For all groups and time periods, boys have higher employment rates than girls, but rates for girls are also lower during this time period. The gaps between SES groups are smaller in the 1996–98 period. The employment rate for 13–14 year-old boys falls from 22.7% in 1982–84 to 10.1% in 1996–98 in the low-SES group and falls from 11.3% to 5.5% in the high-SES group.

The pace of declines in employment rates over the two decades can best be seen in figure 4.1, which shows employment levels for 14- and 16-year-old boys and girls for the entire period 1982–99. The figure shows that employment levels were relatively constant during the 1980s, with some evidence of increasing levels in the late 1980s. The figure clearly shows a substantial downward trend in employment levels for all groups beginning about 1990. It is clear that for all four age and gender groups shown, rapid

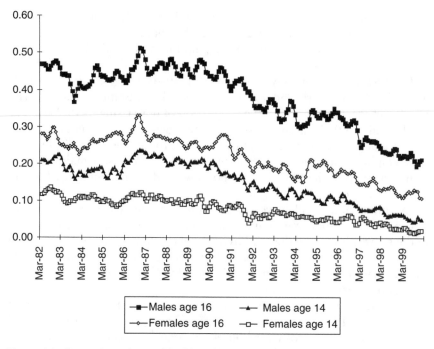

**Figure 4.1** Proportion of 14-Year-Old and 16-Year-Old Males and Females Employed, 6 Metropolitan Areas, 1982–99, Brazil, Three-Month Moving Averages

declines in employment were already underway in the early 1990s, well before the Bolsa Escola and PETI programs began.

While the PME definition of work is supposed to include children with even very low hours of work, most of the children who are reported as working are, in fact, working a substantial number of hours. Table 4.2 presents hours worked by employed children in 1982–84 and in 1996–98. Average hours worked by employed children exceed twenty-eight hours per week in all age groups. Moreover, the underlying month-by-month estimates of average hours worked show very little variation across months of the year. About 80% of the children who are employed are working over twenty hours per week. Even among 10–12-year-olds, work hours are high: in the early 1980s, 23% of employed boys and 39% of employed girls are working at least forty hours per week. By the late 1990s these percentages had shifted to 30% of employed boys and 26% of employed girls ages 10–12.

Figure 4.2 shows the trends over time in employment for 14-year-old boys and girls by socioeconomic status. The lines are remarkably parallel over time, suggesting that employment rates for both high- and low-SES children tend to move up and down together over time. Both groups show substantial declines in employment levels beginning around 1990. The absolute gap between SES groups declines over time, but the proportional

Table 4.2  Hours worked among employed 10–12-, 13–14-, and 15–16-year-old boys and girls, 6 metropolitan areas, 1982–84 and 1996–98, Brazil PME

| | Boys 1982–84 | | | Boys 1996–98 | | |
|---|---|---|---|---|---|---|
| | 10–12 | 13–14 | 15–16 | 10–12 | 13–14 | 15–16 |
| **Average hours worked** | **28.4** | **34.8** | **40.2** | **29.7** | **34.1** | **37.9** |
| Low SES* | 28.9 | 35.0 | 40.9 | 29.4 | 35.1 | 38.4 |
| High SES* | 27.4 | 34.4 | 39.2 | 29.9 | 33.6 | 37.7 |
| Children employed 1 month | 26.0 | 30.9 | 35.2 | 29.5 | 32.2 | 35.3 |
| Children employed 2 months | 29.8 | 33.8 | 37.7 | 28.4 | 33.9 | 36.7 |
| Children employed 3 months | 30.1 | 36.2 | 39.6 | 30.2 | 35.3 | 37.9 |
| Children employed 4 months | 31.2 | 38.7 | 42.9 | 32.5 | 37.0 | 40.1 |
| **Standard deviation of hours** | **14.6** | **14.5** | **12.4** | **12.1** | **11.7** | **9.6** |
| Low SES* | 14.7 | 14.7 | 12.8 | 11.6 | 10.9 | 9.3 |
| High SES* | 14.3 | 14.2 | 11.8 | 12.4 | 12.1 | 9.8 |
| **Percent working at least 20 hours** | **73.7** | **83.4** | **92.8** | **82.8** | **89.9** | **95.8** |
| Low SES* | 74.7 | 83.4 | 92.7 | 84.5 | 91.3 | 96.1 |
| High SES* | 71.6 | 83.3 | 93.1 | 82.0 | 89.2 | 95.6 |
| **Percent working at least 40 hours** | **23.1** | **43.8** | **62.3** | **29.7** | **42.6** | **58.5** |
| Low SES* | 23.5 | 45.2 | 63.9 | 27.3 | 46.6 | 60.2 |
| High SES* | 22.5 | 41.3 | 59.7 | 30.9 | 40.5 | 57.6 |

| | Girls 1982–84 | | | Girls 1996–98 | | |
|---|---|---|---|---|---|---|
| | 10–12 | 13–14 | 15–16 | 10–12 | 13–14 | 15–16 |
| **Average hours worked** | **33.3** | **40.9** | **42.7** | **28.8** | **34.2** | **36.3** |
| Low SES* | 34.8 | 43.0 | 44.7 | 31.6 | 36.6 | 38.8 |
| High SES* | 29.8 | 36.3 | 38.9 | 27.4 | 33.1 | 35.4 |
| Children employed 1 month | 31.5 | 38.1 | 38.7 | 28.5 | 32.2 | 35.1 |
| Children employed 2 months | 32.2 | 40.4 | 41.2 | 26.0 | 36.1 | 35.8 |
| Children employed 3 months | 38.0 | 41.7 | 43.3 | 30.2 | 35.0 | 35.9 |
| Children employed 4 months | 37.6 | 44.4 | 45.4 | 35.2 | 36.8 | 38.1 |
| **Standard deviation of hours** | **16.6** | **16.3** | **14.2** | **14.3** | **12.7** | **11.1** |
| Low SES* | 16.7 | 15.8 | 13.6 | 14.3 | 13.4 | 10.7 |
| High SES* | 15.7 | 16.5 | 14.6 | 14.1 | 12.2 | 11.1 |
| **Percent working at least 20 hours** | **79.9** | **89.3** | **92.6** | **76.7** | **88.4** | **92.6** |
| Low SES* | 82.6 | 91.4 | 94.5 | 87.0 | 90.5 | 94.0 |
| High SES* | 71.4 | 83.3 | 88.4 | 70.8 | 87.0 | 92.1 |
| **Percent working at least 40 hours** | **39.4** | **63.0** | **70.6** | **25.6** | **48.1** | **55.0** |
| Low SES* | 40.8 | 67.2 | 74.8 | 29.1 | 55.1 | 65.6 |
| High SES* | 30.9 | 50.3 | 60.5 | 22.1 | 43.4 | 49.5 |

Note:
    *See note to table 4.1.

differences remain relatively constant, with the low-SES group typically having employment rates roughly double those of the high-SES group. Employment rates for both groups of high- and low-SES status are generally under 10% by the end of the 1990s. For 14-year-old girls, the late 1990s are marked by a rapid decline in employment rates for the low-SES group.

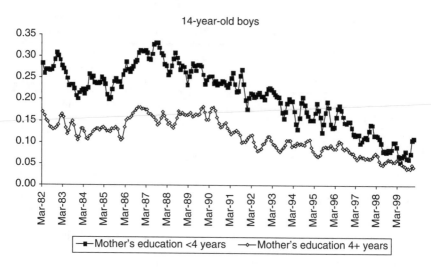

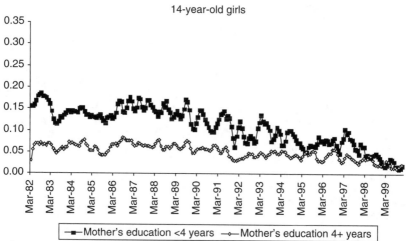

**Figure 4.2**   Proportion of 14-Year-Olds Employed, by Education of Mother, 6 Metropolitan Areas, 1982–99, Three-Month Moving Averages, Brazil PME

## Exit and Entry Rates

While the data presented above provide a good picture of the proportion of children working at any given point in time, they do not tell us anything about the movements of children in and out of employment. From a policy perspective it is important to know whether these employment levels represent a small group of children who work all the time or a larger group of children who rotate in and out of intermittent employment. For example, the 20% of 14-year-old boys working in most months in the early 1980s could represent the same 20% of boys working steadily or 100% of boys each working 20% of the time. The panel structure of the PME data makes it possible for us to analyze child labor transitions—the extent to which children move in and out of employment—and how these employment transitions vary by age, sex, and socioeconomic status and over time.

Table 4.1 includes estimates of monthly transitions in and out of employment. We cannot identify job changes from the PME data, so these measures do not capture transitions from one job to another, only transitions between the state of being employed and the state of being not employed. For each pair of sequential months, the PME data are used to calculate the proportion of children who change status from being employed one month to being non-employed in the following month. We define the exit rate for month $t$ as the number of children who change from employed in month $t$ to non-employed in month $t+1$, divided by the number of children who were employed in month $t$. The entry rate is defined analogously based on those who move from not employed in month $t$ to employed in month $t+1$. Table 4.1 shows that in 1982–84, 2.1% of 10–12-year-old boys who were not working in one month had started working by the following month. The entry rate for older boys was much higher: 6.1% for age 13–14 and 11.9% for age 15–16. The entry rates for boys with low-SES backgrounds were roughly twice as high as the entry rates for high-SES boys.

The exit rates in table 4.1 are much higher than the entry rates because the denominator (the employed population) is much smaller than in the case of entry (the not-employed population). In 1982–84, 39.3% of 10–12-year-old boys who were working in one month were not working in the following month. Exit rates were 26.6% for ages 13–14 and 15.3% for ages 15–16. The entry and exit rates in the 1996–98 period show substantial changes in both entry and exit rates over time. These trends can be seen in more detail in figure 4.3, which presents estimates of entry and exit rates for 14-year-olds for the entire period covered by our data, using three-month moving averages.[10] We focus on 14-year-olds because age 14 is traditionally usually defined by international conventions as the upper limit of childhood. Age 14 is the maximum age of eligibility for Bolsa Escola and PETI.[11]

Figure 4.3 shows that in the early 1980s the probability that a 14-year-old boy who is not working in month $t$ is working in month $t+1$ is around 8–10%. The entry rate for girls is about half as large, around 3–5%. The probability that a working boy leaves employment by the next month is around 25%, with fairly similar estimates for girls. The fact that a gender gap exists in entry rates but not in exit rates suggests that the level of employment observed for a single month is higher for boys because they are more likely to have a spell of employment, not because they have longer spells of employment. Figure 4.3 shows that entry rates fall substantially for both boys and girls over time, falling to levels in the late 1990s that are at least 50% lower than the levels of the early 1980s, with most of the decrease occurring in the 1990s. Exit rates increase over time, roughly doubling between 1982 and 1999.

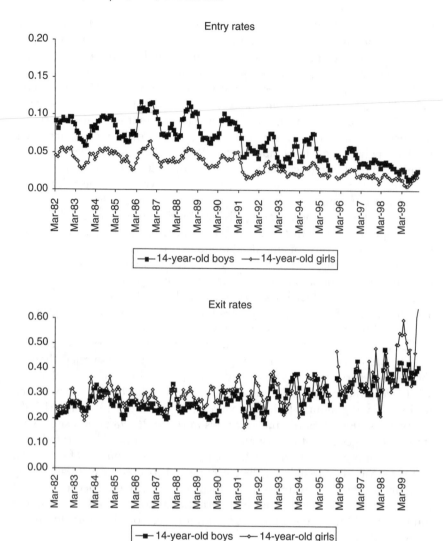

**Figure 4.3** Rates of Entry into and Exit from Employment, 14-Year-Old Boys and Girls, 6 Metropolitan Areas, 1982–99, Three-Month Moving Averages, Brazil PME

Figure 4.4 divides the sample of 14-year-old boys into the two socioeconomic groups defined according to whether the mother has at least four years of schooling. In the early 1980s, the entry rate for the low-SES group is about 12%, while the entry rate for the high-SES group is about 6%. The probability of leaving employment from one month to the next is approximately 25% for both SES groups. The gap in entry rates is falling over time, but as in the case of differences across gender, we see no systematic differences in the exit rates by SES status.

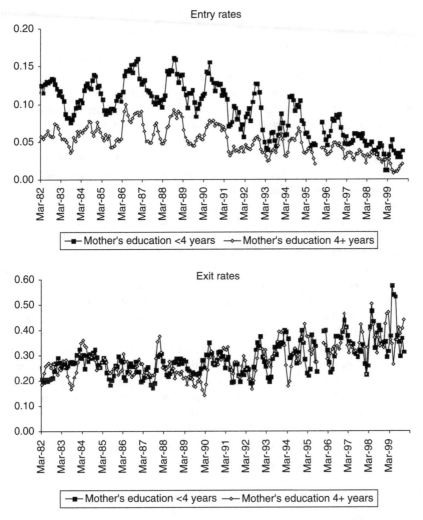

**Figure 4.4**    Rates of Entry into and Exit from Employment, 14-Year-Old Boys, by Mother's Education, 6 Metropolitan Areas, 1982–99, Three-Month Moving Averages, Brazil PME

## The Impact of Entry and Exit Rates on Employment Levels

Changes in child employment over time must be the result of underlying changes in children's propensities to enter employment and to leave employment, as well as how long they stay employed. Our data on transitions allow us to consider whether the downward trend in employment levels over time is driven by decreasing employment entry rates, by increasing employment exit rates, or by both. We can also consider the relative importance of entry rates and exit rates in explaining differences in the level of employment between males and females or between different cities. While our short four-month panels are not adequate for a complete understanding of employment duration, they allow us to infer the broad outlines of children's employment attachment from children's propensity to enter and exit employment.

It is interesting to consider, for example, whether the fact that girls' employment rates are roughly half those for boys, as noted in figure 4.1, is attributable more to differences in entry rates or differences in exit rates. Comparing the top and bottom panels of figure 4.3, it appears that the lower employment rates for girls are explained almost entirely by the fact that girls have entry rates that are half those for boys. Exit rates for males and females are almost identical throughout the 1980s and 1990s. Likewise, entry rates differ widely across socioeconomic status but exit rates are similar. For example, the entry rate for 15–16-year-old boys in 1982–84 is 16.2% for the low-SES group and 8.5% for the high-SES group. However the exit rates are similar at 16.0% and 14.3% respectively. The potential implications of these differences in entry and exit rates across groups will be shown to be important in the design of policies to lower rates of child labor.

Comparing the trends in entry and exit rates in figures 4.3 and 4.4 with the trends in employment rates in figures 4.1 and 4.2, it appears that the decline in employment rates resulted from both increases in exit rates and decreases in entry rates. Entry rates and exit rates fluctuate around a relatively constant trend line during the 1980s, with changes in the trend beginning around 1990. Entry rates fall by roughly 50% and exit rates roughly double from 1982 to 1999 for both males and females. These results may have important policy implications. In looking for the causes of the declining child labor rates in Brazil during the 1990s, it is clear that we should be looking both for factors that reduce the proportion of children who start working and for factors that increase the rate at which children leave employment. The high labor-force mobility rates we estimate mean that child labor in Brazil is not characterized predominantly by a small group of children who drop out of school and then work on a fairly permanent basis. Instead, children who work appear to move fairly rapidly in and out of employment. Previous work has shown that about two-thirds of Brazilian children who work are also reported as being in school, suggesting that work does not necessarily pull children permanently out of school (Levison et al., 2007). Child labor in Brazil appears to be characterized by a high degree of intermittent work, with substantial declines during the 1990s in the probability that children start working and increases in the probability that they move back out of employment once they begin an employment spell.

Although table 4.1 presents employment rates only for the combined sample of children from all 6 cities, there are interesting regional disparities, especially among older children. Levison et al. (2007) show that employment rates for 15–16-year-olds are about 50% higher in the higher-income cities of São Paulo and Porto Alegre than in the poor northeast city of Salvador. This suggests that demand-side effects of greater employment

opportunities may be more important than labor supply effects resulting from low income levels, and it is consistent with the argument of
Barros et al. (1996) that poverty alone cannot explain Brazil's high child
employment rates. Figure 4.5 explores this issue in more detail, showing
the entry and exit rates for 14 year-old boys in the cities of Salvador, São
Paulo, and Porto Alegre.

Comparing São Paulo with Salvador shows that entry rates for 14-year-
olds are fairly similar in the two cities. Exit rates, however, are considerably
higher in Salvador, rising to over 50% by the late 1990s. In other words,
only half of the children who are working in a given month in Salvador in

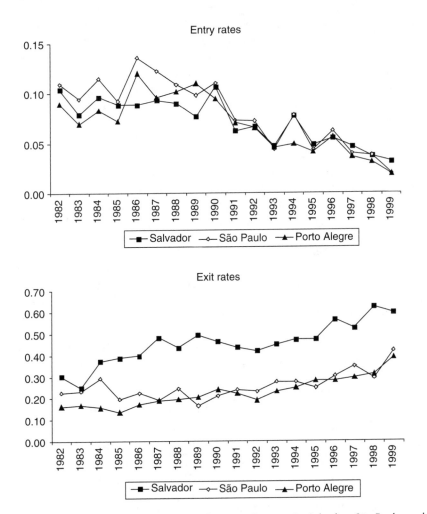

**Figure 4.5**  Rates of Entry into and Exit from Employment in Salvador, São Paulo, and
Porto Alegre, 14-Year-Old Boys, 1982–99, Yearly Averages, Brazil PME

the late 1990s are still working the following month. In São Paulo, the exit rates for both males and females are around 30% in the late 1990s, still a very high degree of labor-force mobility. These patterns suggest that children in São Paulo and Salvador are equally likely to enter employment, but children in Salvador leave their jobs more quickly. This contrasts sharply with the results by SES group and may be further evidence of labor demand effects, with Salvador offering fewer jobs that provide long-term employment for young workers. From a policy perspective it is important to note the high rate at which children leave jobs in Salvador, with only half of 14-year-olds continuing their jobs for more than one month at a time by the end of the 1990s. This may have both positive and negative policy implications. On the positive side, it suggests that labor-force attachment for most child workers is fairly weak, with rapid turnover that may make it easier to keep children from long-term employment activity. On the negative side, it suggests that simply getting children to stop working at one particular job may not have any lasting results. Children appear to move so rapidly in and out of work that programs that pull children out of current jobs may provide only temporary success.

## Undercounting Recent Workers

The high transition rates suggest that an employment survey taken at one particular time is not capturing one group of children who are consistently employed but instead a part of a changing population. In addition, the transition rates imply that the typical measure of an employment rate based on one reference week underestimates the share of children who have been recently employed. Table 4.1 presents three measures of employment: (1) the standard "average proportion employed" based on the activity during the reference week; (2) the "percent employed at least once" over the four reference weeks in a consecutive four month period; and (3) the "percent employed all four months." For example, in the early 1980s, the standard employment rate was 16.9% for 13–14 year old boys in the six cities. However the share of this population observed to be working over the four-month period was over 60% higher at 27.5%. For the two youngest age groups (10–12 and 13–14), approximately twice as many children are employed using the broader measure. In Levison et al. (2007) we examine this intermittency in greater detail and provide multipliers by age group and sex that summarize the difference between employment rates in a reference week vs. a longer reference period.[12] The third measure, "employed all four months," is the best proxy for measuring persistent employment. It is important to note that boys as well as children with lower socioeconomic status display much stronger attachment to the labor market. Approximately twice as many boys as girls are reported as employed all four months, and substantially higher percentages of children are reported as employed all four months among groups with lower socioeconomic status in table 4.1.

One might wonder if the children most likely to be missed in standard calculations, such as children working only one of the four months, are participating in trivial employment activities that can be overlooked because they are unlikely to conflict with school efforts and general well being. This does not appear to be the case. Table 4.2 reports average hours worked by number of months worked. While the average length of hours does increase with the number of months worked, in all groups the average hours worked per week was at least twenty-six, and in most cases more than thirty. In the latter period, among the 13–14 year olds, who were reported to have worked only one month, the average labor market time for girls and boys was thirty-two hours. The lack of a seasonal pattern in intermittency with respect to school vacations also implies that the undermeasurement of child work should be of concern to policymakers. The percentages of children employed for at least one month are qualitatively the same if the samples are restricted to months of the school year. For example, the share of 13–14-year-old boys who worked at least one month, restricting the sample to March-November, is 12.5% for the 1996–98 period; the share for the full sample is 12.0%. For girls, the share is 7.0% during March-November and 6.4% for the full period. The full set of tables in which the sample is restricted to the school year is an appendix table available from the authors on request. The undercounting of employment in standard calculations for Brazil is not driven by the omission of a few hours of work on the weekends or on summer vacations.

A potential weakness of the PME data is that measurement error may lead us to observe apparent movements in and out of employment that do not actually take place. For example, reports of children's employment may change from month to month due to a change in the respondent answering the questions, even if there is no actual change in the child's work activity. This may cause us to overstate transitions both in and out of employment. While all of our estimates may be subject to measurement error, it is important to note that the basic methodology of the PME is constant across cities and across the two decades we analyze in this chapter. It is therefore highly unlikely that measurement error can explain the large changes in entry rates and exit rates over time or the differences we see between groups, such as the higher entry rates for males or the larger exit rates for Salvador relative to São Paulo. While the absolute levels of the entry and exit rates may be measured with error, it seems safe to assume that the large changes we measure over time do reflect actual changes in the labor-force dynamics of Brazilian children.

## Summary and Policy Implications

Using Brazil's exceptionally rich monthly employment survey, we analyze transitions in and out of employment for children and adolescents. We find that child and youth employment is an extremely dynamic process that does not fit the common perception of a consistent set of children persistently attached to long-term jobs. The intermittency of child employment implies that the typical reference period of "last week" in labor surveys seriously understates the number of children working over a longer period. Our results also imply that child workers may be harder to identify than previously imagined, due to the volatility of their activities.

In fact our findings have both negative and positive policy implications. The past few years have seen a proliferation of programs explicitly aimed to reduce child labor in Latin America. Examples include the time-bound programs by the International Labour Organization (ILO) and the Child Labor Education Initiative financed by the U.S. Department of Labor.[13] In the design of these programs by governments and international organizations, it is likely that they have underestimated the number of workers, especially for children under 15. Another negative implication is that simply preventing children from working in a particular job may not free up children's time for attending school since children are often accustomed to moving from one job to another.[14] On the positive side, the results suggest that for many children who can be described as "recent child workers," the apparently normal interruptions in employment provide the potential for interventions to focus on *preventing* new employment activities, which may be easier than asking children to leave specific jobs. The high levels of intermittency also suggest that the cash transfers intended to replace the income earned in the labor market may have a tendency to be set too high since many children do not receive a consistent stream of income. This would imply that the extra cost associated with the underestimate of child workers might be offset by a lower subsidy per child. In general, our results imply that determining eligibility for program funding levels or program participation based on data from a short reference period will result in underfunded programs and the exclusion of large numbers of children who have recently engaged in child labor.

Employment entry and exits rates can be useful inputs for determining optimal benefit levels across different groups. Programs with particular objectives with respect to child labor can better tailor program features depending on the relevant entry or exit rates. For example, the differences in entry rates across gender and SES groups suggest that in urban Brazil, employment *prevention programs* should consider providing higher subsidies to groups with higher entry rates (boys and low-SES groups).[15] While benefit levels for prevention programs should be linked to entry rates, the benefits for *remediation* programs which aim to stop the employment of recently identified child workers should be closely linked to exit rates.[16] In the results for urban Brazil, the similar exit rates across gender and SES groups implies that the subsidy to induce the child to leave the labor force may not need to vary across these groups.

## Notes

Some of the results in this chapter were previously published in Deborah Levison, Jasper Hoek, David Lam, and Suzanne Duryea. 2007. "Intermittent Child Employment and Its

Implications for Estimates of Child Labor." *International Labour Review* 146 (3–4): 217–251. Reprinted with permission.

This research was supported by funding from the National Institute of Child Health and Human Development, Grant R01HDHD031214.

1. Bolsa Escola became part of Bolsa Familia in 2003 and *PETI* was folded into it in 2006 (Lindert et al., 2007).

2. Bolsa Escola is evaluated in chapter 8. PETI is evaluated in chapter 9.

3. A seventh city, Curitiba, was added in 1998. We do not include Curitiba in our analysis.

4. The analysis is restricted to 1982–98, a period in which the questionnaire and survey design do not include any major changes.

5. Sedlacek et al. (1990) provide more details regarding the rotation schedules of the PME survey.

6. The PME asks what all individuals in the household aged 10 and above were doing during the previous week. The responses, listed in a specific sequence, are as follows: work, had a job but didn't work, looked for work, retired, student, domestic tasks, and other. Respondents indicate the first activity on the list that they are involved in. Students who are also working should therefore be indicated as working. Work includes formal and informal work for pay plus unpaid family labor that is normally at least fifteen hours per week. Our measure of employment includes only those who are reported as working or who had a job but didn't work during the previous week (e.g., due to illness or vacation). (IBGE, 1982)

7. Duryea et al. (2007) compare the use of mothers' education with household income as indicators of socioeconomic status in the PME. That chapter shows that the impact of income is very similar to the impact of mothers' education, and discusses a number of problems with the PME income variable. To avoid the problems with the income variable we use mothers' education.

8. No measure of socioeconomic status is without its problems. We use mothers' education because relatively few children have absent mothers; many more fathers are absent. The biggest problem with using mothers' education is that education levels have been increasing over time. In 1982, a much higher proportion of women had fewer than four completed years of education than in 1998. Thus, the group of children in the lower SES group becomes increasingly small and, presumably, increasingly poor relative to the overall population, over time. This implies that the trend of declining employment for the lower SES group would appear even greater if we were able to track a constant proportion of children from poorer households.

9. Two studies use the panel data in the PME to examine the links between children's school and labor behavior with economic shocks (unexpected economic hard times), as opposed to socioeconomic status. For more details see chapter 3 and Duryea et al. (2007).

10. The large monthly variations in figure 4.3 reflect both seasonal movements and monthly volatility due to small sample sizes. The greater volatility in the exit rates reflects the fact that the denominator of employed children in any month is rather small in spite of the large sample sizes, especially at the younger ages and in the later years. Using moving averages makes the trends more easily visible.

11. Recall that the children in the PME samples were not eligible for PETI because PETI had not yet been expanded to urban areas.

12. The chapter also demonstrates that children and adolescents move in and out of employment at much higher rates than adults.

13. There are also country-specific initiatives such as the Programa de Atención Inmediata (PAI) in Costa Rica (Duryea and Morrison, 2004).

14. Moving to less hazardous work should be recognized as a positive outcome.

15. Along with differences in entry and exit rates, consideration should be given to the gender gap in education and unpaid domestic labor within the household as well.
16. The PAI in Costa Rica is an example of a remediation program. Children recently detected as employed are eligible to receive educational scholarships and other assistance.

# How Does Working as a Child Affect Wages, Income, and Poverty as an Adult?

*Nadeem Ilahi, Peter F. Orazem, and Guilherme Sedlacek*

Parents have their children specialize in schooling rather than go to work in part because they expect that children will earn enough as adults to repay the lost earnings as a child. However, children from poor households may not have the luxury of waiting to grow up before entering the labor market. Sending their children to work may be the only option poor parents have to sufficiently raise income to meet current consumption needs, so poor parents forgo the increased future income opportunity to meet basic necessities. One argument for government efforts to limit child labor is that poor parents may under-invest in their children's education relative to the social optimum. Those parents' decisions may not take into account societal returns associated with improved education such as poverty reduction, slower population growth, improved health, reduced crime, and a lower dependence on government transfer programs.

The rationale for government intervention assumes that children who do not work will earn more as adults, and that these future returns are sufficiently high to justify the current loss of income from reduced child labor. However, there is very little empirical research on the impact of child labor on the child's earnings potential as an adult. Empirical estimation is necessary because theory yields ambiguous predictions about the impact of early labor-market entry on lifetime earnings. Child labor need not lower lifetime earnings, and could even increase lifetime earnings for some children.

One way child labor can alter adult earnings is by changing the number of years of schooling children attain. Past studies have shown that a child's years of schooling may be increased or decreased when the child works. Psacharopoulos (1997) found evidence that child labor lowered grade attainment, while Akabayashi and Psacharopoulos (1999) found that child labor lowered measured school achievement per year. Other studies have found the opposite results, however. Because many working children also are in school, some analysts have suggested that child labor and schooling are not mutually exclusive (Ravallion and Wodon, 2000) and may even be complementary activities (Patrinos and Psacharopoulos, 1997). One reason is that child labor may raise household income sufficiently to allow the household to afford to send at least some of their children to school, whether it is the working children or their siblings. Without income derived from working children, these households may not be able to send any children to school.

It is even possible that child labor can raise lifetime earnings of children as adults. Standard theory of earnings initiated by Mincer (1974) argues that work experience raises wages, presumably because human capital is generated through learning by doing. It is possible that returns to a year of work experience dominate the returns to a year of schooling, particularly in developing countries where schools available to poor households often are of poor quality. It also is possible that by increasing current household income, child labor allows the parents to build an endowment of physical assets that can be transferred to the child at maturity. These physical assets may have a greater return in credit-constrained developing countries than do the foregone human capital assets.[1]

This study measures the impact of child labor on adult wages and poverty incidence through each of these potential avenues. Using a unique data set on adult earnings in Brazil, child labor is allowed to affect adult earnings through its impacts on work experience, years of schooling, and human capital attained per year of schooling. Adding up these positive and negative effects, the empirical findings demonstrate that early entry to the workforce reduces lifetime earnings by 13% to 20%. Child labor also raises the probability of being poor later in life by 13% to 31%.

These findings have important policy implications. Reducing child labor can significantly improve children's adult wages, income, and poverty status, so governments can trade-off current costs of child labor eradication programs against future lower costs of poverty programs and/or increased tax returns. Policies that keep working children in school also are supported because the positive effect of increased educational attainment on adult income is larger than the negative effect of child labor on earnings.

## Trends and Tradeoffs between Child Labor and Education in Brazil

As shown in chapter 4, the incidence of child labor in Brazil has decreased over time. The cumulative distribution of the age of workforce entry by birth cohort is presented in figure 5.1. The median age at entry was 12.5 for the cohort aged 40 to 49 in 1996. It increased 1.5 years to age 14 for the cohort aged 20 to 29. Much of the change in average cohort age is due to the decreasing frequency of very early entry into the labor force. One-third of the cohort aged 40 to 49 had entered the labor force by age 10, but the incidence had fallen to 20% for the cohort aged 20 to 29.

The relationship between age of labor-market entry and years of education by birth cohort is illustrated in figure 5.2. The relationship is quite stable across birth cohorts. Overall, as age of labor-market entry increases, years of education completed also increase. However, there is no gain in average schooling by delaying labor-market entry from age 4 to age 10. Over that range, average schooling remains constant at four years. One interpretation of figure 5.2 is that the increasing educational attainment in

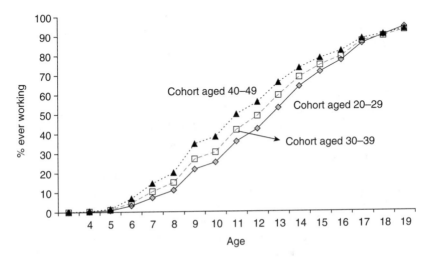

**Figure 5.1**  Cumulative Distribution of Age at Workforce Entry in Brazil, by 1996 Age Cohort

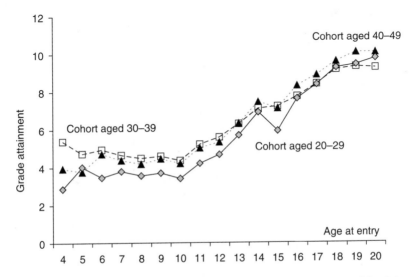

**Figure 5.2**  Educational Attainment by Age-at-Entry in the Workforce in Brazil, by Cohorts

Brazil is due not to increased educational attainment of working children, but to delayed age of labor-market entry for more recent birth cohorts.

There is a strong circumstantial case that early entry into the labor market has adverse consequences for adult income. Table 5.1 reports the probability of being in the lowest income quintile as an adult by years of education and age of labor-market entry. The lowest income quintile in Brazil can be viewed as being extremely poor by international standards. The probability of being extremely poor declines as age of labor-market entry and years of education increase. Child labor appears to be particularly damaging for the 39% of adults who began working before age 13. Of those, 56% are in the lowest two income quintiles, and one-third of them are in the lowest income quintile. However, increasing years of education mitigates the impact of early labor-market entry.

Table 5.2 shows similar adverse impacts of early labor-market entry on wages as an adult. Those who entered before age 13 earned 33% less than those who entered between the ages of 13 and 15. Again, education appears to mitigate the effect. For those with at least four to seven years of education, generally considered sufficient to attain permanent literacy, the adverse effects of early labor-market entry become less clear.

These findings suggest that if a working child remains in school, adult earnings may not suffer. That fact supports the argument that policies restricting child labor could do more harm than good. In Brazilian households that have child workers, child labor represents 17% of urban household income and 22% of rural household income. Given the strong positive effect of household income on child schooling, it is plausible that child labor could self-correct its adverse consequences on adult earnings by inducing additional years of schooling. Econometric estimation is necessary to assess

**Table 5.1**  Proportion of population over 18 in the lowest income quintiles, 1996, by age of labor-force entry and education

| | % of Adults > 18 | Years of Education[a] | | | | | Total |
|---|---|---|---|---|---|---|---|
| | | None | 1 to 3 | 4 to 7 | 8 to 11 | 12 or more | |
| Age at Entry | | | | | | | |
| Before 13 | 39 | 83% | 70% | 51% | 28% | 9% | 56% |
| | | (60%) | (44%) | (25%) | (10%) | (4%) | (33%) |
| 13 to 15 | 26 | 76% | 64% | 42% | 19% | 6% | 36% |
| | | (51%) | (35%) | (18%) | (6%) | (2%) | (17%) |
| 16 to 19 | 24 | 68% | 59% | 42% | 19% | 4% | 27% |
| | | (43%) | (29%) | (18%) | (6%) | (2%) | (11%) |
| After 20 | 11 | 64% | 58% | 43% | 22% | 4% | 24% |
| | | (39%) | (26%) | (18%) | (7%) | (2%) | (10%) |
| Total | 100 | 80% | 67% | 46% | 22% | 5% | 41% |
| | | (56%) | (39%) | (21%) | (7%) | (2%) | (21%) |

Notes:
[a]Numbers in parentheses represent proportions in the lowest income quintile.
Unbracketed numbers represent proportions in the lowest two income quintiles.

Table 5.2 Distribution of wage (R$/Hr.) for population over 18, by age of workforce entry and education, 1996

| | % of Adults > 18 | Years of Education | | | | | |
|---|---|---|---|---|---|---|---|
| | | None | 1 to 3 | 4 to 7 | 8 to 11 | 12 or more | Total |
| Age at Entry | | | | | | | |
| Before 13 | 39 | 0.77 | 1.07 | 1.69 | 2.92 | 7.41 | 1.79 |
| 13 to 15 | 26 | 0.85 | 1.18 | 1.74 | 3.09 | 8.26 | 2.66 |
| 16 to 19 | 24 | 0.96 | 1.39 | 1.62 | 2.53 | 7.3 | 3.03 |
| After 20 | 11 | 1.01 | 1.28 | 1.28 | 2.21 | 8.54 | 4.02 |
| Total | 100 | 0.81 | 1.14 | 1.67 | 2.76 | 7.87 | 2.51 |

whether these positive aspects of child labor outweigh the apparent negatives for lifetime earnings.

## Theory

An implication of the simplified Ben-Porath (1967) model of optimal schooling in chapter 3 is that there is a trade-off between early labor-market entry versus later entry with a longer period of specialization in schooling. It may be that in stage 1 where the child specializes in school (A = 1), the child will gain more academic skills. However, if the child divides time between school and work (0 < A < 1) as in stage 2, the child will be gaining occupational skills that will also have value. There is a strong presumption that for most young children, formal schooling raises lifetime earnings at a faster rate than does occupational training, and so a period of specialization in stage 1 before entering the workforce is optimal. However, this is not necessarily true for all children.

Letting years of schooling completed be designated by $E$; and letting $A$ be the fraction of time devoted to school, the simplest model of the child's lifetime wealth from human capital investments can be summarized by $W = h(E_t, A)$. Hundreds of studies of earnings have confirmed that $h_E > 0$, and so completing more years of schooling is correlated with greater earnings as an adult. It is tempting to presume also that $h_A > 0$, but evidence that wages are higher for children who attend more regularly is not commonly available. Even if children learn more in school when they do not work, it is nevertheless possible that the earnings growth from work experience as a child is still greater than the earnings growth from the gains in cognitive abilities attained in school.

In the Rosen variant of the Ben-Porath model (1977),[2] a child should stay in school as long as the cost of borrowing $r$ is less than the rate of return to an additional year of schooling.[3] However, full-time schooling will not always dominate part-time schooling. As borrowing costs increase, $r$ will eventually rise beyond the rate of return to full time schooling and the best option will be the part-time schooling option. At even higher levels of $r$, the dropout option dominates. Higher values of $r$ would be expected to be associated with lower household income to the extent that poorer households face more constrained credit options, so children in poor households will drop out more readily or split time between school and work. These predictions are borne out in the stylized facts reported in chapter 4.

This model demonstrates that early entry into the labor market could raise lifetime wealth, particularly for children facing poor schools and high discount rates. Whether child labor does in fact raise or lower measured adult wealth indicators requires empirical investigation. This also reinforces why government intervention combating child labor may be socially optimal. If the government's discount rate is less than that of the household, the government would prefer a higher level of schooling investment than the household would select on its own.[4]

## Data

The analysis is based on the 1996 round of the national sample survey of households, *Pesquisa Nacional por Amostra de Domicílios* (PNAD). PNAD, conducted annually by the Brazilian government, is a nationally representative stratified random sample of the Brazilian population designed to monitor the socioeconomic characteristics of the population including education, labor, residency, and earnings. The 1996 survey is particularly suited to the needs of this study in that it includes a retrospective question on age of labor-market entry and information about the parents of a subset of the adult respondents.

This study's empirical estimates of the impact of child labor on lifetime earnings rely on the ability of respondents to recall whether they worked when they were young. In theory, recall bias should be less severe for repeated activities such as work, but it is useful to compare the recall data to contemporaneously collected data on the incidence of child labor. The implied child labor-force participation rates based on recall data are larger than the official rates reported by the International Labour Organization (ILO), as shown in table 5.3.

Two reasons indicate why the retrospective data show a higher incidence of child labor than would contemporaneously collected surveys. The first is that children are likely to enter and exit the labor market, as demonstrated in chapter 4. Consequently, those who first entered the

Table 5.3    Retrospective and contemporaneous measures of the incidence of child labor in Brazil, ages 10 to 14

|  | 1960 | 1970 | 1980 |
| --- | --- | --- | --- |
| Retrospective PNAD 1996[a] | 46.2 | 38.8 | 33.5 |
| Contemporaneous ILO[b] | 22.2 | 20.3 | 19.0 |

*Notes:*
[a]Authors' calculations using data taken from the 1996 PNAD.
[b]Cited in Basu (1999).

labor market at an early age may not have remained in the labor force continuously thereafter. The second is that the retrospective data capture informal and part-time work that may not be captured in contemporaneous survey data. In contrast, the ILO data refer only to full-time work. In his survey of child labor literature, Basu (1999) reported that when ILO estimates were adjusted to include part-time work, the incidence of child labor more than doubled. In fact, the incidence of child labor implied by the retrospective data reported in table 5.3 is nearly twice that of the ILO estimates. Thus, the retrospective data track the contemporaneously collected data quite well.

## Estimation Strategy

There is a long tradition of examining returns to school by using earnings functions. Following Welch (1966), analysis of the returns to education was extended to incorporate returns to school quality. Card and Krueger (1992) used a similar strategy to analyze the effects of school and teacher attributes on lifetime earnings. Child labor can be incorporated into the earnings function framework in the same manner as school quality. To begin, approximate the true structural relationship between education, $E$, and child labor, $C$, as:

$$E(C_i) = \beta C_i \qquad (5.1)$$

where the parameter $\beta$ captures the effects of early labor-force entry on lifetime educational attainment. The coefficient $\beta$ can be positive or negative.

Now consider the complete relationship between earnings (or poverty) as an adult and child labor. We posit a log earnings function:

$$\ln(W_i) = \alpha_0 + \alpha_C C_i + \alpha_E E_i(C_i) + \alpha_{CE} C_i E_i(C_i) + \varepsilon_i \qquad (5.2)$$

where the $\alpha_i$ are coefficients and $\varepsilon_i$ is the error term. Note that the specification in equation (5.2) captures the potential channels through which early entry in the workforce may affect lifetime earnings. The term $\alpha_C C_i$ captures the direct effect of child labor on adult earnings, whether through physical capital endowments inherited from the parents or from work experience. The term $\alpha_E E_i$ represents the returns to full-time investment in schooling (A = 1 in the theory), while $\alpha_{CE} C_i E_i$ captures the difference in adult earnings between full-time and part-time (A < 1) investment in schooling.

Differentiating equation (5.2) with respect to $C_i$ yields the total effect of child labor on earnings:

$$\frac{\partial \ln(W_i)}{\partial C_i} = \alpha_C + \alpha_E \frac{\partial E_i}{\partial C_i} + \alpha_{CE} \overline{C} \frac{\partial E_i}{\partial C_i} + \alpha_{CE} \overline{E} \qquad (5.3)$$

where $\overline{C}$ is the mean rate of child labor and $\overline{E}$ is mean education level.[5] Regrouping terms in (5.3) would give the total effect of child labor on earnings:

$$\frac{\partial \ln(W_i)}{\partial C_i} = \underbrace{\left[ \alpha_C + \alpha_{CE}\overline{E} \right]}_{\textit{direct effect of child labor}}$$

$$+ \underbrace{\left[ \alpha_E + \alpha_{CE}\overline{C} \right]}_{\textit{returns to education}} \times \underbrace{\frac{\partial E_i}{\partial C_i}}_{\textit{effect of child labor on educatio}}$$

(5.4)

The first term in square brackets in equation (5.4) is the direct effect of child labor on earnings. The next two terms capture the indirect effects, that is, through the effects on educational attainment and returns to education.

Measuring the indirect effect of child labor on adult wages requires an estimate of $\partial E_i / \partial C_i = \beta$. One option is to derive a relationship defining the locus of equilibrium points between age of entry into the labor market and years of attained schooling. As figure 5.2 demonstrates, the locus of points has been very stable over time. An alternative is to derive a structural relationship between child labor and educational attainment by empirically identifying factors that shift $C$ but not $E$ and applying instrumental variables. Either method will yield estimates of $\beta$ that can be inserted into (5.4) to derive the indirect effect of child labor on adult earnings through education. As demonstrated below, both options yield similar estimates of $\beta$.

A third alternative is to estimate the total derivative $\partial \ln(W_i)/\partial C_i$ as the coefficient on child labor in an earnings function in which years of education is excluded as a regressor and child labor is treated as exogenous. Treating child labor as a discrete variable in equation (5.2), the coefficient on $C_i$ would be equal to $\alpha_C + (\alpha_E + 2\alpha_{CE})\beta$. In practice, this total derivative estimate is likely to exceed the true value of $\partial \ln(W_i)/\partial C_i$ in absolute value because it will also reflect the likely negative correlation between $E$ and $C$. Nevertheless, this estimate of $\partial \ln(W_i)/\partial C_i$ will serve as a useful reference for the structural estimate based on (5.4).

## Empirical Findings

### Summary Statistics

The sample of adult wage earners is taken as the PNAD respondents over 18 years of age who were out of school. Summary statistics of the samples used in the analysis are presented in table 5.4, which also presents summary statistics for those who started working prior to their thirteenth birthday and those who began working later. On average, the sample who are sons and daughters of the household head were younger, more educated, began working later, and were lower paid than the full sample. Those who began

Table 5.4  Summary statistics for sample of all adults over 18

| | All | | Those Who Started Working before Age 13 | | Those Who Started Working after Age 12 | |
|---|---|---|---|---|---|---|
| | 1 | 2 | 1 | 2 | 1 | 2 |
| Wage (R$ per hour) | 2.51 | 1.49 | 1.78 | 0.88 | 3.02 | 1.78 |
| | (4.73) | (2.31) | (3.30) | (1.35) | (5.47) | (2.59) |
| Educational | 6.52 | 7.31 | 4.45 | 4.92 | 8.00 | 8.40 |
| Attainment (Years) | (4.45) | (4.16) | (3.73) | (3.66) | (4.33) | (3.92) |
| Age at Entry in | 13.92 | 14.73 | 9.88 | 10.11 | 16.77 | 16.84 |
| Workforce | (4.52) | (4.12) | (1.74) | (1.65) | (3.63) | (3.06) |
| Entered Workforce | 0.41 | 0.31 | 1.00 | 1.00 | 0.00 | 0.00 |
| Before Age 13 | (0.49) | (0.46) | (0.00) | (0.00) | (0.00) | (0.00) |
| Age (Years) | 32.34 | 25.05 | 33.60 | 25.01 | 31.45 | 25.06 |
| | (9.11) | (6.61) | (9.26) | (6.88) | (8.90) | (6.48) |
| Female | 0.42 | 0.39 | 0.35 | 0.27 | 0.47 | 0.45 |
| | (0.49) | (0.49) | (0.48) | (0.45) | (0.50) | (0.50) |
| Rural | 0.19 | 0.19 | 0.32 | 0.41 | 0.10 | 0.09 |
| | (0.39) | (0.39) | (0.47) | (0.49) | (0.30) | (0.29) |
| Union | 0.1603 | 0.1081 | 0.1339 | 0.0714 | 0.1788 | 0.1249 |
| | (0.3669) | (0.3105) | (0.3406) | (0.2574) | (0.3832) | (0.3306) |
| Ethnicity: | | | | | | |
| White | 0.5355 | 0.5279 | 0.4734 | 0.4352 | 0.5794 | 0.5703 |
| | (0.4987) | (0.4992) | (0.4993) | (0.4958) | (0.4937) | (0.4951) |
| Black | 0.0674 | 0.0729 | 0.0700 | 0.0783 | 0.0655 | 0.0704 |
| | (0.2506) | (0.2600) | (0.2552) | (0.2688) | (0.2474) | (0.2559) |
| Asian | 0.0042 | 0.0043 | 0.0024 | 0.0020 | 0.0054 | 0.0054 |
| | (0.0645) | (0.0656) | (0.049) | (0.0442) | (0.0735) | (0.0733) |
| Indigenous | 0.0015 | 0.0013 | 0.0018 | 0.0017 | 0.0012 | 0.0011 |
| | (0.0383) | (0.0363) | (0.0423) | (0.0412) | (0.0352) | (0.0338) |
| Dark | 0.3914 | 0.3935 | 0.4523 | 0.4827 | 0.3485 | 0.3527 |
| | (0.4881) | (0.4885) | (0.4977) | (0.4997) | (0.4765) | (0.4778) |
| Age of Household | 43.07 | 55.79 | 42.23 | 56.44 | 43.66 | 55.49 |
| Head | (12.91) | (10.13) | (12.50) | (10.56) | (13.17) | (9.90) |
| Household Head is | 0.18 | 0.30 | 0.14 | 0.29 | 0.20 | 0.31 |
| Female | (0.38) | (0.46) | (0.35) | (0.45) | (0.40) | (0.46) |
| Education of | 5.37 | 3.61 | 3.73 | 1.84 | 6.52 | 4.41 |
| Household Head (Years) | (4.57) | (3.90) | (3.74) | (2.53) | (4.74) | (4.15) |

Notes:
  The numbers in column 1 represent 94,518 individuals in the full sample of adults over 18.
  The numbers in column 2 represent the subsample (N = 25894) who are sons or daughters of the household head.

working at an earlier age were more likely to be male, rural residents, and have a less educated parent.

### Econometric Results

Estimates of equation (5.2), augmented with the other variables in table 5.4 and controls for state of residence, are reported in table 5.5.[6] Four measures

**Table 5.5** The effects of child labor on lifetime wages and poverty, using full sample of adults[a]

| | (1) | (2) | (3) | (4) |
|---|---|---|---|---|
| | | | *POOREST 40%*[c] | *POOREST 20%*[c] |
| | *log (WAGE)*[b] | *log (INCOME)*[b] | | |
| CHLAB ($\alpha_C$) | 0.016* | −0.030** | 0.038** | 0.039** |
| | (0.010)[d] | (0.010) | (0.007) | (0.004) |
| EDUCATION ($\alpha_E$) | 0.108** | 0.110** | −0.052** | −0.025** |
| | (0.001) | (0.001) | (0.001) | (0.000) |
| CHLAB*EDUCATION ($\alpha_{CE}$) | −0.013** | −0.018** | 0.004** | −0.0013* |
| | (0.001) | (0.001) | (0.001) | (0.0007) |
| Age | 0.089** | −0.060** | 0.014** | 0.010** |
| | (0.002) | (0.002) | (0.001) | (0.001) |
| Age$^2$ | −0.001** | 0.001** | −0.0003** | −0.0002** |
| | (0.000) | (0.000) | (0.000) | (0.000) |
| Female | −0.580** | −0.030** | 0.007* | 0.011** |
| | (0.007) | (0.005) | (0.004) | (0.003) |
| Rural | −0.302** | −0.393** | 0.232** | 0.152** |
| | (0.008) | (0.007) | (0.005) | (0.004) |
| Indigenous | −0.187** | −0.137** | 0.064 | 0.044 |
| | (0.071) | (0.068) | (0.049) | (0.034) |
| Black | −0.201** | −0.191** | 0.115** | 0.053** |
| | (0.039) | (0.011) | (0.008) | (0.006) |
| Asian | 0.201** | 0.238** | −0.011 | 0.058** |
| | (0.039) | (0.090) | (0.037) | (0.031) |
| Mixed Race | −0.149** | −0.153** | 0.091** | 0.041** |
| | (0.006) | (0.006) | (0.004) | (0.003) |
| Union | 0.245** | 0.130** | −0.100** | −0.047** |
| | (0.007) | (0.007) | (0.005) | (0.003) |
| Temporary Position | 0.578** | 0.512** | −0.231** | −0.082 |
| | (0.050) | (0.053) | (0.023) | (0.013) |
| Constant | −1.531** | 1.803** | | |
| | (0.038) | (0.036) | | |
| $\lambda$[e] | 0.176** | −0.310** | | |
| | (0.026) | (0.018) | | |
| Direct Effect: $(\alpha_C + \alpha_{CE} \cdot \bar{E} \mid_{C=1})$ | −4.2% | −11.0% | 5.6% | 3.3% |
| Indirect Effect: $(\alpha_E + \alpha_{CE}\bar{C})\dfrac{\partial E}{\partial C}$ | −16.1% | −15.7% | 8.2% | 4.5% |
| Total Effect | −20.3% | −26.7% | 13.7% | 7.8% |
| Log Likelihood | −124601 | −115441 | −44325 | −35212 |
| N | 94321 | 94289 | 94289 | 94289 |

*Notes:*

[a]All specifications include dummy variables for state of residence.

[b]Maximum likelihood variant of Heckman selection model.

[c]Probit coefficients are transformed to be the change in probability of poverty status from a unit change in the regressor.

[d]Standard errors are in parentheses.

[e]Corrects for nonreport of individual wage (column 1) or per capita household income (column 2).

*Significant at the .10 level.

**Significant at the .05 level.

of adult earnings are used as dependent variables: the log hourly wage; log household income; and status in the lowest one- or lowest two-income quintiles. The measure of child labor, CHLAB, takes the value of one if the respondent worked during his first 12 years of life and zero otherwise. This cruder dummy variable is used instead of the reported age at labor-market entry to reduce the measurement error problems associated with retrospective data. The presumption is that adults can more accurately recall working as young children than the actual age at which they initiated work.

A subset of the sample had no wages, either because they were out of the labor force, unemployed, or worked without reported wages. To correct for possible sample selection bias, a maximum likelihood version of Heckman's (1978) correction was implemented. Instruments in the auxiliary equation for the probability of wage work included the number of children and total individuals in the household, regional industry mix, and regional adult unemployment rate and regional per capita income. Household demographic composition, regional unemployment, and per capita income are proxies for individual reservation wage. The industry mix is used to control for the probability of nonwage work. Note that all wage regressions include controls for average wages in the state, so these measures of industry mix reflect variation in the types of work done, holding average wages constant. In practice, the uncorrected and corrected parameter estimates were virtually identical, so issues of selection appear not to have been that critical. Only the selection-corrected estimates are reported to conserve space.

The log wage equations mimic standard results. Wages have a concave pattern over the life cycle. The implied returns to schooling of 10.8% per year were consistent with those reported by Lam and Schoeni (1993) for Brazil when controlling for family background variables. Wages were higher for urban, male, and unionized workers, and were lower for minority groups except Asians. Workers in jobs that were not permanent also were paid a premium.

The parameters of primary interest are $\alpha_C$, $\alpha_E$, and $\alpha_{CE}$. Interestingly, $\alpha_C > 0$, suggesting that at zero years of education, child labor leads to higher lifetime earnings. This is consistent with the presumption that child labor can increase human capital through on-the-job training. However, child labor also makes education less efficient at producing human capital, so $\alpha_{CE} < 0$. However, before proceeding to the numerical estimate of child labor on adult earnings, we need an estimate of the impact of child labor on years of schooling, $\partial E/\partial C$.

### Estimating the Effect of Child Labor on Years of Education, $\partial E/\partial C$

As discussed in the introduction, past studies have disagreed about whether child labor increases or decreases years of education. Such estimates are needed to derive the indirect impact of child labor on earnings through the implied impact on human capital. The equilibrium locus of points in figure 5.2 suggests that for each year the child remains out of the labor market past the age of 10, attained schooling increases by 0.58 years.[7]

Using the sample statistics in table 5.4, the average age of labor-market entry for those who did not work in their first 12 years was 16.77 years, implying 4.77 years of additional specialization in schooling. The implied increase in years of schooling for those who began working after age 12 is $0.58 \cdot (4.77) = 2.8$ years. The corresponding estimate in Psacharopoulos' (1997) study of Bolivian and Venezuelan working children is 2 years of reduced educational attainment.

These are not structural estimates, however. To the extent that years of education and child labor are simultaneously determined, these estimates based on market equilibrium outcomes should overstate the true impact of child labor on years of completed schooling. To address this problem, we made use of a subset of the PNAD sample of adults who were still living with their parents. Because the PNAD collected information on all household members, there is information on household demographics including the number of siblings as well as education and gender of the household head. That subset permits prediction of the incidence of child labor using household attributes and local labor-market conditions as instruments. The predicted probability of child labor was then used in a second-stage estimate explaining variation in completed years of schooling. Those unreported estimates implied that working in the first 12 years of life lowers completed years of schooling by 1.7 years relative to otherwise identical individuals from observationally identical households. The magnitude appears to be reasonable compared to the upper-bound estimate of $\partial E / \partial C = 2.8$ years based on figure 5.2.[8]

## Indirect Effects of Child Labor on Adult Earnings

The direct effect of child labor on life earnings combines two influences, reported as $(\alpha_C + \alpha_{CE} \bar{E} |_{C=1})$ at the bottom of table 5.5. The first effect captures the potential impact of early entry into the labor market on wages through greater years in the labor market. The second effect captures the impact of child labor on returns per years of schooling completed. The negative effect of child labor on returns to education dominates the positive effect on occupational human capital. Consequently, working in the first 12 years of life has a direct effect of reducing adult hourly wages by 4.2%.

Given our estimate of $\partial E / \partial C$ at $-1.7$ years of schooling, we can derive the indirect effect of child labor on adult wages through its impact on attained schooling. This is reported as $(\alpha_2 + \alpha_3 C)\partial E / \partial C$ at the bottom of table 5.5. The impact is significant, reducing adult wages by 16.1%. Consequently, the total effect of early child labor is to reduce adult wages by 20.3%. The implied reduction in adult wages using the biased total derivative estimate is 31.8%, so the structural estimate does not appear too large.

The impact of child labor on household income may be larger or smaller than its impact on individual wages. If child labor increases the probability of unemployment as an adult, then child labor will lower adult income both by lowering payment per hour and by lowering the expected number of hours worked per year. However, child labor may also affect the type of spouse one can attract as an adult. If those who worked as children marry other child workers whose wages were suppressed, then the marriage market will magnify the adverse impacts of child labor on adult poverty. However, if those who attained little education can marry more educated spouses or if more members of the households of child laborers work, then some of the adverse impacts of child labor on adult income may be mitigated.

The second column in table 5.5 regresses per capita household income on child labor measures. The coefficient on child labor $\alpha_C$ turns negative, so that child workers at zero education have household income that is 3% lower than those who did not work in their first 12 years. The penalty of child labor on returns to education also becomes greater so the direct effect of child labor is to reduce adult household income by 11%.

At least some of the negative effects on individual wages appear to be mitigated by household formation. Most notably, women who face a 58% wage disadvantage in column 1 only face a 3% loss of household income, presumably because they can pool income with higher-wage males. However, the adverse effect of child labor on wages is not reduced by pooling incomes within households. The indirect effect of child labor on household income is only modestly smaller than its effect on wages: −15.7%. The total impact of child labor is to reduce adult household income by 26.7%, even larger than the adverse effect of child labor on hourly earnings. The comparable estimate from the biased total derivative estimate is an implied income reduction of 38.9%, so this structural estimate does not appear too large relative to that reduced-form estimate.

The last two columns report the probability that a child laborer is in the bottom one or two income quintiles as an adult. Individuals who worked in their first twelve years of life were 7.8% more likely to be in the lowest income quintile and 13.7% more likely to be in the lowest two quintiles than were otherwise observationally equivalent adults who did not work until age 13 or later. The corresponding upward biased total derivative estimates are 9.5% and 16.9%.

The implication is that adults who worked as children experience a significant and large loss of lifetime earnings. Child laborers are significantly more likely to be poor as adults, both because they have lower human capital and because they marry individuals with low earnings potential.

## Conclusion

This study quantifies the effects of child labor on the wages, income, and poverty status of those same individuals as adults. A procedure was used that incorporated three possible channels through which child labor could affect outcomes. Child labor can alter years of attained education, the returns per year of education, and human capital production outside of school.

The empirical findings suggest that early entry in the workforce reduces years of education and lowers the returns per year of schooling. However, there is some evidence that child labor also may create occupational human capital that can raise an individual's adult wages. Nevertheless, the adverse effects of child labor on the quantity and productivity of schooling swamp any positive effects, so that the overall impact is to reduce adult hourly wages by 20%.

Child workers were 14% more likely to be in the lowest two income quintiles as adults compared to otherwise identical children who did not enter the labor market until after age 12.

The next two chapters review two plausible mechanisms by which child labor leads to these adverse income consequences as an adult. Chapter 6 reviews evidence that child labor perpetuates poverty across generations and chapter 7 presents evidence that child labor lowers cognitive attainment in school. This chapter shows a third way that child labor may lead to adult poverty: because child labor lowers adult household income by an even greater amount than it does hourly wages, it appears that child laborers also marry spouses with lower earnings potential.

Whatever the link between child labor and adult income, policies that delay age of entry into the labor market such as truancy laws or child labor prohibitions may have a significant impact on adult incidence of poverty. While these laws may be expensive to enforce, the enhanced future earnings of children who remain out of the labor force as a result of the laws may provide sufficient revenue to justify the cost. Alternatively, higher future earnings could help justify the expense of providing current poor parents an income transfer conditional on their children not working.

Our findings also support policies that keep children in school even if they work. While child labor reduces the productivity of schooling, the net effect of an additional year of schooling on adult wages is still positive, even if the child works while in school. Consequently, policies that delay dropout even if the child works, such as providing night schools or training at work, may be partially effective at lowering the likelihood of adult poverty for current working children.

## Notes

Work on this paper was completed when Ilahi and Sedlacek were employed at the World Bank. Views expressed are not necessarily those of the World Bank, the International Monetary Fund, or the Inter-American Development Bank.

1. Parsons and Goldin (1989) found that in U.S. households in 1890, child-labor income primarily went toward current household consumption and little if any physical assets were transferred to working children when they reached adulthood.
2. See Orazem and King (2008) for a useful summary of the Rosen optimal schooling problem.
3. Summarizing Rosen (1977), the continuous discounted present value of schooling formula is $V(E_t, A) = (W/r)e^{-rE_t}$ that is maximized at $r = h_E/W$. This formulation assumes there is no direct cost of schooling. As direct costs of schooling are added, optimal time in school decreases (Orazem and King, 2008, 3482), a prediction borne out in empirical tests (Alderman et al., 2001).

4. Jacoby and Skoufias (1997) developed and implemented a strategy for testing whether credit constraints led households to use child labor to smooth income in the face of unanticipated income loss. The studies by Beegle et al. (2006; 2007) and by Eric Edmonds and his coauthors (Edmonds et al., 2005) are more recent studies that demonstrate evidence that poor households face credit constraints in making child schooling and/or work decisions.

5. If child labor is measured as a discrete rather than as a continuous variable, the discrete corollary to (5.3) would be $\Delta \ln(W_i)/\Delta C = \alpha_C + (\alpha_E + \alpha_{CE})(\bar{E}|_{C=1} - \bar{E}|_{C=0}) + \alpha_{CE}\bar{E}|_{C=1}$.

6. To conserve space, the coefficients on the state dummies are not reported in the tables. The full set of results is available on request.

7. The regression pooling the three cohorts of observations from figure 5.2 is

$$\text{Years of Schooling} = \frac{10.13}{(.18)} - \frac{5.95}{(.21)} * D10 - \frac{.58}{(.03)} * (1-D10) * (20 - \text{AGE OF ENTRY}),$$

where D10 is a dummy variable indicating age of entry at 10 or less and (20−AGE OF ENTRY) is the number of years spent in the labor market by age 20.

8. Emerson and Souza (2008) present structural instrumental variable estimates that confirm the fact that child labor and schooling are jointly determined and that exogenous shifts in the probability of child labor reduce years of schooling.

# The Intergenerational Persistence of Child Labor

*Patrick M. Emerson and André Portela F. de Souza*

Many recent economic studies suggest that child labor is both a result of and a strategy to avoid household poverty. If that is the case, then child labor may be viewed not so much as a problem but as a solution to poverty's crushing effects. This means that banning child labor may, in fact, harm the very people it attempts to help (Basu and Pham Hoang Van, 1998). This study explores whether using child labor to avoid poverty can cause it to persist through generations of families. If this is indeed the case, policy makers who hope to achieve long-term reductions in child labor are faced with the new challenge of focusing their attention not only on current child laborers, but future generations as well.

Though there has been some excellent recent theoretical work examining the intergenerational links in child labor and identifying the potential for intergenerational child labor traps (Baland and Robinson, 2000; Basu, 1999; Bell and Gersbach, 2001; Lopez-Calva and Koji Miyamoto, 2000; and Ranjan, 2001),[1] there is a marked absence of empirical work on the topic.

Previous empirical work has focused primarily on isolating the determinants of child labor using survey data (Ray, 2000a; 2000b; Jensen and Neilsen, 1997; Patrinos and Psacharopoulos, 1997; Psacharopoulos, 1997; and Grootaert and Kanbur, 1995). This study asks if the child-labor status of parents impacts the child-labor incidence of their children, and indicates there is strong evidence that it does. It also asks if there is a direct link between the child-labor status of the parents and their children, and again, there is evidence that there is.

## The Intergenerational Child Labor Link

This study begins with the assumption that families prefer to withhold their children from the labor market until they are adults. However, if a family is struggling to survive, they may have to send some or all of their children to work.

This discussion incorporates the essential aspects of previous theoretical work.[2] The recent theoretical literature on child labor and poverty traps incorporates a set of core assumptions: that parents are altruistic toward their children; there is a trade-off between child labor and a child's human capital accumulation; the child's human capital accumulation is an increasing function of schooling; and the credit market is imperfect.

If a family has access to adequate resources, it will choose to invest in the education of its children. However, if the parents cannot keep the family above the subsistence level, and because they cannot borrow against the future earnings of their children, they will choose to send some or all of their children to work to ensure the family's survival. This reduction in schooling causes a loss of overall human capital accumulation and results in lower wages when the children become adults. In turn, those lower wages make those now-adults more likely to send their children to work as child laborers.

This cycle can lead to multiple generations of a family being stuck in what could be termed a child labor trap, which is easily illustrated with a simple figure. Considering the level of adult human capital as a function of the education received as a child, the idea can be expressed as: $h_t = f(e_{t-1})$. Here, $h_t$ is the level of adult human capital in time period $t$ (adulthood) for an individual who reached education level $e_{t-1}$ in time period $t-1$ (childhood). If adult wage is an increasing function of human capital $h_t$, then the level of education of the next generation, that is, the child, $e_t$, will be determined by the parent's human capital level, or $e_t = g(h_t)$. Thus, the child's human capital level as an adult, $h_{t+1}$, will be determined by the parents' human capital level: $h_{t+1} = f(g(h_t))$.

The shape of this function can take many forms; one very plausible form is illustrated in figure 6.1. The rationale for such a shape is easily motivated by what is termed sheepskin effects, or nonlinearities in the returns to education. In other words, the wages one can command from the labor market jump up or at least increase disproportionately upon reaching a certain level of education, such as literacy, grade school certificate, high school diploma, college degree, etc. These types of sheepskin effects can cause the human capital accumulation function of children, which is a function of their parents' human capital, to have an S-shape.

Figure 6.1 assumes the level of human capital an individual is endowed with (that is, an adult with no education) is 1, and the maximum human capital attainable is $\bar{h}$. This figure maps the child's human capital, $h_{t+1}$, as a function of the adult's, $h_t$. The dynamics of this function suggest that there is a critical level of human capital, $h^*$, beyond which a family will continue to increase education through the generations until $\bar{h}$ is reached. A family that is below $h^*$ will continue to slide backward, attaining less and less education generation by generation, until it reaches the no education/all child labor equilibrium. This illustrates the child labor trap.

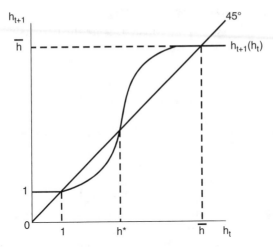

**Figure 6.1**    Child Human Capital as a Function of Parental Human Capital

It should be noted that while this is a plausible and quite likely scenario, other reasons could cause persistence in child labor, although those effects are expected to be less important. They include so-called social norms that dictate parents who worked as children simply send their children to work or feel that working imparts important qualities in children, or that having parents who were child laborers prevents normal returns to education.

## Data and Empirical Strategy

### Data

The data used in this study are taken from the 1996 Brazilian Household Surveys, Pesquisa Nacional por Amostragem a Domicilio (PNAD), conducted by the Brazilian Census Bureau. The survey encompasses approximately 85,000 households in all of Brazil's urban areas and the majority its rural areas, with the exception of the rural areas of the Amazon region.

This study uses a sample of individuals between the ages of 10 and 14 who are considered sons, daughters, or other relatives in the family unit.[3] Each observation consists of information about the characteristics of the children and their parents and families. Due to this criterion, families with single household heads are excluded from the analysis.[4] Finally, the study excludes all observations for which the age difference between the head of the family or spouse and the oldest child is 14 or less.

The child-labor variables for the children are constructed as follows: children were considered working if they worked any hours per week.[5] Children were considered to work full time if they worked twenty hours or more per week. The child-labor variable for the parents is defined as follows: parents who said they began working at age 14 or younger were considered child laborers. Each child's school attendance status, gender, and region of residence was obtained, as were the parents' years of schooling, age, and employment status.[6]

### Empirical Strategy

The study estimates a probit model of the child-labor indicator variable on the parental child-labor status variables and a vector of other controls on the probability that the child was a child laborer. The model does not control for the schooling of the parents nor the income of the family, in keeping with the hypothesis that the intergenerational link is transmitted through adult income, which is a function of schooling.

Next, the study tests for a direct link to child labor. Controlling for family wealth or permanent income, the effect of parental child labor on their children's incidence of child labor should disappear if it is true that child labor only results from familial poverty. Because it is well established that parental education is the most reliable predictor of a family's permanent income, that factor is included as a likely contributor to intergenerational child labor. If there is still an effect after controlling for parental education, it is fairly certain that education is not the entire explanation. The current family income is included to strengthen the test; however, it is possible that the family income variable is likely endogenous.

# The Intergenerational Persistence of Child Labor in Brazil

### Unconditional Probabilities

Table 6.1a presents the proportions of child labor and parents' child-labor status in 1996 for the baseline definitions of child labor for children and parents. In table 6.1a, of all 10- to 14-year-old children in the sample, 13.9% worked and 70.6% of their fathers and 37.2% of their mothers were child laborers. More importantly, in families in which fathers were child laborers, 17.3% of the children were child laborers. On the other hand, in families in which fathers were not child laborers, only 5.9% of the children were child laborers. Similarly, in families in which mothers were child laborers, 24.3% of the children were child laborers; of those whose mothers were not child laborers, around 7.8% of the children were child laborers.

Table 6.1b presents similar figures when child labor is defined as working at least twenty hours a week. In this case, of all children aged 10 to 14, 10.5% were child laborers. Again, children from families in which a parent was a child laborer were approximately three times more likely to be child laborers, compared to those whose parents were not. Although these figures are unconditional probabilities, they suggest the existence of intergenerational persistence in child labor in Brazil.

**Table 6.1a**  Unconditional probabilities of a child working strictly positive hours, given a parent's work status at age 14 or younger

| Son or Daughter Is Child Laborer | | Father Was a Child Laborer | | Mother Was a Child Laborer | | Total |
|---|---|---|---|---|---|---|
| | | No | Yes | No | Yes | |
| No | Number | 7991 | 16833 | 16708 | 8116 | 24824 |
| | Row % | 32.19 | 67.81 | 67.31 | 32.69 | 100 |
| | Column % | 94.1 | 82.72 | 92.19 | 75.72 | 86.07 |
| Yes | Number | 501 | 3517 | 1416 | 2602 | 4018 |
| | Row % | 12.47 | 87.53 | 35.24 | 64.76 | 100 |
| | Column % | 5.9 | 17.28 | 7.81 | 24.28 | 13.93 |
| Total | Number | 8492 | 20350 | 18124 | 10718 | 28842 |
| | Row % | 29.44 | 70.56 | 62.84 | 37.16 | 100 |
| | Column % | 100 | 100 | 100 | 100 | 100 |

**Table 6.1b**  Unconditional probabilities of a child working at least 20 hours per week, given a parent's work status at age 14 or younger

| Son or Daughter Is Child Laborer | | Father Was a Child Laborer | | Mother Was a Child Laborer | | Total |
|---|---|---|---|---|---|---|
| | | No | Yes | No | Yes | |
| No | Number | 8132 | 17690 | 16990 | 8832 | 25822 |
| | Row % | 31.49 | 68.51 | 65.8 | 34.2 | 100 |
| | Column % | 95.76 | 86.93 | 93.74 | 82.4 | 89.53 |
| Yes | Number | 360 | 2660 | 1134 | 1886 | 3020 |
| | Row % | 11.92 | 88.08 | 37.55 | 62.45 | 100 |
| | Column % | 4.24 | 13.07 | 6.26 | 17.6 | 10.47 |
| Total | Number | 8492 | 20350 | 18124 | 10718 | 28842 |
| | Row % | 29.44 | 70.56 | 62.84 | 37.16 | 100 |
| | Column % | 100 | 100 | 100 | 100 | 100 |

## Probit Model Estimations on Child-Labor Indicator Variables

A standard probit model is estimated to consider the effect of parental child labor on the incidence of work among 10- to 14-year-olds. The dependent variable is an indicator that equals 1 if the children usually worked in the labor market. This is regressed on indicator variables that equal 1 if the children's mothers and fathers were child laborers. The model also included the ages of the children and parents; the number of siblings aged 0 to 5, 6 to 9, 10 to 14 and 15 to 17; and indicators for if the children were female, lived in an urban area, or had a parent who was not in the labor market.[7] The results are shown in the first column of table 6.2.[8]

The study found that parental child labor had a strong and positive effect on the probability that children would join the labor force. Female children, those in urban areas, and those with one parent not in the labor market were less likely to work, as were those who had neither parent in the

**Table 6.2**  Child labor persistence. Probit on child labor indicator variable

| Independent Variables | Coefficient | Std. Error | Coefficient | Std. Error | Coefficient | Std. Error |
|---|---|---|---|---|---|---|
| Child Laborer Father | 0.333** | 0.029 | 0.259** | 0.030 | 0.251** | 0.039 |
| Child Laborer Mother | 0.407** | 0.027 | 0.319** | 0.028 | 0.320** | 0.036 |
| Father's Years of Schooling | | | −0.028** | 0.004 | −0.025** | 0.005 |
| Mother's Years of Schooling | | | −0.030** | 0.004 | −0.033** | 0.005 |
| Age of the Child | 0.208** | 0.008 | 0.211** | 0.008 | 0.214** | 0.010 |
| Years of Schooling of the Grandfather (father's side) | | | | | 0.000 | 0.009 |
| Years of Schooling of the Grandmother (father's side) | | | | | −0.008 | 0.009 |
| Years of Schooling of the Grandfather (mother's side) | | | | | −0.001 | 0.008 |
| Years of Schooling of the Grandmother (mother's side) | | | | | 0.002 | 0.009 |
| Female Child | −0.587** | 0.032 | −0.593** | 0.032 | −0.587** | 0.042 |
| Urban | −0.842** | 0.023 | −0.730** | 0.024 | −0.736** | 0.030 |
| Father Not in the Labor Market | −0.172** | 0.045 | −0.236** | 0.046 | −0.251** | 0.062 |
| Mother Not in the Labor Market | −0.270** | 0.027 | −0.361** | 0.029 | −0.361** | 0.036 |
| Father's Age | 0.008** | 0.002 | 0.005** | 0.002 | 0.002 | 0.002 |
| Mother's Age | 0.003 | 0.002 | 0.000 | 0.002 | 0.003 | 0.003 |
| Number of Boys Aged 0 to 5 | 0.059 | 0.022 | 0.033 | 0.022 | 0.001 | 0.029 |
| Number of Boys Aged 6 to 9 | 0.118** | 0.020 | 0.087** | 0.020 | 0.063* | 0.027 |
| Number of Boys Aged 10 to 14 | 0.085** | 0.018 | 0.059** | 0.018 | 0.040 | 0.022 |
| Number of Boys Aged 15 to 17 | 0.036 | 0.020 | 0.012 | 0.020 | 0.038 | 0.026 |
| Number of Girls Aged 0 to 5 | 0.126** | 0.021 | 0.096** | 0.021 | 0.128** | 0.027 |
| Number of Girls Aged 6 to 9 | 0.122** | 0.020 | 0.092** | 0.020 | 0.109** | 0.025 |
| Number of Girls Aged 10 to 14 | 0.078** | 0.018 | 0.049** | 0.018 | 0.028 | 0.023 |
| Number of Girls Aged 15 to 17 | −0.022 | 0.023 | −0.040 | 0.023 | −0.043 | 0.029 |
| Constant | −3.871** | 0.119 | −3.255** | 0.124 | −3.245** | 0.159 |
| Number of Observations | 28805 | | | | 28665 | |
| Chi-Squared (n) | 4018.73(17) | | | | 4094.19(19) | |
| Psuedo R-Squared | 0.230 | | | | 0.1924 | |

Notes:

*Statistically significant at the 5% level.

**Statistically significant at the 1% level.

White's heteroskedastic consistent errors used in all regressions.

labor market.[9] However, the greater the number of siblings aged 5 to 14, the more likely the children were to work.

The third specification reported in table 6.2 shows the results of the regression when the parents' years of schooling were added as dependent variables. As expected, the parents' years of schooling had a strongly negative effect on the children's probability of working; however, the effect of parental child labor remained positive and statistically significant.

The research also estimates a probit model that includes the grandparents' years of schooling as explanatory variables. Column 5 of table 6.2 shows the coefficients from the complete set of regressors. The grandparents' years of schooling became insignificant when the parents' education variables were included, suggesting there is no direct link between grandparents' education and their grandchildren's child-labor status. Although not reported, the study also estimates a probit including grandparents' years of schooling but excluding the parents' years of schooling. In this case, the grandparents' schooling becomes significant; thus, the schooling effect of the grandparents on their grandchildren appears to operate through the education of the parents.

### Probit Model Estimations Including Family Income

Adding family income to the probit specification can cause an endogeneity problem, but considering it as an explanatory variable is useful in determining whether parents' education is an adequate proxy for permanent family income. The family's income minus the income from the observed child is included in the regressions in table 6.3. The first specification includes both the family income variable as well as the parents' education variable; the results are shown in the first column of table 6.3. In this case, the coefficients on both parents' child-labor indicator variables are positive and significant and the coefficients on the parents' education variables are negative and significant. The coefficient on the family income variable is not significant, however. The schooling of the parents is not included in the second specification, shown in column 3 of table 6.3. Here, the coefficients on the parents' child-labor indicator variables are still positive and significant but now the coefficient on the family income variable is negative and significant.

These results are not predicted by the simple model, suggesting (1) the effects of parental child labor may be more complex than the simple human capital relationship posited in the model, and (2) that future research is needed. For example, it is possible that human capital accumulation is not only determined by the amount of education, but also by social norms, preferences, the quality of education, the level of education of siblings, the household environment, etc.

Figure 6.2 compares the probability of working in the labor market for a 12-year-old child of parents who were child laborers and a child of parents who did not work as children. It is assumed that both parents

Table 6.3   Child labor persistence. Probit on child labor indicator variable including family income as explanatory variable

| Independent Variables | Coefficient | Std. Error | Coefficient | Std. Error |
|---|---|---|---|---|
| Child Laborer Father | 0.258** | 0.031 | 0.310** | 0.030 |
| Child Laborer Mother | 0.319** | 0.028 | 0.369** | 0.028 |
| Father's Years of Schooling | −0.026** | 0.004 | | |
| Mother's Years of Schooling | −0.028** | 0.004 | | |
| Age of the Child | 0.212** | 0.008 | 0.211** | 0.008 |
| Female Child | −0.583** | 0.033 | −0.578** | 0.033 |
| Urban | −0.718** | 0.024 | −0.783** | 0.024 |
| Father Not in the Labor Market | −0.244** | 0.046 | −0.230** | 0.046 |
| Mother Not in the Labor Market | −0.363** | 0.029 | −0.314** | 0.028 |
| Father's Age | 0.005** | 0.002 | 0.008** | 0.002 |
| Mother's Age | 0.001 | 0.002 | 0.003 | 0.002 |
| Number of Boys Aged 0 to 5 | 0.037 | 0.022 | 0.052* | 0.022 |
| Number of Boys Aged 6 to 9 | 0.081** | 0.021 | 0.101** | 0.021 |
| Number of Boys Aged 10 to 14 | 0.058** | 0.018 | 0.073** | 0.018 |
| Number of Boys Aged 15 to 17 | 0.011 | 0.021 | 0.032 | 0.021 |
| Number of Girls Aged 0 to 5 | 0.095** | 0.022 | 0.115** | 0.022 |
| Number of Girls Aged 6 to 9 | 0.095** | 0.020 | 0.113** | 0.020 |
| Number of Girls Aged 10 to 14 | 0.047** | 0.018 | 0.065** | 0.018 |
| Number of Girls Aged 15 to 17 | −0.030 | 0.024 | −0.015 | 0.023 |
| Family Income Minus Child Income | −0.00002 | 0.00002 | −0.00012** | 0.00002 |
| Constant | −3.311** | 0.126 | −3.797** | 0.121 |
| Number of Observations | 27791 | | 27926 | |
| Chi-Squared (n) | 3935.88(20) | | 3837.11(18) | |
| Psuedo R-Squared | 0.2384 | | 0.2308 | |

Notes:
*Statistically significant at the 5% level.
**Statistically significant at the 1% level.
White's heteroskedastic consistent errors used in all regressions.

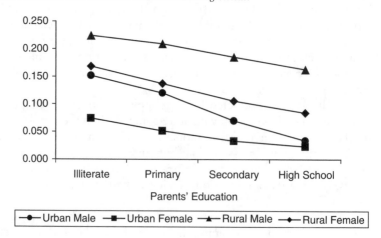

Figure 6.2   The Increased Probability that a 12-Year-Old Child Works Attributed to His/Her Parents Having Been Child Laborers

work, have the same level of education, are 40 years old, and have only one child. The probability differences are constructed separately for sons and daughters in rural and urban areas and use the coefficients from the first column of table 6.2. At any level of parental education, children from families with parents who were child laborers are more likely to be child laborers. This difference decreases as the education level of the parents increases, as expected.

## The Effects of Child Labor on Future Earnings

Child labor also holds the potential to hamper an adults' ability to generate higher earnings. To assess this impact, the study estimates both a simple OLS regression and a Heckman selection model for both mothers and fathers. The specifications regress the log of current earnings on age and age squared, the age at which the parents started work and its square, the grandfathers' years of schooling, the grandmothers' years of schooling, and a race indicator variable. The individual's years of schooling are added in separate specifications. The Heckman estimations attempt to correct for the fact that the study only observed the income of those individuals who self-selected to work as adults; the results would be biased and suspect if the decision to work as an adult is in any way correlated with having been a child laborer. For the selection-bias corrected estimations, the number of sons and daughters aged 0 to 9 years old is added in the first stage regression; see table 6.4 for the results.

For both fathers and mothers, the coefficient on the age they started working is positive and significant in all specifications. In the specification that excludes the years of schooling variables, the age they started to work coefficients are interpreted as the forgone earnings of an individual entering the labor market one year earlier. Further, child labor has a negative impact on current earnings even when the study controls for education and other variables. This means there are negative aspects of having been a child laborer over and above that of losing out on education, again raising questions about the precise effects of parental child labor on children. There do not appear to be positive effects on adult earnings of gaining work experience as a child laborer. The squared term is negative and significant, which means the marginal negative impact of child labor for adults lessens the later the individual enters the labor force.

The results of table 6.4 show that on average, child labor hampers the individual's adult earnings. Emerson and Souza (2002), however, examined this aspect of child labor more closely and found that in some instances (i.e., for particular occupations) child labor may not be harmful. The general idea is that in some professions with strong vocational aspects, individuals may be able to do well as adults. However, these results suggest that though there may be some areas in which child labor is beneficial, they are greatly outweighed by those that are harmful.

Table 6.4  Effect of child labor on log of adult earnings of fathers and mothers. OLS and Heckman model estimates

| Independent variables | OLS | | | | Heckman | | | |
|---|---|---|---|---|---|---|---|---|
| | Coeff. | Std. Error | Coeff. | Std. Error | Coeff. | Std. Error | Coeff. | Std. Error |
| *Father* | | | | | | | | |
| Age Started Work | 0.06132** | 0.00869 | 0.05130** | 0.00766 | 0.06018** | 0.00874 | 0.05101** | 0.00768 |
| Age Started Work-Squared | -0.00070** | 0.00031 | -0.00156** | 0.00028 | -0.00066** | 0.00032 | -0.00155** | 0.00028 |
| Years of Schooling | | | 0.11969** | 0.00166 | | | 0.11944** | 0.00173 |
| Father's Years of Schooling | 0.07389** | 0.00317 | 0.01954** | 0.00290 | 0.07329** | 0.00320 | 0.01949** | 0.00290 |
| Mother's Years of Schooling | 0.07557** | 0.00351 | 0.02178** | 0.00318 | 0.07557** | 0.00352 | 0.02189** | 0.00319 |
| Age | 0.07983** | 0.00601 | 0.05777** | 0.00530 | 0.07634** | 0.00621 | 0.05694** | 0.00553 |
| Age-Squared | -0.00094** | 0.00006 | -0.00064** | 0.00006 | -0.00090** | 0.00007 | -0.00063** | 0.00006 |
| Non-White | -0.44442** | 0.01352 | -0.27841** | 0.01214 | -0.44054** | 0.01367 | -0.27771** | 0.01221 |
| Constant | 3.52783** | 0.15250 | 3.65264** | 0.13444 | 3.62497** | 0.15853 | 3.67701** | 0.14208 |
| Number of Observations | 17950 | | 17925 | | 19571 | | 19543 | |
| R-Squared | 0.3133 | | 0.468 | | | | | |
| Lambda | | | | | -0.182 | 0.075 | -0.047 | 0.088 |
| Chi-Squared (n) | | | | | 7342.63(7) | | 13041.52(8) | |

Mother

| | | | | |
|---|---|---|---|---|
| Age Started Work | 0.09744** (0.00590) | 0.03040** (0.00548) | 0.07096** (0.00651) | 0.01697** (0.00590) |
| Age Started Work-Squared | −0.00208** (0.00014) | −0.00073** (0.00013) | −0.00163** (0.00016) | −0.00053** (0.00014) |
| Years of Schooling | 0.07091** (0.00394) | 0.10580** (0.00224) | | 0.08790** (0.00281) |
| Father's Years of Schooling | 0.06762** (0.00424) | 0.03240** (0.00362) | 0.06404** (0.00422) | 0.03293** (0.00386) |
| Mother's Years of Schooling | 0.14297** (0.01366) | 0.01961** (0.00394) | 0.05807** (0.00457) | 0.01913** (0.00420) |
| Age | −0.00165** (0.00017) | 0.06467** (0.01239) | 0.10366** (0.01434) | 0.03954** (0.01290) |
| Age-Squared | −0.38613** (0.01926) | −0.00070** (0.00015) | −0.00114** (0.0017) | −0.00037** (0.00016) |
| Nonwhite | 1.25984** (0.27920) | −0.27747** (0.01745) | −0.37555** (0.02026) | −0.28780** (0.01837) |
| Constant | | 2.92562** (0.25350) | 2.57553** (0.30262) | 3.89807 (0.27312) |
| Number of Observations | 8943 | 8893 | 13151 | 13093 |
| R-Squared | 0.3047 | 0.4444 | | |
| Lambda | | | −0.547 (0.038) | −0.496 (0.041) |
| Chi-Squared (n) | | | 2019.71(7) | 2818.71(8) |

Notes:
*Statistically significant at the 5% level.
**Statistically significant at the 1% level.
White's heteroskedastic consistent errors used in all regressions.

## Conclusion and Comment on Policy

The results presented in this study suggest that there is a significant relationship between a parent's child labor incidence and years of schooling and those of their children. Children are more likely to be child laborers if their parents worked as children and the less educated their parents are. The educational attainment of grandparents does not directly affect the child's labor status, but there seems to be an indirect impact that is transmitted through the parents' education. These results hold when controlled for family income. In addition, the earlier an individual enters the labor market, the lower his earnings are as an adult. Together, these results paint a striking picture of the intergenerational persistence of poverty and the harmful effects of child labor within dynastic families.

This suggests that the simple persistence model does not explain every way in which parental child labor affects children and that richer models are needed. If this study's results are derived from some unobservable human capital characteristics captured by the parental child-labor variables (e.g., school quality), then the finding essentially captures the intergenerational effects of poverty persistence and is consistent with the theoretical discussion of child-labor persistence. If, on the other hand, the results stem from a difference in the preferences of households in which parents were child laborers or different social norms associated with child labor, the current theoretical child-labor literature is inadequate to fully explain child labor in Brazil.

These results pose complicated challenges for policy makers. If the persistence theory, or a major portion of it, is correct, it may be better to tackle the child-labor problem on a family-by-family basis: if there are limited resources it may be better to target select families to raise each out of the child labor trap. Bell and Gersbach (2001) have examined just such a system in their education model. This type of policy is likely to be politically unpopular but would have lasting long-term benefits.

If child labor is indeed primarily a result of familial poverty, banning child labor can have quite harmful effects (Basu and Pham Hoang Van, 1998) and should be treated with the utmost of caution, and a more challenging policy problem is presented. If, however, poverty is a small part of the story and norms or parental preferences are the major factors, policy solutions such as absolute bans on child labor may be more effective.

This study indicates that both are significant factors. It is easier for policy makers to address policy alleviation than parental preferences, but it is possible to marry the two. Policies such as those that target individual families for conditional income transfers that create incentives to alter behavior and also incorporate educational programs to counteract traditional beliefs that child labor is good for children could affect both avenues at the same time. As this study shows, child labor has lasting and harmful effects on an individual's earning ability as an adult, and the negative effect of the loss of educational attainment is greater than the positive effect of gaining experience as a child laborer.[10] Thus, intervention is both necessary and important.

# Notes

Portions of this chapter previously appeared in Emerson and André Portela F. de Souza. 2003. "Is There a Child Labor Trap? Inter-generational Persistence of Child Labor in Brazil." *Economic Development and Cultural Change*, University of Chicago Press, 51 (January): 375–398. © 2003 by Patrick M. Emerson and Andre Portela F. de Souza. Reprinted with permission.

1. This also is closely linked to the idea of poverty traps such as that illustrated in Galor and Zeira (1993).

2. For a more rigorous theoretical treatment see Emerson and Souza (2000).

3. PNAD assigns each individual to a position or "condition" in the family. They are as follows: (1) person of reference; (2) spouse; (3) son or daughter; (4) other relative; (5) aggregate; (6) pensionist; (7) domestic worker; and (8) relative of the domestic worker.

4. This selection criterion may impose some selection bias if, e.g., children in single-head families are more likely to work. However, similar results were obtained when a full sample of 10- to 14-year-old children was used. In this case the head of the family's characteristics were used instead of the father and mother's characteristics. To capture separate impacts of the father's and the mother's child-labor status and to have a straight interpretation of the coefficients, the results are presented with the sample described in the text.

5. PNAD asks the usual hours worked per week for each individual during the week before the survey.

6. All results in this chapter come from the un-weighted sample. All of the empirical tests in this study were replicated using a weighted sample and obtained qualitatively the same results.

7. The inclusion of the indicator variables of a parent not in the labor market accounts for the fact that for those parents not in the labor market, the age they started to work is unknown.

8. A similar model was estimated for the case when child labor was defined as a child who worked at least twenty hours in the week of reference. The research obtained qualitatively the same results.

9. In the sample, roughly 10% of men and 46% of women were not in the labor market. There seems to be no reason, a priori, to think that these individuals would be more or less likely to have been child laborers. However, the child-labor history of those not in the labor market was not observed and, in the extreme case (they all were child laborers), the negative and significant sign on those not in the labor-market variables for fathers and mothers could counteract the positive coefficient on the parental child labor variable and could mean that the net effect of child labor status is insignificant. Because only 10% of fathers were not in the labor market, it seems very unlikely that this would be the case, but it is potentially a problem for the effect of maternal child labor.

10. This is true for most occupations. See Emerson and Souza (2002).

# The Impact of Child Labor Intensity on Mathematics and Language Skills in Latin America

*Mario A. Sánchez, Peter F. Orazem, and Victoria Gunnarsson*

The previous chapters have shown that working as a child is associated with lower wages and higher incidence of poverty as an adult. Because wages rise with years of education, it is clear that if child labor reduces years of schooling completed, adult wages will be reduced. Numerous studies have linked child labor with lower grade attainment. However, the evidence in chapter 5 suggests that child labor lowers the rate of return per year of education, consistent with the possibility that child labor lowers the amount of human capital produced per grade completed. Although plausible, the link between child labor and student achievement in primary schools is not well understood.

Surprisingly few studies have examined how child labor affects schooling outcomes. Those that do have tended to concentrate on students at the secondary or tertiary school levels in developed countries. Ehrenberg and Sherman (1987) found that working while in college had little impact on grade point average (GPA). However, working while in school did lengthen the time to graduate and increased the probability of dropout. Research performed at the secondary school level presents a similarly mixed message. D'Amico (1984) found that working while in high school lowered study time but had no impact on class rank. Lillydahl (1990) found that part-time work actually increased grade point averages when the job involved less than 13.5 hours per week, although the effect dissipated thereafter. Both D'Amico and Lillydahl found evidence that part-time work improved knowledge of business and economics. Others have found evidence that working longer hours harms academic achievement. Howard (1998) found that A-level grades in England declined when students worked more than fifteen hours per week, and Singh (1998) reported a modest decrease in U.S. achievement test scores as hours worked increased.

The general conclusion from these studies is that there is little evidence that working while in school harms school achievement, provided that the part-time job does not involve too many hours. In fact, part-time jobs can actually enhance learning in subjects that are complementary with work. Where part-time work harms academic achievement, the effect is small. However, it is dangerous to extend these conclusions derived from studies of high school or college students in developed countries to the case of young children working in developing countries. Part-time work may be more disruptive for attaining basic literacy and numeracy than it is of learning at higher levels. The types of jobs performed by older students in developed countries may be more complementary with schooling than the low-skilled, manual work performed by young children in developing countries. Older children also may be more able to absorb the physical demands of combining school and work, whereas younger children may find that labor leaves them too tired to keep up with school.

More recently, researchers have started to examine schooling outcomes n developing countries. Heady (2003), and Rosati and Rossi (2003) have found some evidence that child labor lowers primary school test scores in developing countries. Post and Pong (2000) also found a negative association between work and test scores in samples of eighth graders in many of the twenty-three countries they studied. While these studies suggest that child labor may adversely affect schooling outcomes, various data restrictions may cloud their conclusions. The Rosati and Rossi and Post and Pong studies did not have controls for school attributes, and so their findings may be due to correlation between child labor and missing school quality. The Heady paper did not control for likely joint causality between time in school and in work. None of the studies had information on intensity of work.

Policies designed to limit child labor are predicated, at least in part, on the presumption that part-time work reduces the probability that children will attain literacy and numeracy. On the other hand, some researchers have pointed to the high enrollment rates of child workers as evidence that part-time work and schooling are compatible, presuming that time in school equates to learning, regardless of how time is spent out of school.

Using a unique data set on language and mathematics test scores for third- and fourth-graders in eleven Latin American countries, this study represents a rare attempt to determine which of these presumptions about the effect of child labor on achievement is true, or if both presumptions hold in some locations but not others. The findings are amazingly consistent across countries. Child labor lowers performance on tests of language and mathematics proficiency in every country, even when controlling for school and household attributes. The magnitude of the effect is similar to the percentage reduction in adult wages from child labor reported in chapter 5. The adverse impact of child labor on test performance is larger when children work regularly rather than occasionally. There is only a small advantage in test scores from occasional work versus regular work, so even modest levels of child labor at early ages cause adverse consequences for the development of cognitive abilities. These findings strongly refute the presumptions that child labor may be complementary or neutral with respect to academic performance, provided that the child remains enrolled in school. Instead, child labor consistently makes a year of education less productive in the generation of human capital.

## Methodology

A large amount of literature evaluates the factors that affect children's performance in school. Following Hanushek (1986) and Glewwe (2002), the standard methodology is to relate measures of a student's academic performance, Q, to the attributes of the student's family, F, school, S, and teacher, T, and a measure of the student's ability, A. A measure of the student's time in the labor market, L, can be added to this. The production process can be written

$$Q = f(F, S, T, A, L) \tag{7.1}$$

In practice, family attributes are more important in explaining variation in student achievement in both developed and developing countries. Measures of either the mother's or the father's education and of the income or wealth of the household are typically important in improving the schooling outcomes of their children. Of the school inputs, teacher attributes (teacher education and/or experience) appear to be most important in affecting achievement in developing countries (Hanushek, 1995).[1] Class size does not matter in either developing or developed countries. Other school attributes often have mixed or insignificant effects in developed countries, but school attributes appear to be more important in developing countries. The quality of school facilities, access to textbooks, and expenditures per pupil consistently have positive effects on student achievement (Hanushek, 1995; Kremer, 1995).

Estimates of educational production functions are subject to numerous biases.[2] Among the most common is the lack of adequate control for the student's innate ability. Many studies have attempted to correct for the problem by using two measures of the output measure, Q. If ability has an additive effect on school achievement, the difference between the two output measures will be purged of the ability effect. However, as Glewwe (2002) argues, if measures of F, S, and T only vary slowly over time, the value of using the change in Q as the measure of achievement is minimal. In addition, if there is considerable measurement error in estimates of Q, the level of Q may be measured more reliably than the change in Q.

Less commonly discussed is the lack of measures on the intensity of time or effort spent in school on the part of the child. This is undoubtedly because data sets with measures of the proportion of child time spent in school or at work were not available.

# Data

In 1997, the Latin American Laboratory of Quality of Education (LLECE) carried out the first Comparative International Study on Language, Mathematics and Associated Factors for third- and fourth-graders in Latin America. LLECE initially collected data in thirteen countries: Argentina, Bolivia, Brazil, Chile, Colombia, Costa Rica, Cuba, Honduras, Mexico, Paraguay, Peru, Dominican Republic, and Venezuela. Costa Rica's data did not satisfy LLECE's technical requirements for consistency and was dropped from the study. Later in this study, missing data on child labor in Cuba will cause that country to be dropped from the analysis as well.

The data set is composed of a stratified sample designed to ensure sufficient observations of public, private, rural (communities with less than 2,500 inhabitants), urban (between 2,500 and 1 million inhabitants), and mega-urban (more than 1 million inhabitants) students in each country. The plan called for data to be obtained from 100 schools in each country with forty children per school for a total of 4,000 observations per country. Half of the students were to be in the third grade and half in the fourth grade. The stratified samples were designed to be roughly proportional to the populations of five strata: mega-urban public schools, mega-urban private schools, urban public schools, urban private schools, and rural schools. Rural private schools were not included in the sample design.

For budgetary reasons, LLECE used a priori geographic exclusions to limit the transportation and time costs of data collection. Exclusion criteria varied from country to country; common criteria were very small schools and those in remote, difficult to access, or sparsely inhabited regions. Due to the cost of translating exams, schools with bilingual or indigenous language instruction also were commonly excluded.[3]

The survey used learning tests on language and mathematics with the sample of third- and fourth-graders and self-applied questionnaires with school principals, teachers, and parents (or legal guardians) of the tested children, as well as the children themselves. In addition, surveyors collected information on the socioeconomic characteristics of the communities.

Within each school, the choice of which children to survey and test depended on the number of classes. If there were fewer than five classes of fourth- and fifth-graders, twenty students were randomly selected from third and fourth grade. If there were five or more third- and fourth-grade classes, four classes were chosen, then twenty students were selected from those classes.

## An Overview of the Twelve Countries

Children in the third and fourth grades of selected schools in each of the twelve countries were tested on language (Spanish, except for Brazil, whose students were tested on Portuguese) and mathematics. Table 7.1 presents the average test scores for the two exams by country, along with

**Table 7.1**    Child labor, test scores, and representative characteristics by country

| Country | N | Child Labor[a] (%) | Rural[b] (%) | Private[c] (%) | Poor[d] (%) | Test Score Language | Test Score Mathematics |
|---|---|---|---|---|---|---|---|
| Argentina | 4,224 | 34.4 | 12.4 | 18.9 | 21.4 | 13.5 | 17.5 |
| Bolivia | 4,879 | 56.9 | 25.8 | 32.2 | 35.6 | 10.8 | 15.5 |
| Brazil | 4,374 | 36.4 | 16.2 | 21.7 | 52.9 | 13.0 | 17.2 |
| Chile | 4,646 | 45.7 | 26.5 | 33.7 | 46.8 | 13.0 | 15.8 |
| Colombia | 4,306 | 52.4 | 28.4 | 25.0 | 42.0 | 11.7 | 15.4 |
| Cuba | 3,950 | e | 33.1 | 0 | 4.0 | 17.1 | 26.7 |
| Dominican Republic | 3,729 | 51.8 | 33.1 | 28.2 | 40.3 | 9.9 | 13.1 |
| Honduras | 3,746 | 41.6 | 54.1 | 11.5 | 59.8 | 9.8 | 12.4 |
| Mexico | 5,038 | 43.7 | 34.7 | 19.6 | 24.7 | 11.4 | 16.2 |
| Paraguay | 4,718 | 29.8 | 36.0 | 29.4 | 23.2 | 11.4 | 14.9 |
| Peru | 4,298 | 57.1 | 29.1 | 22.4 | 69.1 | 10.6 | 12.9 |
| Venezuela | 3,691 | 21.4 | 22.5 | 21.6 | 13.0 | 11.5 | 11.8 |
| All Countries | 51,485[f] | 40 | 29.2 | 22.4 | 35.9 | 12.0 | 15.8 |

*Notes:*
[a]Child indicates he works outside the home sometimes or often when not in school.
[b]Child lives in community with population below 2,500.
[c]Child attends private school.
[d]Observer characterizes community socioeconomic status as poor or very poor.
[e]Missing observations.
[f]The potential sample size is attenuated by lack of responses to questions. Children were asked about the amount of time they worked outside the home. Only 36,826 responses were obtained to that question.

representative information on each country sample. The language score has a maximum of 19. The average score across all countries is 12, or 63%. Country averages vary from a low of 9.8 in Honduras to a high of 17.1 in Cuba. Cuba also dominates the mathematics results with an average score of 26.7, more than 53% higher than that of the next highest country. Cuba's academic performance is truly remarkable, given it has the lowest per capita GDP of the twelve countries.[4]

Unfortunately, while the Cuban test scores appear to be an accurate portrayal of the cognitive abilities of Cuban students, the rest of the data appeared unreliable. Only 4% of the Cuban villages were characterized as poor or very poor, out of line with even the most optimistic characterizations of the Cuban economy. More importantly for these purposes, 94% of the Cuban children did not answer the question regarding child labor, so the Cuban data cannot be incorporated into the study. Nevertheless, researchers interested in devising policies to improve school efficiency in poor countries would find it useful to study the Cuban case to determine how they generate such superior outcomes.[5]

In the other eleven countries, just under one-third of the children come from rural areas. Just over one-fifth attend private school. About one-third reside in communities characterized as either low-income or impoverished. Even these simple statistics reveal some interesting patterns. Of eight countries with above-average levels of child labor, six have below-average scores on both exams, and another (Mexico) scores below average on language but not math. Only students in Chile score in the upper half on both exams despite above-average incidence of child labor. All countries with above-average levels of rural population have below-average test scores, except Mexico. The link between poverty and test scores is less apparent. Of six countries with higher-than-average poverty incidence, two (Brazil and Chile) score above average on both exams. There is no particular correspondence between the proportion of students in private schools and average test scores.

Table 7.2 presents the unconditional estimates of the mean test scores for language and mathematics by intensity of child labor. Children were asked

**Table 7.2**  Average language and mathematics test scores by country and level of child labor

| Country | Language Test (Maximum Score = 19) | | Mathematics Test (Maximum Score = 32) | |
|---|---|---|---|---|
| | Unconditional[a] | Conditional[b] | Unconditional[a] | Conditional[b] |
| **Argentina** | | | | |
| Often Working[c] | 12.3 | 12.3 | 16.0 | 16.0 |
| Sometime Working[d] | 13.3**[f] | 13.5** | 17.6** | 17.6** |
| | (8.1%)[g] | (9.8%) | (10%) | (10%) |
| Almost Never Working[e] | 14.5** | 14.1** | 18.9** | 18.0** |
| | (17.9%) | (14.6%) | (18.1%) | (12.5%) |
| **Bolivia** | | | | |
| Often Working[c] | 9.8 | 9.8 | 14.5 | 14.5 |
| Sometime Working[d] | 10.4** | 10.3* | 15.1* | 14.7* |
| | (6.1%) | (5.1%) | (4.1%) | (1.4%) |
| Almost Never Working[e] | 12.3** | 11.6** | 17.2** | 15.6** |
| | (25.5%) | (18.4%) | (18.6%) | (7.6%) |
| **Brazil** | | | | |
| Often Working[c] | 11.4 | 11.4 | 14.6 | 14.6 |
| Sometime Working[d] | 12.1** | 11.8 | 15.9** | 15.8** |
| | (4.3%) | (3.5%) | (8.9%) | (8.2%) |
| Almost Never Working[e] | 14.0** | 13.3** | 18.7** | 17.8** |
| | (22.8%) | (16.7%) | (28.1%) | (21.9%) |
| **Chile** | | | | |
| Often Working[c] | 11.6 | 11.6 | 13.8 | 13.8 |
| Sometime Working[d] | 12.6** | 12.6** | 15.0** | 15.0** |
| | (8.6%) | (8.6%) | (8.7%) | (8.7%) |
| Almost Never Working[e] | 14.0** | 13.6** | 17.0** | 16.5** |
| | (20.7%) | (17.2%) | (23.2%) | (19.6%) |
| **Colombia** | | | | |
| Often Working[c] | 10.3 | 10.3 | 14.2 | 14.2 |
| Sometime Working[d] | 11.5** | 11.7** | 15.6** | 15.8** |
| | (11.7%) | (13.6%) | (9.9%) | (11.3%) |
| Almost Never Working[e] | 12.8** | 12.6** | 16.4** | 16.1** |
| | (24.3%) | (22.3%) | (15.5%) | (13.4%) |
| **Dominican Republic** | | | | |
| Often Working[c] | 9.5 | 9.5 | 12.6 | 12.6 |
| Sometime Working[d] | 9.7 | 9.5 | 13.3** | 13.3* |
| | (2.1%) | (0%) | (5.6%) | (5.6%) |

*Continued*

**Table 7.2** Continued

| Country | Language Test (Maximum Score = 19) | | Mathematics Test (Maximum Score = 32) | |
|---|---|---|---|---|
| | Unconditional[a] | Conditional[b] | Unconditional[a] | Conditional[b] |
| Almost Never Working[e] | 11.1** (16.8%) | 10.6** (11.6%) | 13.8** (9.5%) | 13.1 (4.0%) |
| **Honduras** | | | | |
| Often Working[c] | 9.1 | 9.1 | 11.8 | 11.8 |
| Sometime Working[d] | 9.7** (6.6%) | 9.4 (3.3%) | 12.6** (6.8%) | 11.0 (−6.8%) |
| Almost Never Working[e] | 11.8** (29.7%) | 11.9** (30.8%) | 14.6** (23.7%) | 13.2* (11.9%) |
| **Mexico** | | | | |
| Often Working[c] | 9.6 | 9.6 | 13.8 | 13.8 |
| Sometime Working[d] | 10.6** (10.4%) | 10.7** (11.5%) | 15.1** (9.4%) | 15.4** (11.6%) |
| Almost Never Working[e] | 12.5** (30.2%) | 11.8** (22.9%) | 17.7** (28.3%) | 17.1** (23.9%) |
| **Paraguay** | | | | |
| Often Working[c] | 11.2 | 11.2 | 13.9 | 13.9 |
| Sometime Working[d] | 11.8** (5.4%) | 11.8 (5.4%) | 15.5** (11.5%) | 15.4 (10.8%) |
| Almost Never Working[e] | 13.1** (17.0%) | 13.1** (17.0%) | 17.3** (24.5%) | 18.0** (29.5%) |
| **Peru** | | | | |
| Often Working[c] | 9.1 | 9.1 | 11.6 | 11.6 |
| Sometime Working[d] | 10.1** (11.0%) | 9.7** (6.6%) | 11.9 (2.6%) | 11.8 (1.7%) |
| Almost Never Working[e] | 12.2** (34.1%) | 10.7** (17.6%) | 14.9 (28.4%) | 13.4** (15.5%) |
| **Venezuela** | | | | |
| Often Working[c] | 10.0 | 10.0 | 12.2 | 12.2 |
| Sometime Working[d] | 10.9** (9.0%) | 10.5 (5.0%) | 13.0* (6.6%) | 12.9 (5.7%) |
| Almost Never Working[e] | 11.5** (15.0%) | 11.3** (13.0%) | 14.5** (18.9%) | 13.7** (12.3%) |
| **All Countries** | | | | |
| Often Working[c] | 10.2 | 10.2 | 13.6 | 13.6 |
| Sometime Working[d] | 11.1** (8.8%) | 10.9** (6.9%) | 14.7** (8.1%) | 14.4** (5.9%) |
| Almost Never Working[e] | 13.0** (27.5%) | 12.1** (18.6%) | 17.0** (25.0%) | 15.7** (15.4%) |

Notes:
[a]Simple mean test score over all children in the child labor group in the country.

[b]Based on coefficients of dummy variables for "Sometime" and "Never" from country-specific regressions comparable to the specifications reported in table 7.4. The regressions also included all the school, teacher, and household factors included in table 7.4.

[c]Child almost always works outside the home when not in school.

[d]Child sometimes works outside the home when not in school.

[e]Child almost never works outside the home.

[f]Indicates difference in mean test score from the "often working" group is significant at the .05(*) or .01(**) level of significance.

[g]Percentage difference relative to children who often work outside the home when not in school.

if, when not in school, they worked outside the home almost always, occasionally, or never. Their answers create three child labor groups for each country. The test of the difference in means is between those who often work outside the home and those who sometimes or almost never work.

Across eleven countries and two achievement tests (twenty-two total cases), the pattern never varies. Those who work only some of the time outperform those who work most of the time, and those who never work outperform both. The advantage for children who do not work is large relative to those who work often, averaging 27.5% for languages and 25% for mathematics over those who often work. The advantage for occasional child laborers is much smaller, averaging 8.8% in languages and 8.1% in mathematics. The large gap between children who never work and those who work occasionally suggests that there is a significant opportunity cost in the form of lost cognitive skills when young children work just part of the time.

The questionnaire also elicited information on whether the child often, sometimes, or almost never works inside the home. As shown in Gunnarsson et al. (2006), there was no apparent correlation between school performance and intensity of household work. However, we must be cautious in concluding that work in the home has no adverse impact on cognitive attainment because over 95% of the children reported working in the home sometime or often. It may be that work in the home has a harmful effect, but the lack of variation in child work in the home prevents us from observing the true effect. For the balance of this chapter, we will focus on child work outside the home.

## Regression Analysis

The pattern of unconditional means could be related to other factors that jointly raise child labor and lower test scores, such as poor schools, inadequate teachers, and illiterate parents, all of which would lower expected school productivity and increase incentives to allocate child time to the labor market.

To investigate this, available information on school, teacher, and household attributes was added. Because the information was not available for all children, about 50% of the sample was lost. The greatest cause for missing observations was incomplete data on the parents. It should be noted that none of the qualitative results reported were sensitive to the inclusion or exclusion of individual regressors in the model, so the results are not driven by this particular choice of variable.[6]

The summary statistics for the observations in the regressions are reported in table 7.3. Measures of the school include location (rural versus urban), ownership status (public versus private), whether the school is arranged in single grade or multigrade classrooms, and the number of pupils per classroom. Information on the child's teacher, obtained from a survey of their education and years of teaching experience, is included. Efforts also were

**Table 7.3**  Definitions and summary statistics for variables used to explain test scores

| Variable | Description | Mean | Std. Dev. |
|---|---|---|---|
| *Child Labor* | | | |
| Sometime Working | Dummy variable indicating if child works outside the home occasionally when not in school | 0.33 | 0.47 |
| Almost Never Working | Dummy variable indicating if child rarely works outside the home | 0.43 | 0.49 |
| *School Factors* | | | |
| Rural | Dummy variable indicating if the school is located outside an urban area | 0.29 | 0.45 |
| Public | Dummy variable indicating school is a government school | 0.75 | 0.43 |
| Single Grade | Classroom only includes a single grade | 0.90 | 0.30 |
| Pupils/Classroom | Number of pupils in the classroom | 31.0 | 12.4 |
| *Teacher Factors* | | | |
| Education | Education level of the teacher, indicated by an index in which 0 = none, 1 = secondary, 3 = tertiary | 1.45 | 0.56 |
| Experience | Years the teacher has been teaching | 13.8 | 8.9 |
| *Household Factors* | | | |
| Two Parents | Dummy variable indicating there are two parents or legal guardians in the household | 0.80 | 0.40 |
| Head Education | Average education level of the parents or legal guardians, indicated by an index in which 1 = primary incomplete, 2 = primary complete, 3 = secondary incomplete, 4 = secondary complete, 5 = tertiary incomplete, 6 = tertiary complete | 2.74 | 1.63 |

*Note:*
Sample excludes Cuba and drops observations with missing data on child labor.

made to obtain information on the child's parents through a household survey. This proved expensive and surveyors did not have time to locate parents who were not present at the time of enumeration. Missing parental information costs about 10,000 observations, or one-quarter of the sample. The problem of missing observations is most severe in Honduras, Paraguay, Venezuela, and to a lesser extent, Brazil. Because the results are so consistent across countries with varying levels of missing observations, it does not appear that nonresponse bias is driving the results.

The regressions across the eleven countries (excluding Cuba) are reported in table 7.4. The model explains about one-fifth of the variation in test scores across children. Because country dummy variables are included, it can be concluded that most of the variation in student cognitive abilities are within countries and not between countries.

The results mimic those commonly found in developing countries (Hanushek, 1995). Urban schools outperform rural schools and private schools outperform public schools. Pupil-teacher ratios have no effect, a common finding. Multigrade classrooms outperform single grade classrooms,

**Table 7.4**  Pooled educational production function estimation

|  | Language | Mathematics |
|---|---|---|
| *Child Labor Indicator* (reference = Often Working) |  |  |
| Sometime Working | 0.70** | 0.80** |
|  | (9.11) | (7.12) |
| Almost Never Working | 1.85** | 2.06** |
|  | (24.6) | (18.7) |
| *School Factors* |  |  |
| Rural | −0.91** | −0.39** |
|  | (12.1) | (3.63) |
| Public | −0.85** | −1.77** |
|  | (11.1) | (15.7) |
| Single Grade | −0.10 | −0.30* |
|  | (0.98) | (2.08) |
| Pupils/Classroom | 0.00 | 0.00 |
|  | (1.07) | (0.63) |
| *Teacher Factors* |  |  |
| Education | 0.31 | −0.16 |
|  | (1.15) | (0.42) |
| Education$^2$ | −0.04 | 0.15 |
|  | (0.40) | (1.04) |
| Experience | −0.00 | 0.00 |
|  | (0.39) | (0.25) |
| *Household Factors* |  |  |
| Two Parents | 0.23** | 0.38** |
|  | (3.12) | (3.61) |
| Head Education | 0.18** | −0.07 |
|  | (2.54) | (0.67) |
| (Head Education)$^2$ | 0.05** | 0.12** |
|  | (4.53) | (7.29) |
| *Country Dummies* | Included | Included |
| $R^2$ | 0.21 | 0.18 |
| N | 18375 | 18373 |
| Mean of dependent variable | 11.6 | 14.9 |

*Notes:*
   t-statistics in parentheses.
   *Indicates significance at the .05 confidence level.
   **Indicates significance at the .01 confidence level.

although the effect is small: only 1% to 2% of the mean test score. The conclusions were similar in unreported individual country regressions. Government schools never outperform private schools, although they do equally well in some countries. Rural schools never outperform urban schools in language tests, although in three countries they have an advantage in mathematics. Pupil-teacher ratios and single-grade classrooms have small effects of mixed signs.

Teacher education and experience do not have significant effects in table 7.4, contrary to Hanushek's summary of what has been found in developing countries in general, but consistent with results in the United States.

There is some evidence that teacher education raises student achievement in some countries, but the effect is negligible in most. Teacher experience also had mixed effects.

Household factors have strong effects on student outcomes. Having two parents raises language and math scores by 2% to 3%. The average education of the parents or legal guardians has a positive effect, increasing in magnitude as education increases. A household with parental education equal to the sample mean raises test scores by 7% in language and 5% in mathematics. These findings that household attributes strongly influence school performance in Latin America are consistent with those in other settings. In most of the country-specific regressions, similar positive effects of two-parent households and education of the head are obtained, although the effects are sometimes imprecisely estimated.

The most consistent finding in all the countries and for both test scores, is that child labor harms student performance, even when controlling for family, teacher, and school attributes. The estimated child labor effects for individual countries are summarized in the columns labeled conditional means in table 7.2.[7] All of these estimates are based on regressions of the form reported across countries in table 7.4. Nonworking children enjoy a double-digit percentage advantage in test scores in every country except the Dominican Republic. On the other hand, the advantage of occasional workers over those who often work becomes insignificant in ten of twenty-two possible cases, although the advantage still exists in all but two cases. Therefore, children who work only part-time while in school lose almost as much in terms of lower cognitive achievement as do children who work often outside the home.

Glewwe (2002) found that virtually all of the positive impact of education on wages is through improved mathematics and language skills. The average lost learning as a consequence of being a frequent child laborer relative to not working across all the countries, holding school and home attributes constant, is −18.6% in language ability and −15.4% in mathematical ability. The estimated reduction in adult wages as a consequence of being a child laborer reported in chapter 5 is −20.3%. Consequently, the percentage loss in cognitive skills attributable to working while in primary school is quite consistent with the corresponding percentage loss in wages later in life.

The estimates reported thus far do not account for possible simultaneity between observed child performance in school and the parents' decision of whether to send the child to work. Following the strategy employed in Gunnarsson et al. (2006), we use variation across countries in truancy age and the age at which school starts, and the interaction of these policy measures with the child's age as instruments for endogenous child labor.[8] The results are presented in table 7.5. The child labor equations are estimated as an ordered probit, and so the functional form differs from that in table 7.4. Therefore, we report the least squares coefficients where work outside the home takes values of Never = 0; Sometime = 1; and Often = 2.

**Table 7.5** Ordinary and two-stage least squares estimates of the impact of child labor on test scores

| Variable | Child Labor Exogenous[a] | | Child Labor Endogenous[b] | |
|---|---|---|---|---|
| | Mathematics | Language | Mathematics | Language |
| Sometime Working | −1.519* | −1.284* | −1.842* | −1.390* |
| | (0.080) | (0.050) | (0.139) | (0.090) |
| Proportion[c] | −0.099 | −0.109 | −0.120 | −0.118 |
| Often Working | −2.474* | −2.058* | −2.218* | −1.845* |
| | (0.090) | (0.057) | (0.391) | (0.346) |
| Proportion | −0.161 | −0.174 | −0.144 | −0.156 |
| *Child* | | | | |
| Age | 0.071* | 0.079* | 0.090* | 0.100* |
| | (0.024) | (0.016) | (0.025) | (0.020) |
| Boy | 0.775* | −0.300* | 1.000* | −0.112* |
| | (0.068) | (0.043) | (0.073) | (0.049) |
| No Preschool | −0.532* | −0.326* | −0.505* | −0.312* |
| | (0.084) | (0.053) | (0.081) | (0.052) |
| *Parents/Household* | | | | |
| Parent Education | 0.468* | 0.356* | 0.380* | 0.275* |
| | (0.029) | (0.018) | (0.035) | (0.021) |
| Books at Home | 0.866* | 0.549* | 0.735* | 0.449* |
| | (0.052) | (0.032) | (0.053) | (0.034) |
| *Teacher* | | | | |
| Male | −0.436* | −0.546* | −0.358* | −0.484* |
| | (0.029) | (0.059) | (0.108) | (0.063) |
| Teacher Education | −0.624* | 0.090 | −0.575* | 0.141* |
| | (0.075) | (0.048) | (0.087) | (0.054) |
| *School* | | | | |
| Spanish Enr/100 | −0.031* | 0.025* | −0.039* | 0.016* |
| | (0.007) | (0.005) | (0.007) | (0.006) |
| Inadequacy | −0.421* | −0.342* | −0.359* | −0.289* |
| | (0.039) | (0.024) | (0.043) | (0.023) |
| Math/week (Spanish/week) | 0.008 | 0.008 | −0.004 | 0.003 |
| | (0.014) | (0.007) | (0.015) | (0.008) |
| *Community* | | | | |
| Urban | 0.331* | 0.086 | 0.104 | −0.091* |
| | (0.087) | (0.054) | (0.077) | (0.057) |
| Rural | −1.046* | −1.240* | −1.117* | −1.266* |
| | (0.106) | (0.066) | (0.102) | (0.064) |
| Constant | 15.673* | 10.143* | 15.882* | 10.373* |
| | (0.387) | (0.202) | (0.372) | (0.229) |
| $R^2$ | 0.133 | 0.171 | 0.129 | 0.147 |
| N | 28939 | 34306 | 28939 | 34306 |

*Notes:*

[a]Standard errors in parentheses.

[b]Bootstrapped standard errors in parentheses. Instruments include legal age at which children can start and leave school interacted with child age and indicators of the ability of the government to enforce the law.

[c]Proportional change in test scores associated with moving from the reference group (almost never working) to the ordered child labor group (sometimes working or often working).

Regressions also include dummy variables controlling for missing values.

*indicates significance at the 0.05 confidence level.

We convert the resulting coefficients into the implied proportional disadvantage relative to never working. The implied effect of often working relative to not working is very similar to that implied by table 7.4: −16.1% for language and −17.4% for mathematics. The estimated adverse impact of instrumented child labor on test scores was only modestly smaller: −15.6% for language and −14.4% for mathematics. Children who sometimes work also faced substantial penalties in cognitive performance relative to children who almost never work, scoring 12% lower in both mathematics and language. Therefore, the adverse effects of child labor on cognitive achievement found in this study are robust to alternative assumptions about the endogeneity or exogeneity of child labor.

## Conclusions and Comments

This consistently administered survey of third- and fourth-graders, their parents, and their teachers in eleven Latin American countries reveals a startling fact—the most consistent predictor of test performance in language and mathematics in terms of sign and significance was whether the child engaged in work outside the home. Children who worked occasionally outperformed those who often worked when out of school, but the advantage to part-time workers was small. On the other hand, the advantage in test scores for children who never worked outside the home was 15% to 19%, even when controlling for parental, teacher and school attributes. Nearly identical results were obtained when controlling for the possible endogeneity of child labor. These estimates of the lost cognitive ability associated with child labor are consistent with estimates of the wage loss adults suffer from having worked as a child.

The policy implications are profound. First, there is a cost to having children work while keeping them enrolled in school. Even occasional child workers face a substantial loss of school achievement as a result of their work. As shown in chapter 4, child labor is characterized by high transition rates into and out of the labor force, suggesting that the adverse consequences of occasional work outside the home are spread quite broadly among Latin American children. Second, the lost cognitive ability and the implied adult earnings loss from working as a child are large enough to suggest that the expenses of combating child labor can be recovered in part from higher earnings of the children when they enter adulthood. Furthermore, double-digit gains in cognitive ability attributable to withholding a child from the labor market are enough to raise many out of poverty as adults, to the extent that improvements in cognitive ability have been strongly associated with adult wages.

## Notes

Financial support from the World Bank and the Inter-American Development Bank is gratefully acknowledged. We are indebted to UNESCO and the Laboratorio

Latinoamericano de Evaluación de la Calidad de la Educación for the use of the data. Donna Otto prepared the manuscript. Views expressed are not necessarily those of the World Bank or the Inter-American Development Bank.

1. In the United States, teacher experience also appears important, but teacher education does not matter.
2. See Glewwe (2002) for a comprehensive review of the problems associated with estimating educational production functions.
3. For a detailed description of the a priori exclusions in each country, consult table 7.6 of the Technical Bulletin of the LLECE.
4. Official statistics are not available, but CIA estimates of the Cuban GDP per capita in 2000 was $1,700. That is one-third the per capita GDP of Honduras and Bolivia and about one-seventh the per capita GDP of Argentina.
5. Carnoy (2007) has a recent book evaluating the Cuban advantage that he attributed in part to the low level of child labor in Cuba. However, his finding of low levels of child labor was heavily influenced by his decision to recode the 94% missing child-labor responses to "almost never working," something he felt was consistent with his a priori view that there is little child labor in Cuba (see his Footnote 8, Carnoy, 2007, 189).
6. The authors also reestimated the model using dummy variable interactions to control for missing observations on certain variables. That method resulted in the loss of only 22% of the observations. Qualitative results were not changed.
7. The R-square for individual country estimates were of like magnitude to those reported in table 7.4 for the sample as a whole.
8. A similar strategy was employed by Angrist and Krueger (1991) to control for endogeneity of years of schooling in their study of returns to education.

# IV

# Policy Evaluations

# The Impact of Cash Transfers on Child Labor and School Enrollment in Brazil

*Eliana Cardoso and André Portela F. de Souza*

Bolsa Escola programs give cash grants to poor families with children between the ages of 7 and 14 in exchange for a promise that the families will send their children to school. Households risk losing a month of benefits if their children miss too many days of school per month. The income transfer aims to reduce the current incidence of poverty among disadvantaged households. By requiring more regular school attendance, the programs also aim to increase educational attainment of poor children and thus reduce the likelihood that the children will be poor in the future. The monthly attendance requirement also implicitly aims to reduce child labor by using up child time.

These programs were born in the 1980s at the University of Brasília under the coordination of Professor Cristovam Buarque, but they were not implemented until 1995 by the government of the Distrito Federal. In 1996, the Bolsa Escola received a United Nations prize for innovative development initiatives and became a model for the rest of the country. The expansion was concentrated in metropolitan areas of Brazil. A different program aimed at rural areas, the Program for the Eradication of Child Labor (PETI), also began in 1996.

By 1998, many states and municipalities had replicated the Bolsa Escola program. Using information from the Instituto de Pesquisa Econômica Aplicada, Levinas and Bittar (1999) reported that the program existed in three states (Amapá, Goiás, and Tocantins), in forty-five municipalities in São Paulo, and in nine other municipalities in different states. Adding programs in four other states (Alagoas, Minas Gerais, Mato Grosso do Sul, and Acre) that were not on Levinas and Bittar's list, we estimate that there were sixty-one functioning programs at the beginning of 1999. There were seventeen other nongovernmental programs called Bolsa Escola Cidadã run by the NGO Missão Criança.

These initial programs were under the jurisdiction of individual municipalities. Just before the 1998 elections, the Ministry of Education launched the Minimum Income Program (Programa de Garantia de Renda Mínima) for municipalities with a per capita income and tax revenues below the average of their respective states. The program targeted children between 7 and 14 years old who attended school. In December 1999, the Ministry of Education reported that the program benefited 504,000 families (around 1 million children) in one-fifth of all Brazilian municipalities, with differentiated payments that averaged R\$37 per family per month. It is not known what happened to the decentralized municipal programs after the introduction of the Minimum Income Program. To date, there has been no systematic analysis of the impact of the decentralized programs other than the two case studies discussed below.

The Minimum Income Program disappeared in 2001. In its place, the government substituted the Bolsa Escola Federal. By 2002, 5,545 municipalities (99.7% of all Brazilian municipalities) had joined the Bolsa Escola Federal. The program provided assistance to 5 million children according to the Ministry of Education (2002). As of October 2002, the program had spent R\$1.3 billion from the R\$2 billion budgeted for that year. The Ministry of Education (2002) calculated the operational cost of the program around 7% of distributed benefits. The program pays a monthly stipend of R\$15 per child between the ages of 6 and 15 (up to R\$45) to families with per capita monthly incomes below R\$90. In exchange, the mothers of those families promise to keep all their children in school.

Recently, the federal government instituted the Bolsa Família Program.[1] This program substitutes all income transfer programs (including the Bolsa Escola Federal, the Bolsa Alimentação, and the Auxílio Gas from the previous government; and the Fome Zero created in 2003) into a single benefit program that offers households cash payments in exchange for acceptance of conditions such as school attendance or visits to local clinics. The benefits consist of a monthly basic transfer of R\$ 50 per poor family and a variable transfer of R\$ 15 to R\$ 45 per child under 15 years of age. A family is considered sufficiently poor to qualify for the program if its monthly income per capita is R\$ 100 or less.

One difficulty with this plan is the lack of a trustworthy directory of poor families who are entitled to benefits. The directory inherited from the previous government had been hurriedly completed by municipal governments and was subject to numerous errors. For example, many of the potential beneficiaries have addresses listed as the municipal offices (Ferreira and Lindert, 2003). To rectify this problem, the Bolsa Família Program also will combine all existing lists of recipients under the newly created Ministry of Social Development and Hunger Eradication.

Despite the enthusiasm in Brazil and abroad for the Bolsa Escola program, little is actually known about its costs and benefits. Whereas data from Mexico (chapter 10) and Nicaragua (chapter 11) provide preliminary evidence that these programs can reduce poverty and improve educational outcomes for poor children, the endorsement of Bolsa Escola in Brazil is based on only two cases: those of Brasília Distrito Federal (World Bank, 2002) and Recife.

Brasília was the first installed program. An evaluation of its early progress conducted between 1995 and 1998 suggests that it was more successful than the Recife program. By the end of Cristovam Buarque's administration, the program covered 80% of the targeted families who met a residency requirement and had per capita income below one-half the minimum wage. The program successfully increased school attendance and reduced child labor in recipient households.[2] Part of its success is derived from the relative affluence of Brasília in relation to other municipalities. The Distrito Federal would need only 1% of its budget to benefit all children between the ages of 7 and 14 that belong to families with an income below half the minimum wage. In contrast, Salvador (Bahia) would need 20% of its own budget to obtain the same result (World Bank, 2002).

In contrast to Brasília's 80% coverage rate, Recife's program covered just 2% of the poor families. The program may have had some impact on limiting child labor,[3] but it did not have an impact on schooling outcomes. The children who benefited from the program scored worse on performance tests than those who did not receive the benefit but had the same characteristics of the group benefiting from the program.

Levinas and Barbosa (2001) claim that the vast majority of municipal programs in 1998 and 1999 were similar to the Recife program in that they served only a very small fraction of the poor population. Many municipalities substituted food or cooking gas for cash payments, potentially limiting their program's attractiveness. Some did not offer the program long enough to ensure that children would finish their primary education. In some municipalities, families that received benefits in one year were forced to leave the program the following year to open space for other families.

Both of these evaluations suggest that even the modest evidence of success may be biased. The Recife evaluation lacked baseline data on child labor and dropped families that did not meet the attendance requirements, so it is possible that the results attributed to the transfer are instead due to self-selection. Similarly, the Brasília program did not monitor schooling and child labor of qualified households that refused the program, again leading to the possibility that changed behavior attributed to the program is really due to sorting of households more interested in education into the program while less interested households were left out.

A more rigorous experimental design was applied to the evaluation of PETI, which aimed to eradicate the worst forms of child labor by providing cash grants to families with children aged 7 to 14 and by requiring children to attend both school (80% of the required number of hours) and Jornada Ampliada (an after-school program). By 1999, that program had reached 166 municipalities in eight states and provided assistance to more than 131,000 working children (almost 10% of the working children in Brazil).

As the next chapter reports, and as Pianto and Soares (2003) confirm using national data, PETI reduced child labor and increased schooling. However, there are reasons why the PETI results would not mimic those of the urban Bolsa Escola. First, the after-school program lowers the available time for child labor by doubling the length of the school day. Child labor may be compatible with schooling in urban systems where school lasts only four hours per day. Child labor also is more difficult to target in urban areas because occupations are much more heterogeneous than those in rural areas. Many of the forms of child labor take place in the streets, and data for children selling items, collecting trash, selling drugs, and engaging in prostitution are difficult to obtain. Finally, urban working children may have weaker parental support than do rural working children. Problems of drugs and violence are more severe and may require additional support such as counseling and rehabilitation to generate the same outcomes.

This study uses Brazilian census data to test whether income transfer programs in 2000 affected the child labor and school enrollment decisions of poor households in municipal areas of Brazil. This helps assess whether the findings from Brasília and Recife can be applied to urban poor households in the country as a whole. The chapter finds that income transfer programs had no significant effect on child labor. Transfers had a positive and statistically significant impact on school enrollment. The implication is that the program induces more poor children to go to school, but without reducing participation in the labor market. Apparently, combining the two activities is not difficult with short school days, and the transfers may be too small to provide an incentive to forgo labor income altogether.

## Changes in Child Labor and School Attendance in Brazil from 1992 to 2001

As several chapters in this book have shown, many factors that are tied to household poverty increase the incidence of child labor. Changes in the incidence of child labor or school enrollment could be due to coincidental changes in the distribution of these characteristics rather than the installation of targeted transfer programs. This section summarizes the main findings in Fernandes and Souza (2002). The analysis uses the data from the Pesquisa Nacional por Amostragem a Domicílio (PNAD) of the Instituto Brasileiro de Geografia e Estatística (IBGE). The sample consists of children between 10 and 17 years old: 57,821 boys and girls in 1992 and 60,154 boys and girls in 2002.

Since the early 1990s, child labor in Brazil has declined and school attendance increased. As shown in table 8.1, 36.3% of boys worked in 1992. Employment rates fell to 23.5% by 2001. Among girls, 18.5% worked in 1992 and 12.5% worked in 2001. Over the same time period, enrollment rates for boys rose from 76.1% to 90.6%. Enrollment rates for girls rose from 79.8% to 90.5%. These impressive improvements span the period during which Bolsa Escola programs were first implemented and expanded.

**Table 8.1**  Changes in Child Labor Participation and School Enrollment for Children Aged 10 to 17 in Brazil, 1992–2001, by Gender, Age, and Household Attributes

| Characteristics | Child Labor[a] | | School Enrollment[b] | |
|---|---|---|---|---|
| | Girls | Boys | Girls | Boys |
| Overall | −0.061 | −0.128 | 0.104 | 0.144 |
| *Schooling of Household Head* | | | | |
| 0 to 3 years | −0.075 | −0.135 | 0.146 | 0.196 |
| 4 to 7 years | −0.044 | −0.093 | 0.078 | 0.096 |
| 8 to 10 years | −0.021 | −0.068 | 0.044 | 0.049 |
| 11 or more years | 0.016 | −0.045 | 0.041 | 0.043 |
| *Gender of Household Head* | | | | |
| Male | −0.046 | −0.105 | 0.103 | 0.134 |
| Female | −0.058 | −0.109 | 0.098 | 0.136 |
| *Child's Age* | | | | |
| 10 to 13 years | −0.031 | −0.076 | 0.068 | 0.085 |
| 14 to 17 years | −0.068 | −0.139 | 0.141 | 0.191 |
| *Region* | | | | |
| Rural | −0.071 | −0.124 | 0.170 | 0.222 |
| Urban | −0.043 | −0.101 | 0.085 | 0.110 |
| *Household Size* | | | | |
| Up to 4 People | −0.048 | −0.098 | 0.102 | 0.135 |
| More than 4 People | −0.049 | −0.122 | 0.103 | 0.133 |

*Source:* Fernandes and de Souza, 2002.

*Notes:*

[a]Over the period, child labor participation rates fell from 0.19 to 0.13 for girls and from 0.36 to 0.24 for boys.

[b]Over the period, enrollment rates rose from 0.80 to 0.90 for girls and from 0.76 to 0.91 for boys.

Table 8.1 also shows how the two measures of child time use have changed by various child and household attributes. While there is some variation in the amount of the decline in child labor or the gain in enrollment across different groups, the changes are generally broad-based. The exception is that the biggest decline in child labor and the biggest gain in school enrollment are among households with the least educated parents—those that would be most likely to receive transfers from the Bolsa Escola programs—suggesting that they may have had the desired behavioral effects.

The transfers targeted households with children between the ages of 7 and 14. However, the most pronounced changes in child labor and school enrollment were observed for children between the ages of 14 and 17, even though the children between the ages of 10 and 13 would have been more likely to have received targeted transfers. Similarly, table 8.2 shows that the change in child labor and school enrollment does not vary much between male- and female-headed households or by the size of the family. However, the transfers were targeted disproportionately toward female-headed and large households. The largest improvements were experienced in rural areas rather than urban areas. Although the PETI programs were being implemented at the same time, they were not

**Table 8.2**    Child labor incidence for children aged 10–15 in Brazil, 2000

| State | Number of Working Children Aged 10–15 (in thousands) | Labor-Participation Rate of Children Aged 10–15 (in percent) |
|---|---|---|
| Brazil | 1,479.4 | 8.3 |
| 1. São Paulo | 163.8 | 4.6 |
| 2. Minas Gerais | 156.6 | 8.4 |
| 3. Bahia | 155.5 | 10.2 |
| 4. Ceará | 96.9 | 11.0 |
| 5. Rio Grande do Sul | 89.9 | 9.3 |
| 6. Paraná | 89.9 | 9.2 |
| 7. Maranhão | 84.5 | 11.7 |
| 8. Pernambuco | 83.3 | 9.5 |
| 9. Pará | 79.0 | 10.4 |
| 10. Santa Catarina | 60.2 | 10.8 |
| 11. Goiás | 45.2 | 8.9 |
| 12. Paraíba | 45.1 | 11.5 |
| 13. Piauí | 43.8 | 12.5 |
| 14. Rio de Janeiro | 42.5 | 3.4 |
| 15. Alagoas | 36.8 | 11.0 |
| 16. Espírito Santo | 35.1 | 10.7 |
| 17. Amazonas | 27.5 | 8.0 |
| 18. Mato Grosso | 27.0 | 9.6 |
| 19. Rondônia | 23.5 | 14.0 |
| 20. Rio Grande do Norte | 21.9 | 7.0 |
| 21. Mato Grosso do Sul | 19.3 | 8.7 |
| 22. Tocantins | 18.5 | 13.6 |
| 23. Sergipe | 17.4 | 8.4 |
| 24. Acre | 6.6 | 9.6 |
| 25. Distrito Federal | 4.3 | 2.2 |
| 26. Amapá | 2.8 | 4.7 |
| 27. Roraima | 2.4 | 6.1 |

*Source:* Authors' calculation based on 2000 census data.

as broad-based and they did not cover as many children as did the Bolsa Escola.

The pattern of changes in child labor and school enrollment in table 8.2 is not clearly consistent with the hypothesis that Bolsa Escola programs had an impact. There were presumably other changes occurring in Brazil over the same period that also had an impact on these choices. Disentangling the impact of conditional transfers from other factors will require more careful econometric methods.

## The 2000 Census

The 2000 Brazilian Census is a household-level sample that covers about 12% of the Brazilian population. Similar to the U.S. Census Public Use Sample (PUMS), the micro data sample from the Brazilian census represents the entire country and each municipality, and it includes information on demographics and labor market variables. The advantages of the census over other household surveys in Brazil are that it covers the entire country and it has complete information on social transfers, both conditional and unconditional.

To estimate the incidence of child labor and school attendance in Brazil and its regions, a sample was selected from all children aged 10 to 15 with valid information on child labor and school enrollment. A child is considered enrolled if the respondent answered "yes" to the question, "Does the child attend school or daycare?" A child is considered working if he or she is described as regularly occupied in the labor market or in domestic activities linked to the market. The lower age limit is set at 10 because available information on child labor starts at that age. The 15-year-old cut-off mirrors Brazilian law that allows legal labor market entry after age 15. The sample consists of 2.4 million children (Cardoso and Souza, 2003).

In 2000, approximately 18 million children aged 10 to 15 lived in Brazil; 8.3% were in the labor force (table 8.2). Among the working children in Brazil, 54% lived in urban areas and 46% lived in rural areas. Although the share of working children is higher in rural areas than in urban areas, the absolute number of working children is higher in urban areas than in rural areas. As table 8.2 indicates, there is an enormous difference among states in the number and share of working children. Just over one-half of the working children reside in only six states. São Paulo has the highest number of working children but has a relatively low participation rate. Amapá and Roraima have the lowest number of working children and have relatively low labor participation rates. The highest shares of working children are in Rodonia and Tocantis; the lowest shares are in Distrito Federal and Rio de Janeiro.

According to the figures 92% of the girls and 84.2% of the boys attended school without working. The proportion of children who both worked and went to school was 4.6% for girls and 9.1% for boys. Only 0.8% of the girls and 2% of the boys only worked. The remaining 4.4% of the girls and 4.7% of the boys did not work and did not go to school, although this is likely due to measurement error in responses. The variation in labor participation rates across states is also found in broader regional designations. For instance, 23.6% of boys in Brazil's rural area work, whereas only 6.2% of urban boys work. The corresponding differences in rural versus urban participation rates are not as large for girls but are nevertheless substantial (9.7% rural and 4.1% urban).

Table 8.3 lists the states with the highest child labor participation rates by region and gender. States such as Rondônia have high incidence in both urban and rural areas, while others demonstrate sharper differences in child labor patterns across urban and rural markets. On the other hand, states with high participation rates for boys also tended to have high participation rates for girls. The three states with the highest rural boys' participation rates were also in the top five for girls. Similarly, the three states

**Table 8.3**  Percent child labor participation (CLP) by gender and urban and rural areas for Brazil and for the five highest states, 2000

|  | Urban CLP |  | Rural CLP |
|---|---|---|---|
| *Girls aged 10 to 15* |  |  |  |
| *Brazil (total)* | 4.1 | *Brazil (total)* | 9.7 |
| *Highest 5 states in urban CLP* |  | *Highest 5 states in rural CLP* |  |
| Tocantins | 11.4 | Rio Grande do Sul | 19.7 |
| Goiás | 6.7 | Santa Catarina | 18.4 |
| Mato Grosso | 5.9 | Espírito Santo | 15.4 |
| Mato Grosso do Sul | 5.4 | Alagoas | 13.3 |
| Minas Gerais | 5.3 | Rondônia | 12.5 |
| *Boys aged 10 to 15* |  |  |  |
| *Brazil (total)* | 6.2 | *Brazil (total)* | 23.6 |
| *Highest 5 states in urban CLP* |  | *Highest 5 states in rural CLP* |  |
| Tocantins | 16.26 | Espírito Santo | 35.11 |
| Mato Grosso | 11.36 | Rondônia | 33.79 |
| Rondônia | 10.89 | Rio Grande do Sul | 31.81 |
| Goiás | 10.69 | Paraíba | 31.40 |
| Maranhão | 9.83 | Piauí | 31.24 |

*Source:* Authors' calculation based on 2000 census data.

with the highest urban participation rates for girls were also in the top five for boys.

## Sample Selection and Econometric Tests

Of particular interest to this study was the 2000 census, that gathered information on the values of transfer income received from various assistance programs including the Minimum Income Program, Bolsa Escola, unemployment insurance, and assistance for the handicapped. This study aimed to disentangle the transfers received from the Minimum Income Program and Bolsa Escola from the others to isolate their impact on child labor and school enrollment.

The ideal experiment would observe the same children in both states—with and without income transfers. Those children living in families that received income transfers are the treatment group. The comparison group includes children that could have received the income transfers but did not. The propensity matching score method (Rosenbaum and Rubin, 1983) was used to construct the comparison group. This method balances the observed covariates between the treatment group and a comparison group. Children were assigned to the treatment group if they belong to a family in which the father or mother has a positive value for the income transfer variable. To eliminate the effect of the handicapped aid transfer, all children that live in families where there is at least one handicapped member were dropped from the samples.

The families in the treatment group represent about 2% of all children aged 10 to 15 years old in the Brazilian Census. A random sample of 25% of all 10- to 15-year-old children from families in which parents do not receive public transfers was also added to the treatment group. This is referred to as the "all families" control sample. Sample attributes are detailed in Cardoso and Souza (2003).

This broadest sample undoubtedly includes households that would not normally receive transfers. While that problem is dealt with later using a matching algorithm, three other alternative samples were created: an "only poor families" sample; an "all families with employed parents" sample; and an "only poor families with employed parents" sample. In the "only poor families" sample, a subsample of all children living in poor families was selected, because the Bolsa Escola and Minimum Income programs are supposed to target poor families. A family is considered poor if its per capita income is equal to or less than R$ 100 at 2000 values that represents roughly 55% of the prevailing monthly minimum wage in 2000.

The census does not ask for information on unemployment insurance payments so unemployment insurance cannot be distinguished from the conditional transfers for the complete sample. Unemployment benefits to poor families also act as a partial safety net but do not impose the conditions on school attendance. In an attempt to remove the unemployment insurance effect, two dummy variables were constructed—one for each unemployed parent. The assumption is that the parent receiving unemployment insurance is unemployed.

Because people working in the informal market could work while receiving unemployment benefits, two other treatment samples were constructed to exclude unemployed parents. The "all families with employed parents" sample and the "poor families with employed parents" are sub-samples of children living in families in which neither parent is unemployed and thus cannot collect unemployment insurance benefits.

It is possible that remaining differences in behavior between the treatment and control samples are due to differences in observable child or household attributes. To control for that possibility, child characteristics that could affect the value of time in or out of school (gender, Age, rural location, and ethnicity) were included. Differences in parental attributes that could affect taste for school or the child's productivity in school or at work (years of schooling, age, Race, unemployment dummy, and income minus transfer) also were controlled for.

Family composition can affect the child's value in the home. This study used the numbers of children aged 0 to 5 and 6 to 15 and the number of individuals above 16 to control for household composition. Municipal level variables including the rural proportion and averages and standard deviations of schooling, age, and income net of transfers were used to control for variation across communities in socioeconomic status. For children without a father or a mother, zero values were assigned for absent parent characteristics. Indicator variables for father-absent and mother-absent also were included to reflect possible differences in child labor or enrollment associated with single parent households.

Recognizing that the control sample may not perfectly reflect the distribution of participants in the treatment sample, three observations from the comparison group were assigned to each observation of the treatment group on the basis of predicted propensity scores. These are estimated by a logit model in which the dependent variable is the indicator variable for a child in a family that receives the income transfers and the control variables are the full set of child, parent, household, and municipal characteristics. A control was also added for the political party of the mayor in 2000 because the majority of these transfer programs were decentralized at the local government level before 2001. It is plausible that there were political factors that led a municipality to decide whether or not to adopt a conditional cash transfer program.

Four matched comparison samples were created based on employment and poverty status. The nearest neighborhood criterion was used to identify comparison children. Observations were only kept in the common support following procedures outlined by Dehejia and Wahba (1999). It is important to mention a caveat here. The underlying assumption is that the assignment to the treatment sample is random after conditioning on these observable controls. On this point, see Rosenbaum and Rubin (1983) and Ravallion (2001).

## Results

Table 8.4 shows the estimated effects of the income transfers for the various control samples. The effects are calculated separately for boys and girls. The results are quite robust to the alternative sample definitions suggesting that the matching does a good job of finding close correspondents to observations in the treatment group.

In the first and second columns of table 8.4 the broadest definition of the control sample is used. Enrollment rates for boys are 95% in the treatment group and 92% in the control group. The average treatment effect is an increase of 3 percentage points in school enrollment among boys, and the effect is statistically significant at standard confidence levels. Considering that in the comparison group, only 8% of boys are out of school, a 3-percentage point change is a large effect. A similarly sized effect of the income transfer on enrollment is found for girls.

The estimated effect on child labor is less promising. Child labor incidence falls for boys, but the effect is very small and imprecisely estimated. Furthermore, child labor participation actually rises for girls receiving the transfer by a proportion equal to the decline for boys, so there is no net change in overall child labor participation.

The impact of income transfers on children in four other categories is also measured: those attending school only; those working only; those working and attending school; and those neither working nor attending school. Table 8.4 shows that for both boys and girls, the gain in enrollment

Table 8.4 The effects of transfers on child time use[a]

| | All Families Sample | | Poor Children Sample | | Children with Employed Parents Only | | Poor Children with Employed Parents Only | |
|---|---|---|---|---|---|---|---|---|
| | Treatment | Difference | Treatment | Difference | Treatment | Difference | Treatment | Difference |
| | | | | Boys | | | | |
| School | 0.949 (0.002) | 0.031 (0.002) | 0.946 (0.002) | 0.042 (0.003) | 0.946 (0.002) | 0.034 (0.003) | 0.942 (0.002) | 0.045 (0.003) |
| Work | 0.141 (0.002) | −0.004 (0.003) | 0.144 (0.003) | −0.008 (0.003) | 0.164 (0.003) | −0.004 (0.004) | 0.171 (0.003) | −0.004 (0.004) |
| Only School | 0.827 (0.003) | 0.026 (0.003) | 0.821 (0.003) | 0.040 (0.004) | 0.803 (0.003) | 0.027 (0.004) | 0.793 (0.004) | 0.038 (0.005) |
| Only Work | 0.019 (0.001) | −0.009 (0.001) | 0.019 (0.001) | −0.010 (0.002) | 0.021 (0.001) | −0.012 (0.002) | 0.022 (0.001) | −0.012 (0.002) |
| School and Work | 0.122 (0.002) | 0.005 (0.003) | 0.125 (0.003) | 0.002 (0.003) | 0.142 (0.003) | 0.007 (0.003) | 0.149 (0.003) | 0.008 (0.004) |
| No School and No Work | 0.032 (0.001) | −0.023 (0.002) | 0.035 (0.001) | −0.032 (0.002) | 0.033 (0.001) | −0.022 (0.002) | 0.036 (0.002) | −0.033 (0.003) |
| | | | | Girls | | | | |
| School | 0.961 (0.001) | 0.030 (0.002) | 0.958 (0.002) | 0.038 (0.003) | 0.959 (0.002) | 0.030 (0.002) | 0.956 (0.002) | 0.036 (0.003) |
| Work | 0.074 (0.002) | 0.004 (0.002) | 0.076 (0.002) | 0.006 (0.003) | 0.085 (0.002) | 0.009 (0.003) | 0.090 (0.003) | 0.011 (0.003) |
| Only School | 0.895 (0.002) | 0.020 (0.003) | 0.889 (0.003) | 0.026 (0.003) | 0.883 (0.003) | 0.016 (0.003) | 0.875 (0.003) | 0.020 (0.004) |
| Only Work | 0.008 (0.001) | −0.005 (0.001) | 0.007 (0.001) | −0.006 (0.001) | 0.009 (0.001) | −0.004 (0.001) | 0.009 (0.001) | −0.005 (0.001) |
| School and Work | 0.066 (0.002) | 0.009 (0.002) | 0.069 (0.002) | 0.012 (0.002) | 0.076 (0.002) | 0.014 (0.003) | 0.081 (0.003) | 0.016 (0.003) |
| No School and No Work | 0.031 (0.001) | −0.025 (0.002) | 0.034 (0.001) | −0.032 (0.002) | 0.032 (0.001) | −0.026 (0.002) | 0.035 (0.002) | −0.032 (0.003) |

Notes:
[a]Estimates are the fraction of all children in the subsample engaged in the activity. Standard errors are reported in parentheses.

associated with the transfer comes from three sources: a decrease in the proportion of those only working; an increase in the proportion of those both working and going to school; and a decrease in the proportion of those neither working nor going to school. The negligible impact of the transfer on child labor is due to the increased proportion of those children both working and attending school. It is apparent that increasing school enrollment or attendance does not prevent children from working, presumably because the school day is not long enough to prevent them from working.[4]

Columns 3 through 8 of table 8.4 report similar results using the other control samples. In the sample for "only poor children" the coefficients measuring the impact of transfers on school enrollment rises by about 1 percentage point for both boys and girls. The decline in boys' child labor participation is smaller than 1 percentage point but becomes statistically significant. However, the rise in girls' labor participation leaves the overall child labor participation rate unchanged. Results described above for the "all children" sample remain unchanged when the tests for samples with "children with employed parents" are repeated, as shown in the last four columns of table 8.4. However the increase in child labor participation for girls is now larger in magnitude than the small decrease for boys. In all of these samples the increase in the proportion of children both working and attending school as a result of the transfer suggests that the increase in school time does not limit time available for work.

Additional light is shed on the impact of these transfers by estimating logit models over the matched samples that estimate the comparative static effect of the transfer on the probability of school enrollment and child labor. We also examine whether the magnitude of the effect differs by whether the transfer is made to the mother or the father.[5] The results in table 8.5 are

**Table 8.5** Summary of logit coefficients indicating the effect of income transfers on child labor participation and school enrollment for children aged 10 to 15 in Brazil, 2000

| | Boys | | Girls | |
|---|---|---|---|---|
| Variables | Coefficients | Std. Error | Coefficients | Std. Error |
| *Logit Model of Child Labor Participation* | | | | |
| *Transfers to Father/100* | −0.04 | 0.02 | 0.02 | 0.03 |
| *Transfers to Mother/100* | −0.01 | 0.03 | 0.06 | 0.03 |
| *Logit Model of Enrollment* | | | | |
| *Transfers to Father/100* | 0.18 | 0.03 | 0.15 | 0.04 |
| *Transfers to Mother/100* | 0.45 | 0.05 | 0.51 | 0.06 |
| Number of Observations | 60.449 | | 57.582 | |

*Note:*
Logit equations over the "all families" sample also included controls for the child's age and race; mother's and father's presence; age, education and employment status; household size and income; and attributes of the municipality. Results were similar using the other control samples.

reported only for the primary variables of interest. Findings were similar for all four control samples, so only those from the most complete sample are reported. The full specification is found in Cardoso and Souza (2003).

In the logit models explaining school enrollment, the coefficient on transfers made to mothers is much bigger than the coefficient of transfers made to fathers. The difference is statistically significant, and suggests that transfers directed at mothers have a larger impact on child enrollment than transfers directed to fathers. Nevertheless, transfers to either parent raise enrollment.[6] However, there are no statistically significant effects of transfers to either parent on the probability of child labor for either boys or girls.

## Final Remarks

This research examined the impact of cash transfer programs such as the minimum income program and the Bolsa Escola on child labor and school attendance of poor 10- to 15-year-old children in Brazil. It finds that these programs have a significant but modest (3–4 percentage point) impact on increasing school attendance. The results are the same for boys and girls and are robust to alternative estimation methods and control samples. The study does not find an impact of these cash transfers on child labor.

The results suggest that these transfers may change children's time allocation between school and leisure. The cash transfer program's largest impact is to reduce the incidence of children neither working nor going to school. Some of these children appear to enter school without working, but others combine school with work. It is this latter effect that dominates whatever small reduction there is in the proportion of children who only work.

A possible explanation for the minimal impact of the income transfers on child labor is that the transfers are too small to create an incentive for families to forgo the income from child labor. The average transfer in 2000 was well below half a minimum wage for a father (including unemployment benefits) and around one-quarter of a minimum wage for a mother (including unemployment benefits). Even if such transfers approximated what a child earns working, they would not be enough to convince both parents and children to give up the combination of work and school. This would be particularly true if the income the child derives from work represents a substantial contribution to family income. Kassouf (2001) observes that for 17% of rural households in Brazil, the contribution to family income from working children aged 5 to 14 represents more than 40% of the family income.

Another aspect of the problem is that the average school day in Brazil is only four hours, which means children can fulfill the requirement of the conditional transfer and still work. This problem is avoided in the PETI program analyzed in the next chapter. Finally, even if a small cash transfer can send children to school it does not guarantee that children will learn. Improving the schools themselves will probably have to be part of the solution. However, even with good schools, combining work with school may prevent the learning outcomes that the Bolsa Escola programs must obtain to achieve long-term poverty reductions. Cavalieri (2003) argues that child labor is part of the reason why children in Brazil, chiefly those in the Northeast, perform poorly in school. The Bolsa Escola gains in enrollment through combining school with work may not be enough to declare success.

## Notes

We thank Bernardo Campolina, Edgard Pimentel, and Veridiana Andrade for their research assistance, and Francisco Ferreira, Sergei Soares, Emmanuel Skoufias, and participants in a seminar at the Inter-American Development Bank for discussion and suggestions. We also want to thank the World Bank and the Inter-American Development Bank for financial support.

1. The program was instituted under Law number 10.836 on January 9, 2004. Details on the law can be found at http://www.mds.gov.br/. Last accessed October 22, 2008.
2. It should be noted that the changes were statistically significant but numerically small because enrollment rates were already very high and child-labor rates very low in Brasília even before the program was introduced.
3. Compared to child-labor participation rates for poor children in urban Brazil, the child-labor participation rate for children in the Recife program was relatively low. However, the analysis did not collect baseline information on child labor, so it may be that participating children had atypically low child-labor participation before the program was put in place.
4. It is still possible that the transfer lowers average hours of work, even if it does not change the incidence of child labor, a possibility that should be explored in future research.
5. If household behavior is the outcome of internal bargains and power struggles (Bourguignon and Chiapori, 1994), it is possible that the benefits from the transfer are not shared among all household members.
6. Emerson and Souza (2002) also found evidence of differences in intra-household allocation of resources controlled by fathers and mothers.

# 9

# Limiting Child Labor through Behavior-based Income Transfers: An Experimental Evaluation of the PETI Program in Rural Brazil

*Yoon-Tien Yap, Guilherme Sedlacek, and Peter F. Orazem*

Brazil has maintained a high incidence of child labor despite its relatively high level of income per capita. Brazilian law in the 1990s prohibited children under the age of 14 from working, but the law was not enforced effectively. Although the proportion of working children increased 5 percentage points as children went from age 13 to 14, the increase is small relative to the proportion already working illegally at younger ages. Of all children aged 10 to 13, 6% in urban areas and 33% in rural areas worked at some time in 1996. Complicating enforcement of the child-labor laws is the fact that most children work informally as unpaid family labor. In urban areas, 59% of working children were unpaid; in rural areas, the proportion was 91%. With such informal employment arrangements among household enterprises, it is very difficult to distinguish illegal labor from legal chores.[1]

Without a credible enforcement mechanism, parents cannot be compelled to withhold their children from the labor market if they feel it is in the household's interest for the children to work. Consequently, efforts to limit child labor must alter the parents' incentives to send their children to work. It is commonly assumed that children work because their parents are poor, not because parents are indifferent toward their children's welfare. Baland and Robinson (2000) demonstrate theoretically that credit-constrained households will choose inefficiently high levels of child labor. Consistent with the theory, numerous studies have found that as household income increases, the incidence of child labor falls.[2] This suggests that one way to alter parental incentives with regard to child labor is to transfer income to poor households.

Stronger markets for child labor also induce increased incidence of child labor and lower child enrollment rates.[3] This suggests that another way to lower the proportion of children working is to raise the opportunity cost of child labor. One plausible mechanism is to make time in school a more attractive option. Although it is true that work and school are not necessarily mutually exclusive activities,[4] a child cannot be in school and at work at the same time. Therefore, policies that increase time in school must limit the amount of time potentially available for work.

This study analyzes the effects of the program known as the Programa de Erradicacao do Trabalho Infantil (PETI), or Program to Eradicate Child Labor, which was implemented in poor rural states of northeast Brazil in 1996. PETI provides income transfers to poor households in exchange for an agreement that the child attend school at least 80% of the time. In addition, the child must attend an after-school program that effectively doubles the length of the school day.

Using data on children in PETI municipalities and children in a matched set of control municipalities, this study derives estimates of the program's impact on child schooling, labor supply, academic performance, and hazardous work. The program increased time in school, reduced labor-force participation and hazardous work, and increased academic success for children in the program.

It is possible that by artificially constraining labor supply of program children, the program could raise the return on labor-force participation for children who do not participate in the program. The study finds no evidence that nonparticipating children are more likely to work since the program was implemented. However, those children who did work worked longer hours per week. Consequently, there were some adverse spillover effects on nonparticipants. Nevertheless, the overall municipal impact of PETI, net of any potential adverse impact on nonparticipants, is almost universally in the direction of program objectives. Consequently, PETI appears to be a successful mechanism to speed the decline of child labor in rural areas.

## Background

In Brazil, any effort to significantly reduce child labor must be extended to rural areas, where 96% of the working children reside. In urban areas, 12% of boys and 6% of girls aged 10 to 14 are in the labor force. Incidence of child labor rises from 3% to 10% as age rises from 10 to 13. Child labor participation is four times higher in rural areas, where 48% of boys and 23% of girls, aged 10 to 14, work. Child labor also begins at an earlier age in rural areas, where the probability of working rises from 21% to 43% as age rises from 10 to 13.

In 1996, the Brazilian government initiated the Bolsa Escola program to address problems of poverty, schooling, and child labor in urban areas. That program, which ties income supplements to school enrollment, has had a small positive impact on enrollment rates but little impact on child labor. Bolsa Escola does not prohibit child labor, so the negligible change is in part a design feature. However, the impact also is small in part because child labor is less common in urban areas.

PETI, also implemented in 1996, targets rural areas with high incidence of risky child labor, particularly in agriculture, which accounts for 90% of rural working children. The program is similar to the urban Bolsa Escola in that it ties a transfer payment to school attendance of children aged 7 to 14. However, the program also includes a feature absent in the urban program that directly attacks the likelihood of child labor in the form of an after-school educational program. Program features include:

- Qualified households are required to have per capita income below one-half the minimum wage (roughly equal to U.S. $65/month).[5]
- The households are required to sign a contract stipulating that their children will not work.
- The children must attend school at least 80% of the time.
- The children must attend after-school sessions called the Jornada Ampliada, which roughly double the length of the school day.
- The households receive a monthly income transfer if they fulfill the contract.

The content of the Jornada Ampliada, which was not specified by the program and is subject to local control, varies from academic programs to intramural athletics. The common feature of the after-school program is that it limits the remaining time for children, making it more difficult for them to work. Consequently, the Jornada Ampliada may raise school attainment by limiting child labor, rather than by its program content.

The federal government funds the stipend, or *bolsa*, and pays for part of the after-school program. The local government pays the administrative costs and the remainder of the after-school program costs. Local costs average 25% of the program costs beyond the *bolsa*.

The government has a particular focus on limiting the worst forms of child labor, interpreted as labor that involves health risks. The program was first installed in a few municipalities in Pernambuco, and later expanded to other areas including the states of Bahia and Sergipe. Bahia has the highest child labor-force participation rate of any of the states of Brazil: 38% of the children aged 7 to 14 work. Bahia was targeted because of its child labor in sisal (agave) production. In Pernambuco, 18% of the children work, many in sugarcane production. In Sergipe, where 17% of children are employed, fishing is considered a dangerous activity for children. This evaluation concentrates on those three states.

The states differ in the amount of the transfer associated with each participating child. In Bahia and Sergipe, the *bolsa* is $25 per month for each participating child. In Pernambuco, the *bolsa* is $50 per month for one or two participating children, $100 per month for three or four children, and $150 per month for five or more. In all three states, half of the *bolsa* goes to the schools to pay for after-school programs and half goes to the households as an income transfer. The average *bolsa* per child in Pernambuco is R$37.8 per month, roughly 50% more than in the other two states.

Households are not required to enroll all the children in the specified age group. As a result, it is possible that the participating children in a household gain at the expense of their nonparticipating siblings. Some children may specialize in child labor, even as their siblings specialize in schooling. It is also possible that the program may affect nonparticipant households in the PETI municipalities. If the PETI program is successful in lowering labor-force participation in the qualified households, it may have spillover effects in the nonparticipating sector. By making child labor artificially scarce, child wages may be bid up, leading to increased labor participation for children in nonprogram households.

On the other hand, in Bahia, the Jornada Ampliada was made available to all school children, not just PETI children, so nonparticipating children may benefit from the program as well. In the other two states, the Jornada Ampliada was reserved for participating children. In any event, the possibility of positive or negative spillover impacts on nonparticipating children requires that the impact of the program on all children, and not just the enrollees, be evaluated.

## Experimental Design and Data

Data were collected from six municipalities in each state. The six municipalities were divided into two groups. The treatment group was composed of three municipalities in the PETI program. The control group included three municipalities of like socioeconomic status that were not in the program. In Bahia and Sergipe, the control municipalities had expressed an interest in participating but were scheduled for later implementation due to budget constraints. In Pernambuco, the control municipalities had initially opted not to participate in the program but have since expressed an interest in becoming PETI municipalities. Because states differed in program implementation and selection criteria for control municipalities, the evaluations were conducted separately by state.

From each municipality, 200 households with at least one child aged 7 to 14 were drawn randomly for the sample. Households were excluded if they were too wealthy to qualify for the PETI program, meaning their per capita income exceeded $65 per month. Information was collected on household, parent, and child attributes.[6] Among PETI households, information on the number of participating children and the first year of participation also was obtained.

Five indicators of program impacts on children were collected: school enrollment, labor participation, hours of work, sector of employment, and highest grade attained. These indicators were collected for all of the children in the sample. Comparison of the indicators across treatment and control municipalities will allow assessment of whether the PETI program reduced child labor, lowered the incidence of risky child labor, raised school enrollment, or improved academic performance.

## Sample Means

The initial survey design called for information to be collected from 3,600 households across nine PETI and nine non-PETI municipalities. Complete data were obtained on 3,564 households with 6,772 children between the ages of 7 and 14. The experimental design limited the analysis to households that were poor enough to be eligible for the program, were it to be implemented in that town. This limited the sample used in the analysis to 2,864 households with 5,611 children.

Sample statistics for the three states reported in table 9.1 reveal additional information on the nature of the child labor problem in these states. Virtually all children aged 7 to 14 are enrolled in school, but 17% of those in Pernambuco and Sergipe are also working. In Bahia, the proportion

**Table 9.1**   Sample means for children and households in Pernambuco, Bahia, and Sergipe

| Child Attributes[a] | Pernambuco Mean | Bahia Mean | Sergipe Mean |
|---|---|---|---|
| PETI Eligible | 0.92 | 0.96 | 0.93 |
| Education | 1.99 | 2.33 | 2.11 |
| In School | 0.98 | 1.00 | 1.00 |
| In School and Working[b] | 0.17 | 0.38 | 0.17 |
| Working 10+ Hours/Week | 0.13 | 0.18 | 0.07 |
| Weekly Work Hours (if Working) | 17.90 | 12.53 | 10.97 |
| Weekly Housework Hours | 9.36 | 8.57 | 9.15 |
| Weekly School Hours[c] | 20.14 | 19.30 | 21.94 |
| Age of Workforce Entry (if Working) | 8.29 | 7.44 | 8.67 |
| *Household Attributes*[d] | | | |
| At Least One Child Working | 0.23 | 0.41 | 0.23 |
| At Least One Child Working 10+ Hours/Week | 0.18 | 0.23 | 0.10 |
| Eligible | 0.90 | 0.94 | 0.90 |
| Number of Persons | 6.07 | 5.60 | 5.99 |
| Number of Persons 7 to 14 | 1.95 | 1.80 | 1.90 |
| One-Parent Households | 0.15 | 0.14 | 0.16 |
| Weekly Per Capita Household Income (Net of Program Payments) (R$) | 8.54 | 4.75 | 7.59 |
| Mother Working | 0.29 | 0.56 | 0.36 |
| Father Working | 0.89 | 0.99 | 0.92 |
| Mother's Education | 2.21 | 2.39 | 2.83 |
| Father's Education | 1.39 | 1.34 | 1.82 |
| Mother's Age | 33.61 | 34.90 | 34.36 |
| Father's Age | 35.11 | 35.52 | 33.30 |

*Notes:*

[a] All children aged 7 through 14 living in control municipalities.

[b] "Working" refers to both paid work in the job market and unpaid work in home production of goods and services. "Housework" refers to helping with house cleaning, laundry, and other ordinary household chores.

[c] Includes time in school, school activities, and homework.

[d] All households located in control municipalities.

*Source: Datamerica* survey for the evaluation of PETI 1999.

**Table 9.2** Occupational distribution and weekly hours of working children in Pernambuco, Bahia, and Sergipe

| | Pernambuco | | Bahia | | Sergipe | |
|---|---|---|---|---|---|---|
| Occupation | Proportion % | Mean Hours Worked Per Week | Proportion % | Mean Hours Worked Per Week | Proportion % | Mean Hours Worked Per Week |
| Agriculture (General) | 67.1 | 16.8 | 94.5 | 12.1 | 60.3 | 8.7 |
| Sugarcane | 5.2 | 24.7 | (—) | (—) | (—) | (—) |
| Cattle Breeding | 9.9 | 18.1 | 0.5 | 21.5 | 4.9 | 10.9 |
| Crop Harvest | 2.08 | 19.00 | 2.0 | 10.1 | 0.5 | 15.0 |
| Work in Family Business | (—) | (—) | (—) | (—) | 3.80 | 13.00 |
| Cutting/Carrying Straw/Grass | 1.04 | 17.50 | (—) | (—) | 2.72 | 15.40 |
| Shop Assistant | 2.60 | 32.40 | 1.78 | 23.07 | 2.72 | 12.80 |
| Fishing/Selling Fish | (—) | (—) | (—) | (—) | 13.6 | 15.6 |
| Other | 9.9 | 14.2 | 1.0 | 24.9 | 9.8 | 18.4 |
| Total Working | 100.00 | 17.9 | 100.00 | 12.5 | 100.00 | 11.0 |

*Note:*
  Sample: All working children aged 7 through 14 living in control municipalities.
*Source: Datamerica* survey for the evaluation of PETI 1999.

working is 38%. Children begin working at an average age of 8.1 and work an average of more than ten hours per week. Children also average nine hours of housework per week. Consequently, many children in these states spend as much time working as at school, even though they are on average only 10.5 years of age.

Table 9.2 reports the distribution of occupations for working children in these states. By far the most common enterprise is agriculture, with a few engaged in family-run stores or fishing enterprises. More detailed information on activities within agriculture points to many relatively dangerous tasks including clearing land, caring for livestock, harvesting, and processing. However, the most impressive statistic is the high number of working hours, regardless of occupation. Keeping in mind that these are children aged 7 to 14 it is likely that many are quite tired when they are in school. Little wonder that children already lag behind in school an average of one grade despite being only 10.5 years of age.

## Experimental Design

Figure 9.1 illustrates the design of the analysis. The universe of qualified households in the PETI municipalities was subdivided into two groups. Group A includes all households that participated in the program; group B includes qualified households that did not participate in the program. This

| PETI Municipalities | | Control Municipalities |
|---|---|---|
| A1: Participant Child in PETI Household | A2: Nonparticipant Child in PETI Household | C: Children in Eligible Households in Control Municipalities |
| B: Eligible Nonparticipant Households | | |

**Figure 9.1**  Partitioning the Sample into Eligible Treated, Eligible Untreated, and Controls

may include households that decided not to participate or households that wanted to participate but were excluded. The choice of whether or not to participate was not random, so group B cannot be used as a control for group A.

Children in group A households also can be subdivided into two groups. Group A1 includes all children who are part of the PETI program. However, households were not obligated to enroll all their children, so children in group A households who are not in the program form group A2. Once again, parents undoubtedly did not choose randomly as to which children to include or exclude from the program, so group A2 children cannot be viewed as controls for group A1 children.

Nevertheless, even though they do not receive direct benefits from PETI, children in groups A2 and B may be influenced by the program. Of greatest concern is that PETI will artificially lower the child labor supply, potentially raising child wages and inducing increased labor supply for children in groups A2 and B. However, PETI could benefit those children as well, whether by offering access to the after-school educational program or through demonstration effects that induce nonparticipating households to mimic behavior in the participating households. The evaluation will need to assess spillover effects on nonparticipating children, even if they are not proper controls.

The true controls are the households in group C, which would have qualified for the program but were prevented from participating because their municipality did not have the program. All estimated program effects are changes relative to the measured attendance, child labor, and school outcome measures of the children in group C.

### Methodology

The survey of treatment and control municipalities was conducted in 1999. Let $Y_{99}$ denote an outcome variable measured equivalently in 1999 in both treatment and control municipalities. PETI status is characterized by a sequence of dummy variables, $D_t^P$, $t = 96, 97, 98$, where the t subscript identifies the year of program initiation. Subscript 96 implies 3 years of participation, 97 represents 2 years of participation, and so on. Pernambuco initiated the program in 1996, so only that state can have a three-year effect. Sergipe initiated its program in 1997, and Bahia began its program in 1998. The variation in the length of time the program has been in place will help determine if the program's effects dissipate over time.

$D^B$ is a dummy variable that designates the individual child as a member of group B (the nonparticipating households in the PETI municipalities). $D^{A2}$ is a dummy variable indicating the child is in group A2 (the nonparticipating children in PETI households).

All analyses are reported including covariate controls for heterogeneity in observable household attributes. If PETI and control municipalities were drawn randomly from a universe of homogeneous communities, it would not be necessary to correct for possible covariation between treatment effects and household attributes. However, with only three control municipalities in each state, it is possible that there are underlying differences between control and treatment groups resulting from small sample bias. In fact, joint tests of differences in sample means between PETI and control municipalities rejected the null hypothesis of equality in all three states, although the differences are small numerically.[7]

A second issue is to assess whether assignment into the PETI group A is random in PETI municipalities. A probit model of PETI participation among eligible households is reported in table 9.3. The null hypothesis of random assignment into the PETI program could be rejected, although the pattern of participation by observable household attributes was not always internally consistent. For example, those with higher incomes were more likely to participate, but so were households in which parents were less educated. A few variables indicating distance to school had marginally significant impacts, although the pattern of participation with respect to school proximity was mixed. What is important for the purposes here is that the probit equation confirms that households in group B are different from households in group A. Therefore, households in group B cannot be treated as a control for group A.

## Specification

The sample definitions suggest the following specifications to assess the impact of the PETI program:

I: *Impact on PETI children versus nonparticipating children in the PETI municipalities versus children in the control municipalities:* {A1} vs. {A2 ∪ B} vs. {C}

$$Y_{99} = \alpha_0^I + \alpha_{96}^I D_{96}^P + \alpha_{97}^I D_{97}^P + \alpha_{98}^I D_{98}^P + \beta^I(D^B + D^{A2}) + \gamma_I' Z + \varepsilon^I \qquad (9.1)$$

where Z is a vector of household attributes and $\varepsilon^I$ is an error term. The coefficients $\alpha_t^I$ will estimate the impact of PETI on children within program

**Table 9.3**    Probability of PETI participation among eligible households

|  | dF/dX | Significance |
|---|---|---|
| Bahia | −31.645 | ** |
| Sergipe | −50.140 | ** |
| Average Child Age | 2.388 | ** |
| % Female Children | −5.090 |  |
| Father's Education | −0.455 |  |
| Mother's Education | −3.817 | ** |
| Father's Age | −0.164 |  |
| Mother's Age | 0.201 |  |
| Father's Work Status | 10.790 | * |
| Mother's Work Status | 4.639 |  |
| Number in Family | 2.758 | ** |
| Weekly HH Income | 2.147 | ** |
| Nearest School (0, 1) km | 14.440 | ** |
| Nearest School (1, 2) km | 3.916 |  |
| Nearest School (2, 3) km | −2.481 |  |
| Nearest School (3, 4) km | 26.639 | ** |
| Nearest School (4, 5) km | 11.554 |  |
| N |  |  |
| Global LR Test: (16) | 387.09 |  |
| Log Likelihood | −735 |  |
| Pseudo R-squared | 0.21 |  |

*Notes:*
  Sample: All eligible households in PETI municipalities.
  Coefficients represent percentage point change in the probability of participating in PETI.
  **Indicates significance at 5%.
  *Indicates significance at 10%.
  Significance levels based on standard errors of the underlying probit equation.

*Source: Datamerica* survey for the evaluation of PETI 1999.

households who actually participate in the program. The coefficient $\beta^I$ will capture the spillover effect on nonprogram children in program households and in nonprogram households.

*II. Impact on children in PETI households versus children in nonparticipating households in PETI municipalities versus children in the control municipalities: {A} vs. {B} vs. {C}*

$$Y_{99} = \alpha_0^{II} + \alpha_{96}^{II}D_{96}^{P} + \alpha_{97}^{II}D_{97}^{P} + \alpha_{98}^{II}D_{98}^{P} + \beta^{II}D^{B} + \gamma_{II}'Z + \varepsilon^{II} \tag{9.2}$$

Here, both A1 and A2 children are considered part of the treatment group. A comparison of the estimates between specification 1 and specification 2 will illustrate what is happening to nonprogram children in program households. The sign and magnitude of $\alpha_t^{II}$ gives the impact of PETI on all children in program households, whether or not they participate. If households respond to the program by having some children specialize in schooling while having other children work more, then $\alpha_t^{II}$ will be much closer to zero than was $\alpha_t^{I}$.[8]

*III. Impact on children in PETI municipalities versus children in control municipalities: {A ∪ B} vs. {C}*

$$Y_{99} = \alpha_0^{III} + \alpha_{96}^{III}D_{96}^{PM} + \alpha_{97}^{III}D_{97}^{PM} + \alpha_{98}^{III}D_{98}^{PM} + \gamma_{III}'Z + \varepsilon^{III} \tag{9.3}$$

where $D_t^{PM}$ is a dummy variable reflecting residence in a PETI municipality. The time subscript now represents the year in which the municipality initiated its PETI program rather than the year the household initiated the program.[9] Coefficients on $\alpha_t^{III}$ will measure the impact of PETI on all children in the municipality relative to the control. If there are positive or negative feedback effects of the program on children in group {B}, these will be reflected in $\alpha_t^{III}$.

The advantage of specification III, relative to I or II, is that it reflects the general equilibrium effects of PETI on covered and uncovered children. Because of the possibility of negative feedback effects of PETI on child labor for uncovered children, it is possible to find strong positive effects of the program in I and II, and yet find neutral or negative effects in III. Thus, III is the most complete measure of the program impacts.[10]

# Results

It is important to emphasize that data were only available for a single cross-section in 1999. Consequently, this study relies heavily on the assumption that the municipalities excluded from the program can serve as an adequate control for those in the program, holding constant the covariate measures of observable differences, Z. In other settings, where estimates of program effects using difference-in-differences methods were compared to estimates using cross-sectional differences with covariate controls, results obtained were similar across estimation strategies.[11]

Estimation of specifications I through III is reported in tables 9.4 through 9.8; the tables will be discussed in turn.

## Time in School

The first success indicator examined is the impact of the program on hours in school.[12] Program children must attend school and the after-school program to receive the *bolsa*. As a result, a positive impact on school hours for program children is virtually assured. Of more interest is whether the program reduces school hours for children in groups {A2} or {B}.

Table 9.4 reports the estimated impact of PETI on school hours. A tobit specification is used to accommodate the large number of zero observations. Looking at the effect on participant children in PETI households, average hours in school rose eleven to seventeen hours in Pernambuco, seventeen hours in Bahia, and twelve to fifteen hours in Sergipe. Simply attending the afternoon Jornada Ampliada sessions would increase time in school by about twenty hours per week, so the magnitude of the PETI effect on

**Table 9.4** Tobit estimates of PETI impact on weekly school hours

| Coefficient | Pernambuco | | | Bahia | | | Sergipe | | |
|---|---|---|---|---|---|---|---|---|---|
| | I | II | III | I | II | III | I | II | III |
| $\alpha_{96}$ | 17.49** | 15.66** | 10.02** | | | | | | 4.95** |
| $\alpha_{97}$ | 14.56** | 12.31** | | | | | 14.57** | 9.65** | 1.22** |
| $\alpha_{98}$ | 10.79** | 10.02** | 8.84** | 16.63** | 14.10** | 8.77** | 12.08** | 7.14** | |
| $\beta$ | −1.35 | −0.87 | | 0.81 | 0.77 | | −0.33 | −0.40 | |

*Notes:*
Sample: All program-eligible children. Regressions using pooled sample of eligible and ineligible children (not reported) do not produce different estimates of program effects.
All equations include controls for the covariates listed in Table 9.1.
Coefficients represent change in hours of schooling, school-related activities, or homework.
**Indicates significance at 5%.
Significance levels based on standard errors of the underlying tobit coefficients.

*Source: Datamerica* survey for evaluation of PETI 1999.

school attendance suggests that all of the increase in time in school is due to the Jornada Ampliada. Had attendance in the morning sessions become more regular, PETI would have more than doubled weekly school hours. The longer children participate in the program, the greater the impact of PETI on school time.

The program has no significant impact on local children who are not in the program. Therefore, children will not voluntarily attend the Jornada Ampliada without the subsidy, but they will not reduce time in school, either. There is no apparent adverse impact of PETI on the school attendance of nonparticipating children in the PETI municipalities.

In going from specification I to III, the magnitude of the attendance effect becomes smaller but remains positive and significant. Consequently, any negative impacts on the nonprogram children in the household are not large enough to drive the household average effect to zero. The impact is further reduced when the study moves to the municipality-wide effect in specification III.[13] Nevertheless, the results suggest that in both Bahia and Pernambuco, average time in school rose eight to ten hours (40% to 50%) per week across all eligible children in participating municipalities. The change in school hours is smaller but still positive in Sergipe. There, time in school rose an average of 5% to 23%. The conclusion from table 9.4 is that the PETI successfully increased time in school for program children while imposing no collateral damage on nonprogram children.

### Time in the Labor Market

PETI parents agree not to have their children work, but that agreement is difficult to enforce. However, the Jornada Ampliada limits a child's available time for work. Table 9.5 shows that the probability of working for PETI children fell 4 to 7 percentage points in Pernambuco, nearly 26 percentage points in Bahia, and nearly 13 percentage points in Sergipe. At the same time, probability of work also fell for nonprogram children, albeit by an imprecise amount. In going to the household average estimate II, the effects get smaller, but none change sign or significance. Finally, averaging across all children in the municipality, work probability drops 5 to 6 percentage points in Pernambuco, nearly 18 percentage points in Bahia, and around 4.5 percentage points in Sergipe. That the largest impact is in Bahia reflects two factors: Bahia started with the highest level of child labor, and it was the only state that allowed nonprogram children to attend the Jornada Ampliada. The latter results seem to define that it is the after-school program that is the most important element in combating child labor in these programs.[14]

Child labor-force participation may not be a problem if the child is working relatively few hours. Table 9.6 repeats the exercise in table 9.5, but uses an indicator of whether the child works at least ten hours per week as the labor supply measure. PETI appears to be less successful in lowering the incidence of working long hours than it is in lowering the probability of working overall. This suggests that PETI is more successful at

**Table 9.5** Probit estimates of PETI impact on the probability of child labor

| Coefficient | Pernambuco | | | Bahia | | | Sergipe | | |
|---|---|---|---|---|---|---|---|---|---|
| | I | II | III | I | II | III | I | II | III |
| $\alpha_{96}$ | −7.02** | −5.49** | −6.01** | | | | | | |
| $\alpha_{97}$ | −4.13 | −2.36 | | | | | (—) | −10.74** | −4.47 |
| $\alpha_{98}$ | −3.77** | −4.96** | −4.97** | −25.93** | −24.77** | −17.56** | −12.75** | −10.27** | −4.59** |
| $\beta$ | −2.76 | −1.99 | | −4.70* | −4.82* | | −2.99 | −2.51 | |

*Notes:*
Sample: All program-eligible children. Regressions using pooled sample of eligible and ineligible children (not reported) do not produce different estimates of program effects.
All equations include controls for the covariates listed in table 9.1.
Coefficients represent percentage point change in probability of child labor.
**Indicates significance at 5%.
*Indicates significance at 10%.
(—) = coefficient not estimable. Variable perfectly predicts that child is out of labor force.

*Source: Datamerica* survey for evaluation of PETI 1999.

**Table 9.6** Probit estimates of PETI impact on the probability of a child working at least 10 hours per week

| Coefficient | Pernambuco | | | Bahia | | | Sergipe | | |
|---|---|---|---|---|---|---|---|---|---|
| | I | II | III | I | II | III | I | II | III |
| $\alpha_{96}$ | −5.40** | −4.39** | −5.46** | | | | | | |
| $\alpha_{97}$ | −3.74** | −2.26* | | | | | (—) | −2.56 | 0.24 |
| $\alpha_{98}$ | −3.97** | −4.11** | −3.14** | −9.48** | −8.29** | −4.54** | −5.04** | −2.55** | 0.17 |
| $\beta$ | −0.99 | −0.52 | | 3.44* | 3.38* | | 1.82 | 2.25* | |

*Notes:*
Sample: All program-eligible children. Regressions using pooled sample of eligible and ineligible children (not reported) do not produce different estimates of program effects.
All equations include controls for the covariates listed in table 9.1.
Coefficients represent percentage point change in probability of child labor.
**Indicates significance at 5%.
*Indicates significance at 10%.
(—) = coefficient not estimable. Variable perfectly predicts that child is out of labor force.

*Source: Datamerica* survey for evaluation of PETI 1999.

removing part-time child workers from the labor force than it is at removing more dedicated child laborers from their jobs. The probability of working at least ten hours fell from 5 to 9 percentage points for children in the program, depending on location and length of time the program was in place. Nonprogram children were not affected in Pernambuco, but there was an increased probability of working more than ten hours among nonprogram children in Bahia and Sergipe. In Sergipe, the spillover increase in labor supply behavior for nonprogram children is large enough to outweigh the small benefit to program children so that the municipality-wide probability of working at least ten hours is unaffected by PETI. In Bahia and Pernambuco, the probability of working ten hours or more drops by 4.5 and 3.1 percentage points, respectively.

Overall, PETI lowers child labor-force participation, but it is less successful in limiting the probability of working ten hours or more. There is evidence that in Bahia and Sergipe, some children increase their specialization in labor while others participate in the PETI. Unreported regressions suggest that across all children, average hours worked dropped one to two hours per week as a result of PETI. Relative to sample averages reported above, that means PETI lowered total hours worked by children by nearly 50% in all three states.

### Success in School

The Jornada Ampliada does not have a prescribed curriculum, so its value may differ across states and municipalities. Reports indicate that the program varies from sessions that are closely integrated with the regular teacher to a complete lack of integration between the two. Nevertheless, as shown above, PETI did increase average time in school and lower hours of work. The *Jornada* may improve academic performance merely by adding available time for study or by reducing child exhaustion through reduced child labor.

Absent available standardized tests, one measure of academic performance is whether children pass the grade. Child labor has been linked closely to grade retardation in Brazil, so grade attainment should improve if PETI is successful. The measure of grade attainment is grade-for-age (GFA), defined as

$$\text{GFA} = \frac{\text{Education}}{\text{Age} - 7}, \text{Age} > 7 \quad = 0 \text{ otherwise} \quad (9.4)$$

Despite PETI's relatively short implementation period, GFA should rise in PETI municipalities, particularly those which have had the program the longest.

Estimates of the effect of PETI on grade-for-age are reported in table 9.7. Participating children had significant gains in all three states. The gains

Table 9.7  Ordinary least squares estimates of PETI impact on grade-for-age

| Coefficient | Pernambuco | | | Bahia | | | Sergipe | | |
|---|---|---|---|---|---|---|---|---|---|
| | I | II | III | I | II | III | I | II | III |
| $\alpha_{96}$ | 0.16** | 0.11** | 0.13** | | | | 0.24** | 0.16** | 0.03 |
| $\alpha_{97}$ | 0.14** | 0.11** | | 0.11** | 0.07** | 0.07** | 0.02 | 0.01 | 0.00 |
| $\alpha_{98}$ | 0.14** | 0.12** | 0.05 | 0.04 | 0.04 | | 0.01 | 0.01 | |
| $\beta$ | −0.08* | −0.08* | | | | | 0.01 | 0.01 | |

*Notes:*

Sample: All program-eligible children.

All equations include controls for the covariates listed in table 9.1.

Coefficients represent percentage change in years of education attained per year of age.

**Indicates significance at 5%.

*Indicates significance at 10%.

Significance levels based on standard errors of the underlying tobit coefficients.

*Source: Datamerica* survey for evaluation of PETI 1999.

remain significant but smaller when nonparticipant children in the household are included in treatment group A. In Pernambuco, as a result of PETI, there is an apparent decrease of 0.08 grades per year of age in grade-for-age among nonparticipants. There is no evidence of collateral harm to nonparticipants in Bahia or Sergipe. The total impact on PETI municipalities is positive in all three states. The effect is significant in Bahia and in the Pernambuco municipalities that implemented PETI in 1996.

It would be useful to know why the Jornada Ampliada enhanced the educational experience of PETI children. As the program is expanded and various academic plans for the *Jornada* are tried, analysts may be able to identify which types of after-school programs best enhance academic performance. As noted above, however, simply lowering the incidence of child labor may have improved academic performance.

### Hazardous Work

The main motivation of the PETI program is to reduce the incidence of dangerous work. Using detailed information on the incidence of injuries reported by child occupation, working children were placed in one of four risk categories. Risk level is coded as 1 if the child is not working, 2 if the occupation has an accident rate less than one-fourth of a standard deviation above the average accident rate, 3 if the accident rate falls between one-fourth and one-half of a standard deviation above the mean, and 4 if accident rates are above that.

The evaluation of the PETI impact uses an ordered probit analysis to estimate the change in probability of being in risk categories 1 through 4; the results are reported in table 9.8. Because the impact on occupational hazards is spread over four coefficients, a summary measure of the change in risk is derived

$$\delta = \sum_{i=1}^{4} i \cdot \left( P_i \middle| D_t^P = 1 - P_i \middle| D_t^P = 0 \right) \tag{9.5}$$

The term in parentheses is the difference in the probability of being in risk group i between those in the PETI group and the control. These probability changes are weighted by their associated risk level, i. The resulting measure, $\delta$, may be interpreted as the change in average risk level in the population. If $\delta < 0$, occupational risk falls.

The significance test refers to whether the associated dummy variable coefficient is significantly different from zero. All but one of the PETI coefficients is significant, but none of the coefficients on nonparticipant status is significantly different from zero. The implication is that risk fell significantly among participating children without any significant collateral damage on nonparticipating children.

In all states, the probability of being in the lowest risk group rises and the probability of being in risk groups 2 through 4 falls. The pattern holds

**Table 9.8**   Ordered Probit Estimates of PETI Impact on Hazardous Child Labor

| Specification | Pernambuco | Sig[a] | P(1)[b] | P(2) | P(3) | P(4) | δ |
|---|---|---|---|---|---|---|---|
| I | $\alpha_{97}$ | ** | 12.99 | −93.40 | −56.89 | −49.67 | −0.21 |
| | $\alpha_{98}$ | ** | 7.31 | −52.59 | −32.03 | −27.97 | −0.12 |
| | $\alpha_{99}$ | ** | 5.59 | −40.22 | −24.50 | −21.39 | −0.09 |
| | β | | 2.09 | −15.04 | −9.16 | −8.00 | −0.04 |
| II | $\alpha_{97}$ | ** | 8.54 | −63.86 | −37.66 | −31.06 | −0.14 |
| | $\alpha_{98}$ | * | 4.50 | −33.65 | −19.84 | −16.37 | −0.07 |
| | $\alpha_{99}$ | ** | 7.03 | −52.56 | −30.99 | −25.57 | −0.12 |
| | β | | 1.33 | −9.94 | −5.86 | −4.84 | −0.02 |
| III | $\alpha_{97}$ | ** | 8.08 | −53.95 | −38.14 | −28.80 | −0.14 |
| | $\alpha_{98}$ | | | | | | |
| | $\alpha_{99}$ | ** | 6.63 | −44.24 | −31.28 | −23.62 | −0.11 |
| Specification | Bahia | | | | | | |
| I | $\alpha_{99}$ | ** | 43.08 | −56.72 | −76.83 | −133.56 | −0.48 |
| | β | | 2.70 | −3.55 | −4.81 | −8.36 | −0.03 |
| II | $\alpha_{99}$ | ** | 36.80 | −48.38 | −64.03 | −120.41 | −0.41 |
| | β | | 2.75 | −3.61 | −4.78 | −9.00 | −0.03 |
| III | $\alpha_{99}$ | ** | 21.35 | −26.11 | −40.10 | −68.83 | −0.24 |
| Specification | Sergipe | | | | | | |
| II | $\alpha_{98}$ | ** | 17.17 | −62.86 | −121.95 | −107.00 | −0.26 |
| | $\alpha_{99}$ | ** | 10.70 | −39.17 | −75.99 | −66.67 | −0.16 |
| | β | | 0.37 | −1.36 | −2.63 | −2.31 | −0.01 |
| III | $\alpha_{98}$ | ** | 6.89 | −24.80 | −49.02 | −44.04 | −0.10 |
| | $\alpha_{99}$ | | 3.76 | −13.54 | −26.77 | −24.05 | −0.06 |

*Notes:*
[a]Significance level at the associated dummy variable coefficient in the ordered probit equation.
[b]Estimated change in the probability of being in the lowest occupational risk group.
Sample: All program-eligible children.
All equations include controls for covariates listed in table 9.1.
For Sergipe, estimates of specification I failed to converge.
**Indicates significance at 5%.
*Indicates significance at 10%.

not only for PETI participants, but for nonparticipant children as well. Consequently, there is no evidence that nonparticipant children entered risky work as participant children left risky jobs.

In Pernambuco, the average risk level in the absence of PETI was 1.39. Among treatment children, the change in risk scores, δ, fell between 0.1 and 0.2 points. The impact across all children in PETI households is somewhat smaller. However, when the municipal effect is measured, the magnitude remains at −0.2 over three years and −0.1 over one year. Consequently, ending average risk drops to between 1.2 and 1.28 in PETI municipalities.

Bahia has the largest risk in the absence of the program and experienced the largest average risk decline. Children in PETI households experienced sharp reductions in risk level of more than 0.4 points, with no apparent increase in risk for children in nonparticipant households. The municipal effect is −0.24, so the average risk drops to 1.36.

Sergipe has the smallest reduction in risk when evaluated at the municipal level, although it had the lowest initial level of risk. Average risk fell by 0.06 points over one year and by 0.1 points over two years.

## Conclusions

PETI attempted to combat child labor through two interventions. The first was to create the Jornada Ampliada, an after-school program with the potential to complement the regular school academic program. The second was to provide a subsidy, or *bolsa*, to poor households whose children attended the *Jornada* at least 80% of the time. Budget constraints and/or parental disinterest meant that only a subset of qualified children could receive the *bolsa*. Consequently, there was a possibility that the program would benefit participating children but would have adverse child labor and education consequences for nonparticipating children.

An evaluation based on experimental design principles found that the program had a positive impact on children who participated in the program. They spent more time in school, less time at work, less time in risky work, and progressed in school at a faster rate. In Bahia and Sergipe, the PETI program appears to have caused a slightly higher probability for nonparticipant children to work more than ten hours per week. In Pernambuco, nonparticipating children appear to have had slightly greater difficulty progressing to the next grade. In no case, however, were the adverse effects large enough to outweigh the positive effects on participating children. The positive effects appear to be largest in the longest-running programs.

Although the incidence of child labor has decreased as per capita incomes have increased, it has persisted in rural areas and in those where household incomes have stagnated. While government policies aimed at improving school quality have been implemented worldwide, it is doubtful that improving schools alone will reduce child labor. Poor households may not be able to afford to remove their children from the labor force, even if schools offer better services. Indeed, in Brazil, most working children also are enrolled in school.

In Bahia, which allows all children to attend the *Jornada*, some nonparticipating children did in fact increase time in school. The effect is modest, however, and suggests that just adding the after-school program is not enough to reduce child labor. Adding the targeted income transfer appears to be necessary to obtain the dramatic increases in voluntary time in school. On the other hand, a truancy law could be enforced if the after-school program were made a regular part of the school day. The PETI experience suggests that by increasing time in school, whether voluntarily or through government mandate, child labor can be reduced.

# Notes

Donna Otto prepared the manuscript. Research was conducted while Yoon-Tien Yap was in residence at the World Bank. The views in this chapter do not necessarily reflect those of the Inter-American Development Bank, the World Bank, the International Monetary Fund, or their member countries.

1. Moehling (1999) found that in the United States, minimum age work rules were not effective in limiting child labor in the United States between 1880 and 1910, but Lleras-Muney (2002) found that state compulsory attendance laws increased school enrollments between 1915 and 1939. Truancy laws are easier to enforce because, unlike child labor, school attendance is easily monitored. As a consequence, compulsory schooling laws appear to alter child time use (Angrist and Krueger, 1991).

2. See chapters 2–3. For other examples, see Grootaert and Patrinos (1999), Jensen and Nielsen (1997), Tzannatos (2003), Beegle et al. (2006; 2007) and Edmonds et al. (2005).

3. Rosenzweig and Evenson (1977) and Levy (1985) found that higher child wages led to increased child-labor participation and decreased enrollments. King et al. (1999a) found that stronger local child-labor markets increased the incidence of school dropout.

4. E.g., Ravallion and Wodon (2000) found only weak substitutability between child labor and child time in school.

5. Over the sample period, the Brazilian real was pegged to the U.S. dollar, so there is a one-to-one conversion from Brazilian to U.S. currency.

6. Data were collected by Datamerica.

7. F-tests corrected for clustering were 6.16 in Pernambuco, 4.63 in Bahia, and 2.74 in Sergipe. All are significant at the 0.05 confidence level.

8. This study could not estimate a separate effect of group {A2} versus groups {B} and {A1} because Datamerica did not identify which children in group {A} participated and which did not. They did identify which households had universal participation, however. Consequently, estimation of specification I is conducted over the sample of households in which all children were in PETI or all children were out of PETI. This problem does not affect specifications II or III.

9. In Pernambuco, municipalities signed on in 1996 and 1998. Some households entered the program in 1997, but they will be considered as treated in 1996 for the municipal effect defined by specification III. They will be considered as treated in 1997 for the child and household effects defined by specifications I and II.

10. Schultz (2004) also used estimator III in his evaluation of the PROGRESA program in Mexico.

11. See Kim et al. (1999) or Schultz (2004) for examples.

12. One also could estimate the impact on enrollment, but virtually all children were already enrolled.

13. There is no municipal effect for 1997 because all municipal programs were installed in either 1996 or 1998. Some households enrolled in PETI in 1998, but they would be incorporated into the 1996 municipal group.

14. This result is consistent with findings elsewhere that child labor laws by themselves are ineffective, but truancy laws that require children to be in school do affect child labor. The difference between the two is that child-labor laws are hard to enforce, but child attendance is easily monitored.

# 10

# The Impact of PROGRESA on Child Labor and Schooling

*Emmanuel Skoufias and Susan W. Parker*

Over the past few years within Latin America, a number of new antipoverty programs have been introduced specifically to increase investment in human capital. Their success is measured in particular by education, but also by health and nutrition. In general, these programs represent a significant departure from previous antipoverty policies within the region, for they are based on the premise that a fundamental cause of poverty and of its intergenerational transmission is the lack of investment in human development. A distinguishing characteristic of these programs is the provision of cash transfers on the condition that poor families take their children out of work and send them to school.

In 1997, the federal government of Mexico introduced one of the first programs of its kind as a part of the country's renewed effort to break the intergenerational transmission of poverty. The program, known as Programa de Educación, Salud y Alimentación (PROGRESA), or the Education, Health, and Nutrition Program, provides cash transfers to increase families' investment in human capital as defined by education, health, and nutrition. PROGRESA makes cash transfers conditional on children's enrollment and regular school attendance as well as clinic attendance. The transfers, which are given directly to the mothers of the families, correspond to an average increase of 22% in the income levels of the beneficiary families. The program also includes in-kind health benefits and nutritional supplements for children up to age 5 and for pregnant and lactating women. PROGRESA has grown rapidly and now covers 2.6 million extremely impoverished families in rural areas, corresponding to about 40% of all rural families in Mexico.

This study conducts a detailed analysis of PROGRESA's impact on the schooling, work, and time allocation of children between the ages of 8 and 17. It addresses the following questions: Does the program reduce child labor? Does it increase participation in school activities? Does the latter occur at the expense of children's leisure time? How do the program's effects vary by age group and gender?[1] The empirical analysis relies on data from a quasi-experimental design that evaluates the program's impact on a sample of communities that receive PROGRESA benefits (treatment) and comparable communities that receive benefits at a later time (control).

The analysis consists of two parts, based on a progressively broader definition of what constitutes work. The first uses data from various survey instruments used to evaluate PROGRESA and applied to both the treatment and control groups before and after program implementation. This allows the study to estimate PROGRESA's impact using the double difference estimator, commonly acknowledged as the preferred estimator for program evaluation. Information is available on household labor-market participation, income, expenditures, and wealth, as well as children's school attendance. The second part uses a module on time use, carried out about a year after program implementation. It contains information on time allocated to eighteen different activities during the previous day and examines of the impact of PROGRESA on leisure as well as time allocated to market, domestic, and farm work.

Empirical studies using data from other countries find that the marginal effect of an unconditional income change is surprisingly small on both school enrollment (Behrman and Knowles, 1999) and child labor (Nielsen, 1998). This suggests that unconditional cash transfer programs (which increase household income) can have only a limited effect on school enrollment or child labor participation. Cash or in-kind transfer programs that are conditional on school enrollment may be more effective at achieving this dual objective. Ravallion and Wodon (2000), for example, find that the Food for Education program in Bangladesh, which provides rice to families in exchange for sending their children to school, lowers the incidence of child labor and increases boys' school enrollment by 25%. This implies that most of the increased attendance of boys takes place at the expense of leisure.

## PROGRESA and an Economic Model of Investments in Human Capital

In Mexico, the design of PROGRESA represents a significant change in social programs. In contrast to previous poverty alleviation programs in Mexico, PROGRESA targets the household level to ensure that it reaches those in extreme poverty. Also unlike earlier social programs, PROGRESA contains a multisectoral focus, intervening simultaneously in health, education, and nutrition. Its integrated nature reflects a belief that addressing all dimensions of human capital simultaneously has greater social returns, since school attendance and performance often are adversely affected by poor health and nutrition. PROGRESA gives benefits exclusively to mothers, recognizing their potential to address the family's immediate needs.

*Specific Benefits*

PROGRESA provides financial educational grants to children under the age  of 18 who are enrolled between the third grade of primary school and the third grade of secondary school (table 10.1). The grant amounts increase  as children progress to higher grades, reflecting the income children would contribute if they were working. The grants are slightly higher for girls than for boys at the junior high level.[2] For boys, they range from 90 pesos (about U.S. $9) in the third grade of primary school to 290 pesos (U.S. $30) in the third grade of secondary school. Girls receive the same stipend in primary school, but their grant rises to 335 pesos (U.S. $35) by the time they reach the third year of secondary school.

PROGRESA also provides basic health care to all family members through the Ministry of Health and IMSS-Solidaridad, a branch of the Mexican Social Security Institute, and a fixed monetary transfer (135 pesos each month) for improved food consumption and nutritional supplements.

The program's objective is to provide incentives for increased human capital contingent on the beneficiary families fulfilling certain obligations. The educational grants are linked to school attendance: if a child misses more than 15% of school days in a month (for unjustified reasons), the family will not receive that month's grant. Similarly, families must make scheduled visits to health care facilities to receive the support for improved nutrition.

This section presents a simple household decision-making model that highlights the costs and benefits associated with investing in the human capital of children. The impact of the cash transfer on child time in school differs depending on whether the child is initially in or out of school.

The vertical axis of figure 10.1 depicts the quantity of other goods available for household consumption, whereas the horizontal axis measures the time a child devotes to schooling, S. Full attendance occurs when the child devotes all non-leisure time to school, including school-related homework (i.e., $S = T$ where $T$ denotes the amount of time available after excluding

**Table 10.1**  Monthly amount of educational grant (pesos), second semester 2000

| Grade | Boys | Girls |
|---|---|---|
| Primary | | |
| 3rd Year | 90 | 90 |
| 4th Year | 105 | 105 |
| 5th Year | 135 | 135 |
| 6th Year | 180 | 180 |
| Secondary | | |
| 1st Year | 260 | 275 |
| 2nd Year | 275 | 305 |
| 3rd Year | 290 | 335 |

*Source:* PROGRESA staff.

A    —   Child initially not attending.
C    —   Child initially attending beyond Smin.
T    —   Maximum amount of child time available excluding leisure.
Smin  —  Program's required school attendance.

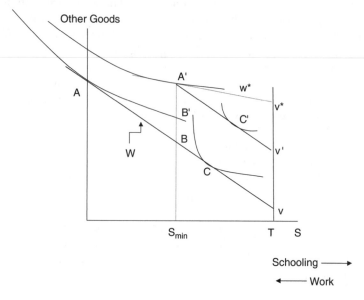

**Figure 10.1**    The Effect of Conditional Cash Transfers on Children's School Attendance and Work

leisure time which for simplicity is assumed to be fixed). The vertical line of height $V$ at the value of $S = T$ denotes the maximum amount of other household goods available when a child devotes all her time to school rather than work. When a child divides her time between work and school, the opportunity set of the household is described by the line $TVA$. The negative slope of this line is given by the real market wage $W$ for child labor, which describes the trade-off in the market between the consumption of other goods and schooling (or work).[3]

Let $S_{min}$ denote the 85% attendance rate required by the PROGRESA program. Eligibility for the PROGRESA benefits causes the budget line in the region between points $T$ and $S_{min}$ to shift up and increases the non-labor component of income upward to $V'$. $V' - V$ equals the maximum amount of benefits the household can obtain from the program; the feasible budget constraint of an eligible family is now described by the line $TV' A'BA$ which is discontinuous at the point $S_{min}$.

Differences in family non-earned income and market opportunities may determine why some children are enrolled or not enrolled in school. It is assumed that the income opportunities of households are identical; consider the case of two different types of households represented by two different indifference curves. The household denoted by the tangency at point

$C$ represents those with a child attendance rate close to 100% ($S > S_{min}$) and a child who works only a very small fraction of the time. The indifference curve that crosses the vertical axis at point $A$ represents a household with a child who does not attend school at all ($S = 0$) and devotes all of her free time to market work.

The discontinuity of the household budget constraint combined with the assumption of utility maximization implies that a minimum conditional cash transfer (CCT) will induce households to send their children to school. Let $B'$ denote the point of intersection of the indifference curve of household $A$ with the vertical line at $S_{min}$. The vertical difference $B' - B$ then represents the minimum cash transfer that will make household $A$ just indifferent between complying with the 85% attendance requirement and keeping the child out of school. A CCT less than $B' - B$ is insufficient to induce the household to enroll the child in school because by having its child work, the family receives a higher level of utility. In figure 10.1, it is implicitly assumed that the size of the CCT, $V' - V$, is greater than the minimum amount, $B' - B$, needed to induce household $A$ to enroll the child in school and comply with the 85% attendance requirement. Consequently, household $A$ finds it advantageous to enroll the child in school.

As can be inferred from this figure, program participation is likely to affect households differently depending on their location on the budget line before program administration. Household $C$ ($C'$ under the program), for example, can represent households with children of primary school age in which the enrollment rate is close to 95% or households with children of secondary school age who regularly attend school even before the administration of the program. Because the conditions are not binding, the program will likely have only a pure income effect represented in figure 10.1 by the parallel upward shift in the portion of the budget constraint between points $T$ and $S_{min}$. For these households the impact of the program may concentrate on increasing the time they devote to school, such as spending more time studying.[4]

In contrast, consider household $A$. Initially, it is very hard for this household to attribute any income and substitution effects to the program because the final equilibrium point $A'$ is not a tangency point. Yet, by linearizing the budget constraint (Killingsworth, 1983), it becomes apparent that household $A$'s participation results in both substitution and income effects that tend to reinforce each other. The cash transfer component leads to a pure income effect that increases schooling, while the condition that the child devote at least 85% of her time to school leads to a price effect. On the basis of standard economic theory, the price effect may be further decomposed into a substitution and income effect. At the final equilibrium point $A'$, the lower shadow wage rate $W^*$ ($< W$) represents the lower price of schooling as a result of the program, while the total increase in household income as a result of the program may be considered to be the cash transfer $V' - V$ plus the implicit extra income $V^* - V'$ earned as a result of the lower price of schooling.

In other words, program participation is likely to affect households differently, depending on their constraints and preferences (or locations on the budget line) before the administration of the program. In households for which the program constraints are binding, income and substitution effects can reinforce the program's impact. In households for which the constraints of the program are non-binding, the program will likely have only income effects. Given the heterogeneity of households' preferences and constraints, the extent to which the program has a significant impact on the human capital and work of children can only be determined through empirical analysis.

## Data, Empirical Specification, and Results

The sample used to evaluate PROGRESA consists of repeated observations of 24,000 households from 506 localities in the states of Guerrero, Hidalgo, Michoacan, Puebla, Queretaro, San Luis Potosi, and Veracruz. Of the 506 localities, 320 were randomly assigned to the treatment group ($T = 1$) and 186 were assigned as controls ($T = 0$). The localities serving as the control group began receiving PROGRESA benefits by December 2000.[5]

The data in this report were taken from the Survey of Household Socioeconomic Characteristics (ENCASEH) and the Evaluation Survey of PROGRESA (ENCEL), designed specifically for evaluation purposes. ENCASEH, an economic census, was used to select which households in the eligible communities were eligible to participate in PROGRESA.

School enrollment is defined according to those households that say their children attend school; the question is identical over the different rounds of analysis. In this study, working includes paid and unpaid labor. Home production activities are not included in this definition of work, but the analysis incorporates a work definition that includes domestic chores.

The time use module included information on eighteen activities carried out during the previous day for all individuals aged 8 or older. The analysis first constructed overall measures of leisure time, defined as the difference between twenty-four hours and the time spent on all reported activities. Three different types of work were considered: market, farm, and domestic. Participation and hours spent in each activity were analyzed, as were participation and time spent in school.

Even before PROGRESA was implemented, 95% of boys under age 12 were enrolled in school and fewer than 5% worked. After age 11, school enrollment rates dropped steadily to 20% by age 17. By age 13, 20% of boys worked, and the rate rose to 70% by age 17. At early ages, participation was generally dominated by unsalaried work that was primarily self-employment and helping in family businesses. Only by age 14 did the percentage of boys in salaried work begin to exceed unpaid work activities.

A similar schooling pattern existed for girls, with 95% participating until age 12, when a steady decline toward 20% by age 17 began. However, in contrast to boys, labor-force participation of girls increased very slowly with age. By age 17, less than 20% of girls were working. At that age, two-thirds of the girls were neither in school nor working, so their primary time was spent on home production activities.

## Measuring Eligibility

The regressions here focus only on families eligible for the program. The study used the sample of all eligible households, whether or not they received any benefits. Thus, the estimated program effect includes the operational inefficiency with which the program operated. Using the terminology of Heckman et al. (1999), the program impact estimates provide an idea of the mean direct effect of the offer or the intent to treat. For this reason it should be noted that these are lower-bound estimates of the program's impact on households that actually received the treatment.[6]

## Impact on Labor-Force Participation and School Enrollment of Children

The baseline data set (ENCASEH) was first collected in November 1997. Changes in behavioral outcomes were collected in November 1998, June 1999, and November 1999.[7]

Mean school attendance for boys and girls was practically the same between treatment and control areas before PROGRESA implementation. By November 1998, the mean attendance rate of boys in treatment villages was noticeably higher than the mean attendance rate in the villages not yet covered. Although mean attendance rates rose slightly in the control villages, the increase in the mean attendance rate in treatment villages was considerably higher. The same pattern can be observed in the mean school attendance of girls in the same age category. The mean school attendance rates in the treatment areas appeared to remain more or less stable at the higher level over successive survey rounds.

In contrast to mean school attendance, there were differences between treatment and control villages in labor-force participation rates before PROGRESA was introduced. In November 1997, the labor-force participation rates for both boys and girls were lower in control villages than treatment villages. By November 1998, labor-force participation rates of boys and girls in both treatment and control villages appeared to decrease and remained at that lower level for the remaining rounds.

Quantitative estimates of a program's impact vary depending on the data available and the assumptions one is willing to make about the unobserved counterfactual state (i.e., behavior in the absence of the program).[8] "Before-and-after" and "cross-sectional difference" estimators can be used. However, the "before-and-after" estimator attributes to the program all increases in school attendance rates including those that would have occurred without the program. The "cross-sectional difference" estimator assumes there are no pre-existing differences between the control and the treatment group, an assumption that is violated in our sample.

A third estimator, considered by the evaluation literature to be the most preferable, is the difference-in-differences or double difference (2DIF) estimator, which essentially measures impact by subtracting any pre-program differences between treatment and controls from the mean differences observed between individuals in treatment and control villages after the start of the program.

To the extent that it was feasible, the quasi-experimental design of PROGRESA involved randomization of communities into treatment and control groups to ensure that both were comparable in both observable and unobservable characteristics (Gomez de Leon et al., 1994). However, it is possible that some systematic differences were still present when comparing differences of means of individuals between treatment and control localities. The data suggest that there are some pre-program differences in the mean labor-force participation rates of boys and girls. To account for this, regression methods were used to compare the means of key outcome variables conditioned on individual observed and unobserved characteristics.

The empirical equation for participation in work (school) is specified as:

$$
\begin{aligned}
Y(i,t) = {} & \alpha + \beta_T T(i) + \beta_{R2}(R2) + \beta_{R3}(R3) + \beta_{R4}(R4) \\
& + \beta_{TR2}(T(i) * R2) + \beta_{TR3}(T(i) * R3) \\
& + \beta_{TR4}(T(i) * R4) + \sum_{j=1}^{J} \theta_j X_j(i,t) + \eta(i,t)
\end{aligned}
\tag{10.1}
$$

where $Y(i,t)$ the work (school) outcome indicator for individual i in period t, $\alpha$, $\beta$, and $\theta$ are fixed parameters to be estimated, $T(i)$ is a binary variable taking the value of 1 if the household belongs in a treatment community and 0 otherwise (i.e., for control communities), R2, R3, and R4 are binary variables equal to 1 for the second, or third, or fourth rounds of the survey, respectively, after the initiation of the program and equal to 0 otherwise, X is a vector of household and village characteristics, and $\eta$ is an error term summarizing the influence of random disturbances.[9]

The different intercept terms, $\beta_{Ri}$, capture temporal changes in probability of working for reasons unrelated to PROGRESA. The coefficient $\beta_T$ allows the conditional mean of participation in work or school to differ between eligible households in treatment and control localities before the initiation of the program. A test of the significance of $\beta_T$ also serves the role of a test of the randomness in selection of localities. If there were a truly random selection of localities into control and treatment, the conditional mean of the outcome indicator should be identical across treatment and control households/individuals.

The coefficients $\beta_{TR}$ associated with the interaction of the treatment dummy $T(i)$ with the dummy variables indicating the round of the survey yield the 2DIF estimate of the program's impact in each round. This will determine whether impacts are constant, decreasing, or increasing over time, and whether there are seasonal effects. The coefficients $\beta_{TR}$ also provide an estimate of the impact of the various income and substitution effects within households induced by program participation.

For a better understanding of how the 2DIF estimator measures program impact, consider equation (10.1) above for the simple case in which there are only two survey rounds: one after the start of the program, denoted by R2 = 1, and one before the start of the program, denoted by R2 = 0. The conditional mean values of the outcome indicator for treatment and control groups before and after the start of the program are as follows:[10]

$$\left[E(Y \mid T = 1, R2 = 1, \mathbf{X})\right] = \alpha + \beta_T + \beta_R + \beta_{TR} + \sum_j \theta_j X_j \qquad (10.2a)$$

$$\left[E(Y \mid T = 1, R2 = 0, \mathbf{X})\right] = \alpha + \beta_T + \sum_j \theta_j X_j \qquad (10.2b)$$

$$\left[E(Y \mid T = 0, R2 = 1, \mathbf{X})\right] = \alpha + \beta_R + \sum_j \theta_j X_j \qquad (10.2c)$$

$$\left[E(Y \mid T = 0, R2 = 0, \mathbf{X})\right] = \alpha + \sum_j \theta_j X_j \qquad (10.2d)$$

The 2DIF estimator provides an estimate of the program's impact that is net of any pre-program differences between treatment and control households and/or any time trends or aggregate effects in changes of the values of the outcome indicator. Specifically,

$$\begin{aligned} \beta_{TR} = 2DIF &= (a - b) - (c - d) = (a - c) - (b - d) \\ &= \left[E(Y \mid T = 1, R2 = 1, \mathbf{X}) - E(Y \mid T = 0, R2 = 1, \mathbf{X})\right] \\ &\quad - \left[E(Y \mid T = 1, R2 = 0, \mathbf{X}) - E(Y \mid T = 0, R2 = 0, \mathbf{X})\right]. \end{aligned} \qquad (10.3)$$

The vector $\mathbf{X}$ of control variables consists of parental characteristics such as age, language, and education of the mother and father.[11] Also included are variables measuring the number of household members by age and gender, a marginality index that summarizes the level of economic development in the village, and distances to the municipality capital and closest secondary school. These capture differences in schooling or work outcomes that are due to differences in locality or household factors unrelated to program implementation.[12]

The clustering of the households within villages implies that the household-specific error terms $\eta(i,t)$ are likely to be correlated within each village (as well as across time). Failure to account for such a correlation may lead to a considerable bias in the estimated standard error of the program impact; thus, the regression models account for the clustered nature of the sample and report robust standard error estimates for the impact of the program.

The estimates are obtained by estimating equation (10.1) using separate probit equations explaining the incidence of child work and enrollment.[13] Given the large number of regressions, only the results of PROGRESA's impact are reported.

Table 10.2 presents the results of PROGRESA's impact on child labor-force participation. The sample was split into two groups: children aged 8 to 11 (primary school age) and children aged 12 to 17 (secondary school age). Secondary school-age children are more likely to be out of school and subject to both income and substitution effects toward additional time in school. Consistent with that premise, other research shows that the highest educational impacts of PROGRESA are at the secondary level (Schultz, 2004; Coady and Parker, 2004).

The results are presented, showing the initial level of labor-force participation and the impact estimates for each round of ENCEL after program implementation. The estimates represent the marginal effects of being in a household eligible for PROGRESA benefits on the probability of being in the labor force.

Table 10.2 shows PROGRESA's clear negative impacts on children's labor-market participation. Beginning with the overall group of boys aged 8 to 17, PROGRESA yielded consistently negative impacts on work in every round of ENCEL, accounting for a reduction of approximately 10% to 14% in the probability of working. In November 1999, for example, there was a reduction of 3 percentage points in the probability of working for boys aged 8 to 17, whose overall participation rates prior to the program were 22.4%.

Among boys aged 12 and 13, PROGRESA reduced the probability of working from 15% to 20%. For boys aged 14 and 15, the effects show a

**Table 10.2**  The impact of PROGRESA on the probability of working: Boys and girls

|  | | Difference in Difference Estimates | | | | | | |
|---|---|---|---|---|---|---|---|---|
|  |  | Boys | | | | Girls | | |
|  | Pre- | Impact | | | Pre- | Impact | | |
| Age | Program | | | | Program | | | |
| Group | Level | Nov. 98 | Jun. 99 | Nov. 99 | Level | Nov. 98 | Jun. 99 | Nov. 99 |
| *All work* | | | | | | | | |
| 8 to 11 | 0.0620 | −0.013 | −0.009 | −0.011 | 0.0353 | −0.005 | −0.003 | −0.000 |
|  |  | [−2.0] | [−1.4] | [−1.3] |  | [0.8] | [−0.6] | [−0.5] |
| 12 to 17 | 0.3775 | −0.032 | −0.033 | −0.047 | 0.1317 | −0.018 | −0.011 | −0.023 |
|  |  | [−1.6] | [−1.6] | [−2.1] |  | [−1.7] | [−1.0] | [−1.8] |
| 12 & 13 | 0.1715 | −0.016 | −0.025 | −0.038 | 0.0870 | −0.015 | −0.011 | −0.007 |
|  |  | [−1.0] | [−1.6] | [−2.2] |  | [−1.6] | [−1.1] | [−0.7] |
| 14 & 15 | 0.4058 | −0.045 | −0.041 | −0.042 | 0.1495 | −0.032 | −0.023 | −0.038 |
|  |  | [−1.7] | [−1.5] | [−1.4] |  | [−2.3] | [−1.5] | [−2.4] |
| 16 & 17 | 0.6299 | −0.028 | −0.016 | −0.052 | 0.1727 | 0.007 | 0.017 | −0.020 |
|  |  | [−0.8] | [−0.4] | [−1.3] |  | [0.3] | [0.7] | [−0.8] |

*Notes:*

1. The coefficients reported are the marginal effects of the PROGRESA program on the probability of working.
2. t-values reported in brackets are based on robust standard errors that account for clustering of individuals within villages.
3. See text for a detailed description of the other control variables used in the regression.

significant reduction of about 15% of the probability of working only in the first after-program round, which is insignificant in posterior rounds. For boys aged 16 and 17, there is no significant reduction in the probability of working.

Among girls, despite their overall lower participation prior to the program, there also are significant reductions associated with PROGRESA, particularly in the first after-program round. Work participation fell approximately 14% in the first round and maintained that level thereafter. As with boys, the analysis shows larger effects on girls aged 12 to 17, especially among girls aged 14 and 15. Among girls aged 12 and 13, the effects are again significant only in the first round, and show a reduction in participation equivalent to that from the pre-program level of about 17%. For girls aged 14 and 15, the effects are consistently large, showing a reduction in the probability of work ranging from about 20% to 25%, depending on the round. The effects are not significant for girls aged 16 and 17.

Table 10.3, using the same sample, shows negative impacts on child work are matched by positive and significant impacts on the probability of school enrollment. In general, the percent of increase in schooling is larger than the decline in child labor-force participation for the same age group.

The relative gain in school enrollment for boys is only marginally larger than the decrease in child labor participation. This is consistent with the presumption that boys increase school time mainly by withdrawing from the labor force, rather than combining school with work. In similar

Table 10.3  The impact of PROGRESA on the probability of being enrolled in school: Boys and girls

| | | *Difference in Difference Estimates* | | | | | | |
|---|---|---|---|---|---|---|---|---|
| | | | *Boys* | | | | *Girls* | |
| *Age Group* | *Pre-Program Level* | *Nov. 98* | *Jun. 99* | *Nov. 99* | *Pre-Program level* | *Nov. 98* | *Jun. 99* | *Nov. 99* |
| 8 to 11 | 0.9363 | 0.013 [1.8] | 0.011 [1.6] | 0.018 [2.7] | 0.9402 | 0.003 [0.1] | 0.006 [.01] | −0.003 [0.3] |
| 12 to 17 | 0.5678 | 0.043 [2.4] | 0.032 [1.8] | 0.058 [2.8] | 0.4807 | 0.078 [4.3] | 0.075 [3.8] | 0.095 [4.3] |
| 12 & 13 | 0.8128 | 0.025 [1.5] | 0.023 [1.3] | 0.033 [1.8] | 0.7184 | 0.058 [3.1] | 0.067 [3.2] | 0.075 [3.7] |
| 14 & 15 | 0.5263 | 0.063 [2.3] | 0.053 [2.1] | 0.050 [1.7] | 0.4312 | 0.092 [3.4] | 0.101 [3.4] | 0.109 [3.7] |
| 16 & 17 | 0.2780 | 0.026 [0.9] | 0.009 [0.3] | 0.054 [1.9] | 0.2070 | 0.031 [1.3] | −0.002 [−0.1] | 0.018 [0.7] |

*Notes:*
1. The coefficients reported are the marginal effects of the PROGRESA program on the probability of attending school.
2. t-values reported in brackets are based on robust standard errors that account for clustering of individuals within villages.
3. See text for a detailed description of the other control variables used in the regression.

programs, such as Bangladesh's Food for Education program, the lower incidence of child labor was found to account for 25% of the increase in boys' school enrollment, implying that the program cuts children's leisure time (Ravallion and Wodon, 2000). The lower incidence of child work due to PROGRESA appears to account for about two-thirds of the increase in school enrollment for boys by November 1999.

In contrast to boys, PROGRESA's estimated marginal effects on girls' probability of school enrollment are considerably higher than those on the probability of girls' participation in the labor force. In fact, the estimated effect of PROGRESA on schooling is much larger for girls than for boys, as in Schultz (2004). Given that the labor-force participation of girls already is quite low, these results suggest that most of the girls' increased school enrollment probably occurs by girls combining domestic work with school. This will be addressed by closer investigation of the time use survey later in this report.

The reduction in the probability of working is similar for boys and girls, although given the higher pre-program participation rate of boys in work, the absolute reductions for boys are larger. The study shows generally large increases in school enrollment, particularly among girls. Whereas for boys, the increases in school enrollment are similar to the reductions in work, for girls, the increases in school enrollment are much larger than their reduction in work, suggesting either that girls reduce their leisure time, or that other types of work are reduced.

### Impact on Leisure and Time Use

Because the time use module was only used once, approximately one year after program implementation, the double difference estimator used to measure labor-market participation cannot determine the impact on leisure and time use. Instead, the program's impact is measured by comparing conditional means between treatment and control households in a post-program round. This implies that it cannot be determined whether or not there are significant differences in the dependent variables of interest prior to the program (e.g., participation and hours spent in the work activities). However, the estimates of equation (10.1) indicate the study was unable to reject the hypothesis that there are no significant differences in the mean values of these variables among individuals in treatment and control localities prior to program implementation (i.e., $\beta_T = 0$ in equation [10.1]). This suggests that the selection of the localities is sufficiently random, so even post-program comparisons between treatment and controls can yield unbiased estimates about the program's impact.[14]

Based on the sample of eligible households, the leisure time of individual $i$ denoted by $L(i)$ is described by an equation as follows:

$$L(i) = \alpha_0 + \gamma T_i + \sum_{j=1}^{J} \theta_j X_j(i) + \eta(i) \tag{10.4}$$

where T(i) represents a binary variable equal to 1 if individual i lives in a treatment community and 0 otherwise, and Xj(i) represents the vector of J control variables for individual i (described above). Equation (10.4) is estimated using Ordinary Least Squares (OLS). Note that since there is one round of data for time use, the impact of PROGRESA is measured by a dummy variable indicating whether the family lives in a treatment community or a control community. Specifically, the coefficient $\gamma$ provides an estimate of the cross-sectional difference in the conditional mean leisure between children in treatment and control communities, that is,

$$\gamma = \left[ E(L \mid T = 1, \mathbf{X}) - E(L \mid T = 0, \mathbf{X}) \right]. \tag{10.5}$$

Participation in activities is analyzed, using a probit model of the form:

$$P^A(i) = \alpha + \gamma T(i) + \sum_{j=1}^{J} \theta_j X_j(i) + \eta(i) \tag{10.6}$$

where $P^A(i)$ is a binary variable taking the value 1 if individual i participates in activity A and 0 otherwise, and the rest of the variables are as specified above.

The analysis of the program's impact on the daily hours spent on activities is somewhat more complicated by the censoring of hours at zero for children not participating in different work activities. Heckman's (1979) two-stage method for correcting for selection bias was used to account for the censoring at zero. Thus, to find the program's impact on the hours spent on each activity, the study estimates an equation of the form:

$$H^A(i) = \alpha + \gamma T(i) + \sum_{j=1}^{J} \theta_j X_j(i) + \delta \lambda(i) + \eta(i) \tag{10.7}$$

where $H^A(i)$ and $\lambda(i)$ represents the inverse Mills' ratio calculated from the first stage probit equation for participation in activity.

Market work consists of all salaried work and that corresponding to a business or selling products. Farm work is defined as working on land (including but not limited to on family land) and caring for animals. Domestic work consists of making family purchases; making clothes for family members; taking family members to school, work, the health center, or hospital; cleaning the house; washing and ironing clothes; cooking; fetching water or firewood; disposing of trash; and caring for small children, the elderly, or sick individuals. Leisure is defined as total hours in a day minus time spent in all work activities and non-work areas such as transportation.

Note that the reference period for the time use questions refers only to time spent in the activity during the previous day. This is not ideal because for some children, the survey may refer to a day which was not typical. Additionally, many activities may be infrequent. However, this method was used to reduce recall bias, given the large number of activities included in the questionnaire.[15] Therefore, the format implies that the impacts on these variables must be interpreted with caution.

In the case of schooling, children may be enrolled but did not attend the previous day. As a result, school participation will be underestimated. Of all children reporting they were enrolled in school, about 15% reported zero hours spent in school the previous day. The time use survey was conducted in the June 1999 ENCEL, a period near the end of the school year when there may be greater seasonal demand for child work. It is perhaps unfortunate that this same period was when the only time use module was carried. There is no mechanism to adjust for possible seasonal variation in time use if absenteeism is higher at the end of the school year. It also is possible that these remote villages end the school year earlier than the mid-July guideline set by the Ministry of Education. To ensure the study excluded interviews when school was no longer in session, all interviews carried out after July 4 were excluded. Similar seasonal biases should exist in both the treatment and control villages, so some of the concerns should be mitigated by the evaluation design.

Table 10.4 indicates PROGRESA does not appear to have significant effects on leisure time of boys in all age groups. Among girls, PROGRESA has a negative and significant effect on leisure time, but the magnitude of the effect is quite small. The average impact is a loss of about 0.2 hours of leisure per day, suggesting the large impact of PROGRESA on increasing school enrollment of girls resulted only partially from a reduction in leisure time. However, some of the increase must have resulted in a reduction of time spent in work or home production activities.

Table 10.5 presents the impact of PROGRESA on participation in and hours dedicated to school and work by type (market, farm, and domestic) and examines the effects by age group. However, sample size problems

Table 10.4    The impact of PROGRESA on leisure: Boys and girls

| Age Group | Boys | | Girls | |
|---|---|---|---|---|
| | Pre-Prog. Daily Hours | Impact | Pre-Prog. Daily Hours | Impact |
| Leisure Children | | | | |
| 8 to 17 | 17.37 | −0.018 [−0.2] | 17.74 | −0.196 [−2.4] |
| 12 & 13 | 17.38 | −0.113 [−0.7] | 17.55 | −0.317 [−1.9] |
| 14 & 15 | 16.82 | 0.020 [0.1] | 17.37 | −0.211 [−1.0] |
| 16 & 17 | 16.80 | 0.204 [0.8] | 18.00 | 0.010 [0.0] |

Note:
t-values reported in brackets.

suggest placing more emphasis on the aggregated results over all children aged 8 to 17 or older children aged 12 to 17, rather than those further disaggregated by age group.

PROGRESA significantly increased school participation among boys aged 8 to 17. In unreported regressions, the impact was largely concentrated on boys aged 12 and 13, which is broadly consistent with previous studies (Schultz, 2004) and (Behrman et al., 2000). There was no significant impact on average time spent in school. Overall work participation was significantly reduced for boys aged 8 to 17. The work reductions are practically identical in magnitude to the increase in schooling, which provides evidence that boys in these communities find school and time in work to be strong substitutes. It also is important to note that average hours dedicated to work were not affected, suggesting PROGRESA primarily increased school enrollment in terms of the number of children in

**Table 10.5**   The impact of PROGRESA on time use—work and school—of boys and girls

| Age Group | Boys | | | | Girls | | | |
| | Participation | | Daily Hours | | Participation | | Daily Hours | |
| | Pre-Prog. Level | Impact | Pre-Prog. Level | Impact | Pre-Prog. Level | Impact | Pre-Prog. Level | Impact |
|---|---|---|---|---|---|---|---|---|
| *School* | | | | | | | | |
| 8 to 17 | 0.68 | 0.022 | 6.07 | 0.073 | 0.64 | 0.04 | 6.03 | 0.121 |
| | | [1.9] | | [1.5] | | [3.4] | | [2.5] |
| 12 to 17 | 0.57 | 0.042 | 6.3 | 0.038 | 0.51 | 0.065 | 6.3 | 0.111 |
| | | [2.5] | | [0.5] | | [3.5] | | [1.5] |
| *All Work (Market + Domestic + Farm)* | | | | | | | | |
| 8 to 17 | 0.47 | −0.023 | 3.82 | −0.148 | 0.52 | −0.032 | 3.42 | −0.112 |
| | | [−1.9] | | [−1.3] | | [−2.5] | | [−1.1] |
| 12 to 17 | 0.55 | −0.035 | 4.7 | −0.26 | 0.63 | −0.032 | 4 | −0.202 |
| | | [−2.2] | | [−1.7] | | [−2.0] | | [−1.5] |
| *Market* | | | | | | | | |
| 8 to 17 | 0.09 | −0.006 | 7.47 | −0.169 | 0.02 | 0 | 7.47 | −0.436 |
| | | [−1.8] | | [−1.0] | | [−0.1] | | [−1.2] |
| 12 to 17 | 0.15 | −0.021 | 7.6 | −0.168 | 0.05 | 0 | 7.58 | −0.912 |
| | | [−2.3] | | [−1.0] | | [0.0] | | [−2.4] |
| *Domestic* | | | | | | | | |
| 8 to 17 | 0.34 | −0.02 | 2.87 | −0.016 | 0.48 | −0.04 | 2.87 | −0.076 |
| | | [−1.7] | | [−0.3] | | [3.2] | | [−0.8] |
| 12 to 17 | 0.37 | −0.024 | 1.65 | −0.034 | 0.58 | −0.043 | 3.31 | −0.161 |
| | | [−1.6] | | [−0.4] | | [2.6] | | [−1.3] |
| *Farm* | | | | | | | | |
| 8 to 17 | 0.18 | −0.006 | 2.01 | −0.119 | 0.09 | 0 | 2 | 0.287 |
| | | [−0.7] | | [−0.7] | | [−0.1] | | [1.4] |
| 12 to 17 | 0.21 | −0.015 | 4.11 | −0.163 | 0.1 | −0.004 | 2.11 | 0.541 |
| | | [−1.2] | | [−0.7] | | [−0.5] | | [1.9] |

*Note:*
t-values are reported in brackets.

school and reduced the number of children who are working. It does not necessarily reduce the hours worked by children who work and attend school.

PROGRESA lowered participation in market work for boys aged 8 to 17. Consistent with the data on schooling participation, the largest reductions appeared to be concentrated among boys aged 12 and 13, who experienced a 40% reduction in their probability of market work. However, average hours of market work were unaffected. Compared to other types of work, the results show a reduction in participation in domestic work for boys. With respect to farm work, the coefficients are all negative but none are significant at conventional levels, implying there is no evidence that PROGRESA reduced farm work for boys.

The estimates on school participation are much larger for girls than boys. In fact, among girls aged 8 to 17, PROGRESA's average impact on schooling is almost twice the estimate for boys. For girls aged 12 to 17, the program increased enrollment from 51% to 58%.

PROGRESA also lowered the probability of work for girls. Decomposing the analysis by type of work, PROGRESA had little impact on reducing market work for girls. More important is the significant reduction in the probability of working at home. However, while all the estimated coefficients are negative, there are no precise estimates of the reduction in average hours of domestic work. Again, it appears that PROGRESA successfully increased school participation and reduced child work, but there is little impact on reducing the hours of children who continue to work.

## Conclusions

Estimates based on double difference models before and after the implementation of PROGRESA show important reductions in children's labor force for both boys and girls. Labor force participation by all children between the ages of 12 and 15 has been reduced by as much as 15% to 25%, depending on the probability of working prior to the program.

According to the time use module, children of secondary school age are particularly more likely to attend school and spend more time on school activities. Boys of secondary school age show strong reductions in participation of market work and domestic work. On the other hand, girls of all ages show reductions in participation and/or hours spent in domestic work.

PROGRESA also lowered the time girls spent on domestic chores. This study is one of the first to demonstrate that subsidizing school enrollment can reduce the time spent in domestic work. That PROGRESA is associated with both increasing enrollment and reducing domestic work implies that domestic work competes with time spent on school, although many girls nevertheless combine both domestic work and school. Market work, as has been shown, is a much more important deterrent to school attendance for boys than for girls, in accordance with the higher level of participation of boys relative to girls.

For boys, the reductions in work are largely comparable with the increases in schooling. For girls, the reductions in work are significantly less than the increases in schooling. This would seem to confirm that while child labor is an important deterrent to school for both boys and girls, it is less of a deterrent for girls. Again this is likely related to the trends shown earlier, that while many girls participate in domestic work, many work only a few hours, permitting them to combine school and work. Girls' overall leisure time has shown small decreases with PROGRESA, consistent with the lower reductions in work than the increases in school.

These findings indicate that work is an important deterrent to school, particularly for boys, in the poor, rural areas of Mexico where PROGRESA operates. The estimated increase in the educational attainment of children is about 10% in the total years of completed schooling. Because additional schooling is associated with higher wages on average, these children will be expected to earn 8% more when they reach adulthood as a result of the added time in school (Schultz, 2004).

A separate analysis of the program's costs suggests that it is generally cost-effective. For example, for every 100 pesos allocated to the program, 8.9 pesos are absorbed by administration costs (Coady and Parker, 2004). Given the complexity of the program, this level appears to be quite small. It is certainly lower in comparison to the costs associated with the roughly comparable tortilla and milk subsidy.

It also appears that conditional transfer programs are more effective than alternative interventions on the supply side. For example, other research shows that if additional schools were built so that all children would reside no more than four kilometers from their junior secondary school, the impacts on secondary school enrollments would be less than one-tenth the size of those from PROGRESA. Thus, the impact estimates combined with the cost effectiveness of the program suggest that a CCT such as PROGRESA effectively induces poor rural families to invest in the human capital of their children.

The findings in this study also appear to validate the design feature of PROGRESA, which provides grants for attending school and thus substitutes for children's contributions through work. PROGRESA's impact on child labor is not only relevant in the context of this evaluation, but also as a test of a basic assumption behind PROGRESA: children do not attend school because their parents take them out of school to send them to work. This hypothesis has been convincing enough to motivate a number of other Latin American countries to adopt or consider adopting similar programs. The analysis here shows a large degree of support for the idea that schooling and work are incompatible and that work can be reduced through subsidizing schooling.

## Notes

This is an abridged version of a paper that originally appeared as Emmanuel Skoufias and Susan W. Parker, 2001. "Conditional Cash Transfers and Their Impact on Child

Work and School Enrollment: Evidence from the PROGRESA Program in Mexico."
*Economía* 2 (1) (Fall): 45–96. Reprinted with permission.

1. It should be noted that there is a handful of studies concerned with the impact of PROGRESA on schooling. Schultz (2004) and Behrman et al. (2005) focus on the program's impact on schooling and continuing in higher school grades using only a binary indicator of whether a child is in school, and do not consider work at all. Behrman et al. (2000) focus on the program's impact on child achievement test scores, while Coady and Parker (2004) evaluate the cost effectiveness of the schooling impact of the program. Demombynes (2001) is the only study that considers work in addition to schooling and is discussed further in the chapter.

2. In poor areas of Mexico, girls tend to drop out of school earlier than boys, so the grants are intended to help reverse this tendency.

3. It is assumed that the opportunity cost of child schooling is the fixed market wage for child labor. The assumption of a perfectly competitive labor market can be replaced by (or combined with) the assumption that children work at home producing commodities that are perfectly substitutable with purchased commodities with no additional complications (Skoufias, 1994).

4. It should be noted that the program also may have important dynamic effects by increasing the probability that children continue on to higher grades in school. These dynamic effects of PROGRESA are explored by Behrman et al. (2005).

5. For more discussion of the advantages and disadvantages of experimental designs and a test of the randomization of the sample of control and treatment localities used to evaluate PROGRESA, see Behrman and Todd (1999).

6. See Parker and Skoufias (2000) for estimates of the impact of the mean effect of the program on those who actually receive treatment.

7. This study uses ENCASEH rather than the ENCEL-March 1998 survey as its baseline of labor-market participation because the March 1998 survey did not include information on labor-force participation. The labor-market participation questions in ENCASEH and the remaining evaluation surveys are identical.

8. For a more detailed and rigorous discussion of the relative merits of impact estimators, see Heckman et al. (1999).

9. Given that the variables used to evaluate the impact of the program on schooling and child labor are binary variables, the study adopted a reduced-form approach instead of attempting to decompose the impact of the program into Hicks/Slutsky substitution and income effects. These effects are meaningful and best estimated empirically when data are available for hours of schooling and work (Heckman, 1978). For an analysis that decomposes the impact of PROGRESA into income and substitution effects, in spite of the binary nature of the dependent variables, see Demombynes (2001).

10. Expressions (10.2a)–(10.2d) rely on the assumption that sample of households randomized at the household level, $\left[ E\left( \eta \mid T, R2, X \right) \right] = 0$, for $T = 1,0$ and $R2 = 0,1$. Though unable to test this assumption directly, Behrman and Todd (1999) examine whether the distributions of the values of more than 300 variables collected by the 1997 ENCASEH survey are identical between treatment and control localities.

11. Missing variable dummies also are included in the regressions for the cases in which data are not available (for instance, because the father no longer lives in the household).

12. If the randomization process is successful, these factors would be equal across treatment and control villages and will have no effect on the measured impact of PROGRESA.

13. The study also estimated the model using a bivariate probit model that allows for correlated disturbances and confirmed that the main results do not change.

14. Behrman and Todd (1999) tested the hypothesis that the locality means of key variables are equal between treatment and control localities, and could not reject it.
15. The study does not correct for the possibility that an individual may perform two tasks simultaneously. Consequently, the estimates of time spent in each activity may overstate total work time, and the residual estimate of leisure may be understated. This should not bias the estimated impact of PROGRESA on time use unless PROGRESA changes the probability of multitasking.

# 11

# Education and Child Labor: Experimental Evidence from a Nicaraguan Conditional Cash Transfer Program

*John A. Maluccio*

Education levels in Nicaragua are dismal. One-third of adults over the age of 25 have no formal education and another one-third have never completed primary school. Although increasing school coverage and stable political conditions in the 1990s spurred improvements, the net primary enrollment ratio, at 78%, remained one of the lowest in Latin America in the late 1990s (World Bank, 2001a, Annex 16). Unsurprisingly, these poor educational outcomes were accompanied by a high incidence of child labor, particularly among boys. In 1998, 27% of boys aged 10 to 14 in rural areas were working an average of thirty hours a week (World Bank, 2001a, Annex 25). These initial conditions and continued poor outcomes, despite improvements in school supply, are primary concerns for the economic development of Nicaragua and have led the government to consider different approaches, including interventions with demand-side components.

One of these was the pilot Red de Protección Social (RPS), or Social Safety Net, a government program to reduce both current and future poverty via cash transfers to households living in extreme poverty in rural Nicaragua. The transfers were conditional, requiring evidence that the household had undertaken prescribed actions to improve the human capital development of their children. The program's stated objectives included supplementing household income for up to three years to increase expenditures on food, increasing the healthcare and nutritional status of children under age 5, and reducing school desertion during the first four years of primary school.

Cash transfer programs similar to RPS have been implemented in several Latin American countries, including the Programa Nacional de Educación, Salud y Alimentación (PROGRESA) in Mexico (now called Oportunidades), after which RPS was modeled, and the Programa de Asignación Familiar (PRAF) in Honduras.[1] One reason for their popularity is their integrated approach, which encompasses various dimensions of human capital such as nutritional status, health, and education. As such, these programs are able to influence many of the key indicators highlighted in national poverty reduction strategies.

The government of Nicaragua initiated RPS in 2000 as a two-year pilot with a budget of U.S. $11 million, representing approximately 0.2% of the country's GDP and 2.5% of recurrent government spending on health and education. As a condition of the Inter-American Development Bank loan financing the project, and to assess whether the program merited expansion in the same or an altered form, the government solicited an evaluation of the pilot phase of RPS. The International Food Policy Research Institute (IFPRI) conducted the evaluation. In late 2002, the program expansion was approved for three more years with a budget of U.S. $22 million, but in 2006 with a change it government in Nicaragua it was discontinued.

## The Red de Protección Social

### Program Design

The pilot phase of RPS was implemented in two stages. In the first, the program benefited all of the approximately 6,000 households in twenty-one so-called census *comarcas*[2] (hereafter localities), which were selected from six municipalities in the northern part of the Central Region of Nicaragua. In the second stage, approximately 4,000 additional beneficiary households from different localities in the same six municipalities were selected using household-level targeting mechanisms. This chapter examines education- and child-labor-related effects of the program on beneficiaries during the first year for the first stage of the pilot phase in which only geographic, locality-level targeting was used.

RPS had two main components:

(1) Health, nutrition, and food security: Each eligible household received a bimonthly cash transfer, known as the *food security transfer*, contingent upon attendance at bimonthly (every other month) health educational workshops and upon bringing their children under age 5 for scheduled healthcare appointments.

To ensure adequate supply in these poor, rural communities, RPS trained (and paid) nongovernmental organizations to provide the healthcare services to beneficiary households free of charge. In the workshops, mothers were trained in household sanitation and hygiene, nutrition, reproductive health, and breastfeeding. Other services were directed toward children, and included growth monitoring; vaccination; and provision of anti-parasites, vitamins, and iron supplements. Children under age 2 were seen monthly while those between the ages of 2 and 5 were monitored bimonthly.

(2) Education: RPS gave each beneficiary household a bimonthly cash transfer, known as the *school attendance transfer*, contingent upon enrollment and regular school attendance. In addition, for each eligible child, the household received an annual cash transfer for school supplies, uniforms and shoes, known as the *school supplies transfer*, contingent upon enrollment. Unlike the school attendance transfer, which was a fixed amount per household (regardless of the number of children in school), the school supplies transfer was a per-child transfer.

In rural Nicaragua it is common for schools' parents' associations to request contributions to support the teacher and the school. Therefore, there was also a small cash transfer, known as the *teacher transfer*, to cover this contribution. This token amount was given to each beneficiary child, who in turn delivered it to the teacher. The teacher could keep one-half while the other half was earmarked for purchasing additional school supplies. Only the delivery of the funds to the teacher was monitored.

Table 11.1 summarizes the eligibility requirements, demand- and supply-side benefits, and conditions or co-responsibilities for the different components of RPS.

In the localities where there was only geographic targeting, nearly all households were eligible for the food security transfer, and the transfer was a fixed amount per household. Households with children between the ages of 7 and 13 who had not yet completed the fourth grade of primary school also were eligible for the program's education component of the program.

The amounts for each transfer were initially determined in U.S. dollars, then converted into Nicaraguan *Córdobas* in September 2000, just before they began distributing the various *bonos*. Table 11.1 shows the original annual dollar amounts and their *Córdoba* equivalents. On its own, the food security transfer represented about 13% of total annual household expenditures in beneficiary households before the program. A household with one child benefiting from the education component would receive additional transfers of about 8%, yielding a total transfer of approximately 21% of total annual household expenditures.[3] This is the same percentage as the average transfer in PROGRESA, but about five times as large as the transfers given in PRAF. In contrast to PROGRESA and PRAF, which indexed transfers to inflation, the nominal value of the transfer remained constant for RPS (Caldés et al., 2006). As a result, inflation caused the real value of the transfers to decline about 5% during the first year.

To enforce compliance with program requirements, beneficiaries did not receive a transfer when they failed to carry out any of the conditions shown in table 11.1. During the first year of operation, about 10% of beneficiaries were penalized at least once and therefore did not receive a full transfer. The program allowed households to receive a partial transfer if they complied with the health requirement and not the education requirement, or vice versa. It also was possible for households to be removed from the program. Possible causes for expulsion included (1) failure to collect the transfer in two consecutive pay periods, (2) more than twenty-seven unexcused

**Table 11.1** RPS eligibility, benefits, and co-responsibilities

| | Health, Nutrition, and Food Security (Food Security Transfer) | Education | |
| --- | --- | --- | --- |
| | | School Attendance Transfer | School Supplies Transfer |
| **Eligibility** | All households | All households with children aged 7 to 13 who have not completed fourth grade of primary school | Each child aged 7 to 13 who has not completed fourth grade of primary school |
| **Transfers (Demand Side)** | | | |
| Scheduled Transfer | C $480 bimonthly per household all year (U.S. $37) | C $240 bimonthly per household all year (U.S. $19) | C $275 per child at beginning of school year (U.S. $21) |
| Expected Annual Transfer | C $2,880 (U.S. $224) | C $1,440 (U.S. $112) | C $275 (U.S. $21) |
| **Transfers and Services Provided (Supply Side)** | | | |
| Teacher/School Transfer | — | C $10 bimonthly per beneficiary student delivered by student to teacher. Teacher keeps half and remainder purchases school supplies (C $60 or U.S. $4.75 annually) | — |
| Health Education Workshops | Bimonthly | — | — |
| Child Growth Monitoring | Monthly (0 to 2 years) Bimonthly (2 to 5 years) | — | — |
| Provision of vaccinations, anti-parasites, vitamins, and iron supplements | According to Ministry of Health guidelines | — | — |
| **Co-responsibilities (Conditions) for Receiving Transfer** | | | |
| | 1. Attend bimonthly health education workshops | 1. Enrollment | — |
| | 2. Bring children to prescheduled healthcare appointments | 2. Regular attendance (85%, i.e., no more than five absences every two months without valid health reason) | — |
| | 3. Adequate weight gain for children under 5 | 3. Deliver *teacher transfer* to teacher | — |

school absences during the school year for a single child, (3) failure of a student in the program to be promoted to the next grade, (4) falsifying information during any part of data collection, or (5) falsely reporting fulfillment of co-responsibilities. Less than 1% of households were expelled from the program during the first year of operation. When it was learned that some, but not all, schools practiced automatic promotion, enforcement of the grade promotion condition was deemed unfair and was not enforced. This change highlights the importance of careful consideration and monitoring of co-responsibilities in the design of a conditional cash transfer program, as well as flexibility during its implementation.

Only the designated household representative could collect the cash transfers and, where possible, RPS designated the mother as the household representative. This strategy mimicked the design of PROGRESA and PRAF, and is based on evidence that resources in the hands of women often lead to better outcomes for child well being and household food security (Strauss and Thomas, 1995). As a result, more than 95% of the household representatives were women. These representatives attended the workshops and were responsible for ensuring that the other co-responsibilities were fulfilled.

Although centrally administered within the Emergency Social Investment Fund (FISE), with its multi-sector approach across education, health, and nutrition, RPS required bureaucratic cooperation at various levels. Committees composed of delegates from the health and education ministries, representatives from civil society, and RPS personnel coordinated activities at the municipal level. This coordination proved important in directing supply-side responses to increased household demand for health and schooling services. At the locality level, RPS representatives worked with local volunteer representatives known as *promotoras* (beneficiary women chosen by the community) and local school and healthcare service providers to implement the program. The volunteer *promotoras* were charged with keeping beneficiary household representatives informed about upcoming healthcare appointments for their children, upcoming payments, and any failures in fulfilling the conditions.

## Program Targeting and Design of the Evaluation

Rural areas in all seventeen departments of Nicaragua were eligible for the pilot phase. The focus on rural areas reflected the distribution of poverty in Nicaragua—of the 48% of Nicaraguans designated as poor, 75% reside in rural areas. The government selected the departments of Madriz and Matagalpa for the pilot on the basis of need and their capacity to implement the program. Approximately 80% of the rural population of Madriz and Matagalpa was poor, and half of those extremely poor (Maluccio, 2008). In addition, these departments had easy physical access and communication, relatively strong institutional capacity and local coordination, and reasonably good coverage of health posts and schools in the majority of their poor communities (Arcia, 1999). The Nicaraguan education system consists of six years of primary school and four years of secondary school. In rural areas, however, it is common to find schools that provide only four years of primary school and in some cases fewer. By purposely targeting areas with existing educational and health facilities, RPS could avoid devoting a disproportionate share of its resources during the pilot to increasing the supply of educational and health services.

In the next stage of geographic targeting, six out of twenty municipalities were chosen within the selected departments for their participation in a FISE-run participatory development program. The goal of that program was to develop the capacity of municipal governments to select, implement, evaluate, and monitor social infrastructure projects such as school and health-post construction. Therefore, it is possible that the municipalities had atypical capacity to carry out RPS. Nevertheless, these municipalities were appropriately targeted on the basis of poverty. Between 36% and 61% of the rural population in each of the chosen municipalities was extremely poor and between 78% and 90% was poor or extremely poor (Maluccio, 2008). Though they were not the poorest municipalities in the chosen departments, the proportion of impoverished people living in these areas was much higher than the national average.

In the final stage of geographic targeting, a marginality index based on information from the 1995 National Population and Housing Census was constructed for all fifty-nine rural localities in the selected municipalities. The index was a weighted average of a set of poverty indicators in which higher index scores were associated with more impoverished areas (World Bank, 1995; Arcia et al., 1996). The indicators (and their associated percentage weights) were family size (10%), access to potable water (50%), access to latrines (30%), and illiteracy rates (10%) (Arcia, 1999). The forty-two localities with the highest scores were selected for the pilot phase's first stage. These localities were ordered by their marginality index scores and stratified into seven groups of six each. Three localities from each group were randomly selected for inclusion in the program, leaving the other three as controls for the evaluation. Thus, there were twenty-one localities selected in the intervention group and twenty-one distinct localities with similar levels of poverty in the control group. Maluccio and Flores (2005) describe the design of this social experiment, known as a community-based randomized trial.

## Methodology and Data Sources

### Methodology

To measure program impact, it is necessary to estimate the counterfactual, what would have happened had the program not been implemented. The problem is that a single area, household, or individual cannot simultaneously undergo and not undergo the intervention. The most powerful way to construct a valid estimate of the counterfactual is to randomly select beneficiaries from a pool of equally qualified candidates. Recipients and non-recipients will have the same observed and unobserved characteristics, on average. A further advantage to such a randomized design is that the program impact is easy to calculate and, as a consequence, easy to understand.

Household- and individual-level data were collected before and after RPS was implemented in both the intervention and control localities. This enables the use of the double difference method to calculate average program impact of the intent to treat. The resulting measures can be interpreted as the expected impact of implementing the program in a similar population elsewhere.[4]

Before presenting the estimated impacts of the program, there are two important aspects of RPS that need to be highlighted. The first is that the program was in its pilot phase, and as such the outcomes for the pilot may differ from the outcomes for an expanded program. As with most pilots, RPS underwent an initial learning period (with its attendant setbacks) and undertook a variety of activities that would not need to be repeated in an expansion (e.g., preparing training materials), possibly reducing its effectiveness. At the same time, the selection of municipalities was conditioned on the likelihood of success as described above, so that the observed outcomes might exaggerate the likely outcomes from program expansion to other, less favorable, areas. Moreover, as with any new program, there was the potential for observed behavioral changes to result, in part, from the novelty of the program—the Hawthorne effect. Finally, expansion of the program could introduce new advantages and disadvantages associated with scaling up and economies of scale. All these factors suggest a degree of caution in forecasting exactly what would happen were the program to be extended as is to other municipalities and departments.

A second important feature is the design of RPS, which provided a package of services in which all beneficiary households were eligible for the food security transfer, regardless of whether they also benefited from the educational transfers. Therefore, it is not possible to isolate the effects of the education component of the program without further assumptions; all the observed effects, even those that pertain specifically to educational outcomes, are the result of the program as a whole.

### Data Sources

This analysis uses a household panel survey with measurements before and after the program was implemented, in both intervention and control localities. A baseline survey was conducted before the start of the program, in August and early September 2000. It was a stratified random sample of 1,585 households, approximately 13% of the household population in the study area. In October 2001, a follow-up survey revisited all the original baseline households, successfully re-interviewing 1,494 households (94%).[5] All relevant households from each survey round, regardless of whether they were interviewed in both waves, were included in the double difference analyses that follow. Results were substantively unchanged whether or not the analysis was conducted with or without sample weights to correct for the stratified sample design and whether or not it included controls (via locality fixed effects) for the fact that the randomization was at the locality, and not the household, level.

## Results

### Schooling and Child Labor at Baseline

Before the start of RPS, the enrollment rate in the program area for the target group, those aged 7 to 13 who had not yet completed fourth grade of primary school, was 71%. This overall average, while demonstrating a large potential for improved outcomes, masked important differences by the children's age and level of household well-being. Figure 11.1a shows enrollment rates by age in the completely shaded portion of the bars.[6] (The unshaded areas represent the impact of RPS and will be discussed later.) For the targeted children, enrollment peaks at 82% for 9-year-olds but declines to 51% by age 13. Thus, even at its peak, there was substantial room for improvement. In addition, the age pattern (initially rising) indicated that of those children who eventually attend school, many start late. A possible effect of the program would be to improve age-appropriate starts as well as increase overall enrollment.

Figure 11.1b shows the enrollment rates for the same children by household expenditure group (extremely poor, poor, and nonpoor)[7] and by gender. These simple comparisons indicate that resources play a role in the decision to enroll children. Indeed, children living in households in the lowest per capita expenditure decile in the sample were more than one-third less likely to have enrolled than those living in the wealthiest decile (not shown). Although not controlling for the many other factors that

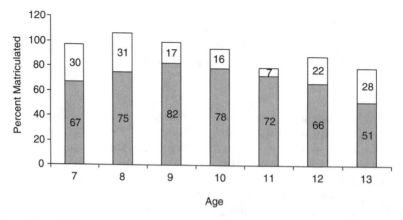

**Figure 11.1a**  RPS Average Impact on Enrollment for 7- to 13-Year-Olds Who Have Not Completed Fourth Grade, by Age.

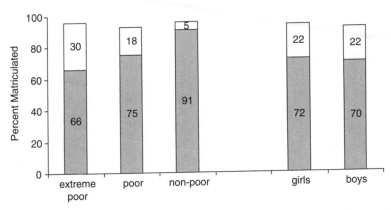

**Figure 11.1b**   RPS Average Impact on Enrollment for 7- to 13-Year-Olds Who Have Not Completed Fourth Grade, by Expenditure Group and by Gender.

affect enrollment, this evidence still suggests there was potential for a cash transfer program to influence enrollment rates. There were no differences between the enrollment rates for boys and girls.

Figures 11.2a and 11.2b show very similar patterns for regular attendance in the baseline survey, collected approximately three months before the end of the academic year. Children are defined as regularly attending if they indicated they were still enrolled and had either missed three or fewer days in the past month or had missed more, but due to illness. As with enrollment at the beginning of the year, attendance rises to age 9 and declines thereafter. The percentage of children still in school toward the end of the academic year was on average 12 percentage points lower than the percentage enrolling, indicating that dropout was common. Again, it is evident that there was substantial room for improvement. Finally, the large advantage in enrollment for children in nonpoor households did not seem to carry through to attendance (figure 11.2b). Hence, even children from wealthier households stood to benefit from the program.[8]

Figure 11.3 shows the extent to which children were working before the start of RPS as the entire bar with the total percent indicated above the bar. All individuals were asked whether work was their primary activity in the previous week and, if not, why they did not work. The most relevant possible reasons for children not working were that they were in school or that they were disabled. If the primary activity was not work, the children were further prompted about other activities in the previous week. They were considered to be working if work was a primary activity or secondary activity, with positive hours worked. Nearly all child workers were agricultural laborers or unskilled helpers, and typically worked without pay.

While children under age 10 rarely reported working, from age 10 upward they were increasingly likely to work; 45% of 13-year-olds in the sample reported working (figure 11.3a). Average hours worked also

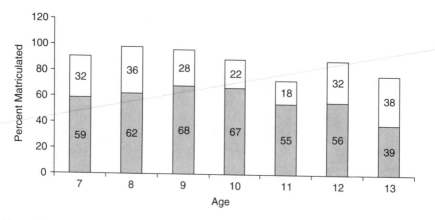

**Figure 11.2a**   RPS Average Impact on Attendance for 7- to 13-Year-Olds Who Have Not Completed Fourth Grade, by Age.

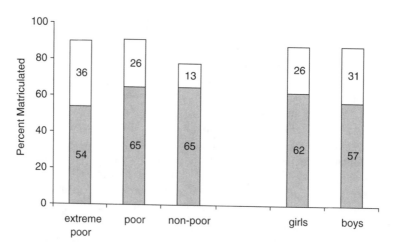

**Figure 11.2b**   RPS Average Impact on Attendance for 7- to 13-Year-Olds Who Have Not Completed Fourth Grade, by Expenditure Group and by Gender.

increased with age (not shown). There was no obvious relationship between working and the economic well being of the household, however (figure 11.3b). This undoubtedly reflects the likelihood that child labor increases household expenditures, this study's measure of well-being. Boys were substantially more likely to report working. By age 13, only one-quarter of the girls reported working, compared to nearly 60% of the boys. Conditional on working, boys also worked longer hours, averaging twenty-five hours per week compared to sixteen hours for girls. Given the questionnaire's orientation toward economically productive activities outside the home, the difference between boys' and girls' reported likely work reflect in part the underreporting of girls' domestic activities within the home.

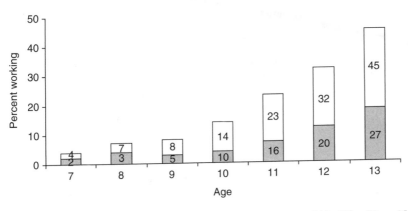

**Figure 11.3a**  RPS Average Impact on Work for 7- to 13-Year-Olds Who Have Not Completed Fourth Grade, by Age.

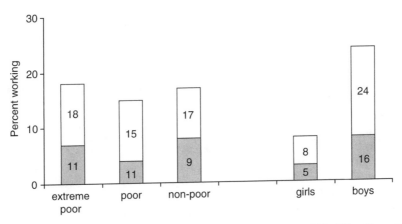

**Figure 11.3b**  RPS Average Impact on Work for 7- to 13-Year-Olds Who Have Not Completed Fourth Grade, by Expenditure Group and Gender.

## Double Difference Results on Schooling and Child Labor

RPS induced an average net increase in enrollment of 22 percentage points for the target population of children aged 7 to 13 who had not yet completed the fourth grade of primary school (table 11.2). Before the program, enrollment rates in intervention and control areas for this age group were very similar, with approximately 70% of eligible children enrolling. With the program in place, enrollment rose to nearly 95%.

As a first step toward examining what underlies the average impact of 22 percentage points, the study considers program impact by age. The results are shown in figure 11.1a, in which the bottom, completely shaded portion of each column is the initial situation described earlier, and the unshaded top portion is the double difference estimated average program impact. In all cases, this impact was positive.[9] With the exception of those

**Table 11.2**  RPS average impact on enrollment for 7- to 13-year-olds who have not completed fourth grade

|  | RPS | Control | Difference |
|---|---|---|---|
| Follow-up (2001) | 94.5 | 76.4 | 18.1*** |
|  | [880] | [852] | (3.1) |
| Baseline (2000) | 69.2 | 73.0 | −3.8 |
|  | [967] | [886] | (5.2) |
| Difference | 25.4*** | 3.4 | 22.0*** |
|  | (3.4) | (1.9) | (3.9) |

Notes:

   Standard errors correcting for heteroskedasticity are shown in parentheses (StataCorp, 2001); number of observations are shown in brackets.

   ***Indicates significance at the 1% level.

Source: RPS baseline (2000) and follow-up (2001).

aged 11, the program impact was statistically significant for each year and tended to be larger where there was more potential at the outset, that is, where the initial enrollment levels were lower.[10] Enrollment rates in the intervention areas are now between 90% and 100%, and no longer vary by age.

   Figure 11.1a shows that gains were made in enrollment by reaching both younger children, who for the most part had not yet attended school, as well as older children, who had completed some schooling but had abandoned it before the program started. A potential concern for the group of older children was that they would be returning to the lower grades. If so, this would lead to more mixing of younger and older children, potentially resulting in classroom disruption. Nearly all (80%) of the overall improvement in enrollment came from younger children, however, and most of the older children who returned to school were returning to the third and fourth grades. Moreover, both the average and standard deviation of child age-by-grade remained constant before and after the program, indicating little change in overall classroom composition. Figure 11.1b presents results for enrollment and attendance by household expenditure group and gender. Clearly, the extreme poor and poor are benefiting most. The effects for boys and girls were identical.

   The program's effect on attendance was even larger than on enrollment, with an average impact of 29 percentage points. The impact was again significant for all ages except 11, and the effects were generally larger for those age groups with lower initial attendance rates (figure 11.2a). As with enrollment, the extreme poor and poor benefited the most (figure 11.2b). Nonetheless, the nonpoor also experienced large and significant gains in attendance.

   The final aspect of the impact of RPS on education considered here is grade progression. Unlike the enrollment and attendance results just presented, the impact of RPS on grade progression is measured as a first difference, because two years of information are required to calculate progression.

The estimated impact is thus the difference between the percentage of students continuing in the intervention areas minus the percentage continuing in the control areas. Overall, and by grade (except for third to fourth), the effects are significant and show an average improved retention rate of 8% (table 11.3). An unanticipated additional benefit of the program was the large effect on those making the transition from fourth to fifth grade. This was despite the fact that enrollment in the fifth grade was not one of the conditions for receiving the education transfer. Unfortunately, it is not presently possible to determine why this is occurring. It may be due to potentially long-lasting changes in attitudes toward education, or it may merely reflect confusion about the program requirements on the part of beneficiaries. Examining grade progression for all four grades at once for the different expenditure groups (table 11.4) shows that as with the other

Table 11.3    RPS average impact on percentage of students aged 7 to 13 continuing in school, by grade

|  | Grade 1 to Grade 2 | Grade 2 to Grade 3 | Grade 3 to Grade 4 | Grade 4 to Grade 5 |
|---|---|---|---|---|
| RPS | 96.0 | 95.6 | 95.0 | 91.7 |
|  | [346] | [159] | [141] | [121] |
| Control | 87.8 | 88.3 | 88.8 | 79.6 |
|  | [336] | [197] | [125] | [98] |
| Difference | 8.2*** | 7.3*** | 6.2 | 12.1** |
|  | (2.1) | (2.8) | (3.4) | (4.8) |

Notes:
   Standard errors correcting for heteroskedasticity are shown in parentheses (StataCorp, 2001); number of observations are shown in brackets.
   ***Indicates significance at the 1% level.
   **Indicates significance at the 5% level.
Source: RPS baseline (2000) and follow-up (2001).

Table 11.4    RPS average impact on percentage of students aged 7 to 13 continuing in school, by expenditure group

|  | Extreme Poor | Poor | Nonpoor |
|---|---|---|---|
| RPS | 94.2 | 95.4 | 96.5 |
|  | [326] | [328] | [113] |
| Control | 84.9 | 84.4 | 92.6 |
|  | [410] | [251] | [95] |
| Difference | 9.3*** | 6.9** | 3.8 |
|  | (2.2) | (2.3) | (3.2) |

Notes:
   Standard errors correcting for heteroskedasticity are shown in parentheses (StataCorp, 2001); number of observations are shown in brackets.
   ***Indicates significance at the 1% level.
   **Indicates significance at the 5% level.
Source: RPS baseline (2000) and follow-up (2001).

measures, the largest impacts of the program were concentrated among the extreme poor.

RPS had a massive impact on enrollment and attendance in the intervention areas. Although only about one-third of the rural localities in the selected municipalities were included in the pilot phase, increases in enrollment could be seen even in the aggregate municipal-level data compiled by the Ministry of Education. In the six municipalities combined, there was an increase of about 5% in enrollment in grades one to four between 1999 and 2000, before the program. The increase was nearly 18% between 2000 and 2001, far higher than what occurred in the rest of the country for that period.

While schools were generally available in the program area as a result of the targeting described above, a number of steps were taken to accommodate the large changes in enrollment as the program developed—principally, increasing the number of sessions per day and increasing the number of teachers. RPS supported local communities in their efforts to solicit additional teachers from the Ministry of Education. For most rural schools, this was a straightforward process, because they operate under an autonomous system with substantial local control.[11] In one RPS municipality with a smaller proportion of autonomous schools, however, it was more difficult to increase the number of teachers. In some cases, this problem was resolved when beneficiary parents agreed, at the suggestion of RPS, to contribute part of their transfers to help pay for a new teacher. In other cases, staffing problems were not resolved. Probably reflecting these problems, enrollment rates were the lowest in those areas, though they were still 90% on average. In sum, the overall level of enrollment left little room for improvement, and supply does not appear to have been a major constraint. This achievement, however, required active intervention and coordination on the part of RPS.

Among those not enrolling, economic reasons were cited in nearly half the cases, and work was specifically cited for about 10% of the cases. For those who dropped out during the year, work was cited as the main cause 20% of the time. The need to work plays a role in schooling decisions, though apparently not the dominant one.

Examining the impacts of RPS on reducing child labor among the target population, figure 11.3a shows the program's impact on the percentage of children working by age in the intervention areas.[12] The unshaded portion of each column represents the reduction in those reporting work after one year of the program. The percentage of children working was lower after the program for every age group. Only in the case of 12- and 13-year-olds, however, did the program significantly decrease the percentage of children working. This is not surprising because among the younger age groups, very few were working to begin with, so while there appear to have been changes of 50% or more, it was not possible to estimate them precisely. The double difference estimator shows a significant 9-percentage-point decrease in the number of children working when restricted to ages 10 to

Table 11.5   RPS average impact on percent working of 10- to 13-year-olds who have not completed fourth grade

|  | RPS | Control | Difference |
|---|---|---|---|
| Follow-up (2001) | 9.3 | 17.8 | −8.4*** |
|  | [397] | [411] | (2.6) |
| Baseline (2000) | 27.1 | 27.8 | −0.6 |
|  | [480] | [443] | (3.9) |
| Difference | −17.8*** | −10.0*** | −8.8** |
|  | (2.7) | (2.6) | (3.7) |

Notes:
    Standard errors correcting for heteroskedasticity are shown in parentheses (StataCorp, 2001); number of observations are shown in brackets.
    ***Indicates significance at the 1% level.
    **Indicates significance at the 5% level.
Source: RPS baseline (2000) and follow-up (2001).

13 (table 11.5). Note that in both the intervention and control areas, the percentage of children working declined significantly. This likely reflects a general economic downturn in the program area as the result of severe drought and depressed international coffee prices, both of which led to substantial declines in well-being within the control group (Maluccio and Flores, 2005). The percentage of children working declined about the same amount within each of the three expenditure groups (figure 11.3b). Finally, while the impact on education outcomes was the same for boys and girls, the impact on reported work for boys was three times as large as for girls (figure 11.3b).[13]

Not only did the percentage of children reporting work decrease, but for those who did work, hours worked declined substantially. The double difference calculation (not shown) indicates a significant average decrease of about ten hours of work in the previous week (for both boys and girls), yielding an average of fifteen hours of work per week. For those who continued to work, they did so less intensively, permitting more time for schooling.

A final way to examine changes induced by the program is to consider the percentages of children who were (1) in school exclusively, (2) working exclusively, (3) both in school and working, or (4) neither in school nor working. Figure 11.4a shows the distribution of children among these categories before and after the program (for the intervention areas only). For comparison, among children between the ages of 10 and 14 in rural Nicaragua in 1998, 69% were in school exclusively, 7% were exclusively working, 9% were doing both, and 15% were doing neither (World Bank, 2001b, Annex 25). Exclusive schooling increased substantially (from 59% to 84%) with RPS at the expense of the other categories, in particular of doing neither (i.e., children who were neither economically active nor in school before the program) (figure 11.4b). This finding is consistent with these children having lower opportunity costs of time than those who had

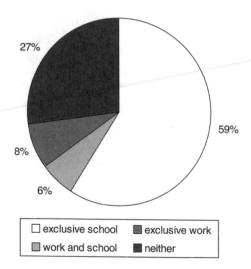

**Figure 11.4a** Schooling and Work for 7- to 13-Year-Olds, RPS Baseline Intervention Areas Only.

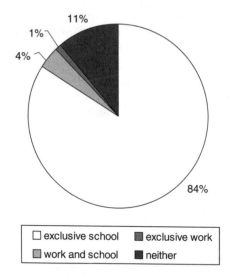

**Figure 11.4b** Schooling and Work for 7- to 13-Year-Olds, RPS Follow-up Intervention Areas Only.

been working. While schooling in general rises with the program, it is exclusive schooling that saw the largest gains.

## Conclusion

There is little doubt that RPS had a significant and substantial impact on enrollment and attendance during its first year of operation. The evidence presented here, based on a randomized community-based trial carried out to evaluate the program, provides strong support for the effectiveness of RPS. Moreover, all signs indicate that the program simultaneously led to a substantial reduction in child labor within the target population. While this chapter was being processed, analysis continued using a third round household survey carried out in 2002. After two years of operation, esti- mated double difference average impacts of the program (relative to 2000) were similar to those reported here (Maluccio and Flores, 2005). As seen in some other contexts (Edmonds, 2008), then, it is possible for a cash trans- fer program aimed at education to reduce child labor, even during a general economic downturn such as occurred in Nicaragua during this time. This is an important finding given the recent expansion of such programs to more than twenty-five countries worldwide.

The preponderance of evidence and the experimental design also suggest that the limited expansion of the program elsewhere in Nicaragua (until it was discontinued in 2006), was likely to have been equally successful. It would be unwise, however, to assume that the changes observed in the pilot would be replicated exactly as presented here. Scaling up from a pilot program could have introduced a variety of potential differences in the outcomes. In partic- ular, the involvement of RPS in facilitating the supply-side response in educa- tion would have needed to be continued or made unnecessary.

A number of questions, however, regarding the efficacy of conditional cash transfer programs such as RPS remain. Since RPS was designed to last three years in a beneficiary locality, after which the demand-side incentives ceased, one question is whether the substantial effects persisted after the program exited those areas. Also, careful consideration of the cost effec- tiveness of the program—enabling comparison with other approaches with the same objectives—would represent a valuable future research direction.

## Notes

This research began as part of the evaluation of the Red de Protección Social by the International Food Policy Research Institute. The author thanks the Red de Protección Social team, particularly Mireille Vijil for constant support, Natàlia Caldés for research assistance, and David Coady, Rafael Flores, Peter F. Orazem, Ferdinando Regalia, and Guilherme Sedlacek for many helpful comments.

1. Skoufias (2005) presents an overview of PROGRESA and its impacts; IFPRI (2000) provides background on PRAF.
2. Census *comarcas* are administrative areas within municipalities that include one to five small communities averaging 100 households each.
3. The percentage is lower, however, when one uses the national average of total annual household expenditures (13%) or the national rural average (18%) because the pro- gram targets poorer areas, described later in the text.
4. Ravallion (2001; 2008) provides a useful, and enjoyable, discussion on this and related evaluation tools.
5. Maluccio and Flores (2005) describe the sample size calculations and baseline and follow-up samples in more detail; figures reported there differ slightly since in this paper an earlier release of the data was used for the analyses.

6. I.e., the (weighted) average of $I_0$ and $C_0$.
7. Households are classified into poverty groups based on their per capita annual total expenditures before the program (including own-production) and using the 2001 updated Nicaraguan poverty lines. The extreme poverty line is C $2,691 (U.S. $202) per capita per annum and the poverty line is C $5,157 (U.S. $386). Maluccio and Flores (2005) provide details.
8. Even the nonpoor households in RPS are generally in the bottom two-thirds of the Nicaraguan income distribution and so are near-poor.
9. Note that while this is a convenient way of summarizing the program effects, it is not possible to interpret the sum of the two parts of each column as the enrollment rate after the program. This fact becomes evident, e.g., in the subgroup of 8-year-olds, for whom the sum is higher than 100%.
10. The smaller estimated effect for age 11 (and subsequent lack of significance) is due to an imbalance at the outset in which the intervention areas had a somewhat larger enrollment rate that then translates into a smaller estimated effect in the double difference. It is therefore unlikely that it reflects any behavioral responses to the program.
11. In the early 1990s, a school reform was undertaken to devolve control from the central government to local schools or, in some rural areas, to clusters of schools (King et al., 1999a).
12. The estimated effects on work by age are first differences ($I_1 - C_1$). Because of the small percentages of young children who are working, precise estimation of double differences was possible only for older children.
13. This finding, similar to the finding that boys were more likely to work than girls, likely reflects in part how the questions about work were designed.

# V

# Conclusions

# 12

# Policy Options to Eradicate Child Labor and Promote Education in Latin America

*Zafiris Tzannatos, Peter F. Orazem, and Guilherme Sedlacek*

Latin American countries have been pioneers in the use of Conditional Cash Transfers (CCTs) as a means of combating poverty. In the first decade of the twenty-first century, at least twenty-two developing countries have had at least one type of CCT program in place; and some having more than one. Over half are found in Latin America.[1] Other countries are planning their own schemes based on the Latin American experience, including developed countries. In 2007, New York introduced "a program, which is based on a similar effort in Mexico,"[2] whereby poor families would receive cash for family members meeting any of a series of criteria. Thus, CCT use is expanding, and it is useful to review the evidence of whether, where and how they are likely to succeed.

This concluding chapter has three missions. First, it summarizes the theoretical foundation for using CCTs to effect social change. Second, it reviews evidence presented in this volume and elsewhere of how CCTs have affected child labor and education, the subject matter of this volume. Finally, it lists the likely future use of CCTs in Latin America and elsewhere. We conclude that CCTs can be an important component of policies that aim at poverty reduction and human development. Nevertheless, there are potential challenges for their success: the need to expand social services as demand for these services increases; the need to marry these CCT programs with potentially competing government social and infrastructure services; and the political economic constraints associated with expanding and contracting government services that are yet to be resolved.

## Theoretical Consideration for Targeted CCTs

CCTs tie the receipt of public assistance to a household's fulfillment of behavioral objectives that are thought to have social benefits. Targeted transfers are programs that identify a subpopulation that can qualify for the program, typically on the basis of low income or measured socioeconomic status. Our use of the CCT terminology will presume that the program is targeted toward the poor.

There are two avenues by which the CCT can attack poverty. First, the targeted transfer aims to provide poor households with a minimum level of consumption that directly raises a household's socioeconomic standing. Second, the conditions stipulate that receipt of the benefit requires that the household maintains some minimum level of participation in some socially desirable activity. In the setting examined in this volume, the desired activity is to participate in school and/or to refrain from child labor.

The two objectives are linked. The direct receipt of the transfer provides an infusion of resources that can improve the household's short-term access to necessities. Furthermore, it can help insulate the household from short-term income shocks from job loss or crop failures that have been shown to affect large fractions of children (chapter 4) and that pressure poor households to withdraw their children from school (chapter 3). By lowering household exposure to income shocks, the transfer reduces the need to use increased child labor and reduced school attendance to smooth the household's income stream during bad times.

The second avenue is aimed at reducing poverty in the long-term by inducing behaviors that will increase the child's stock of human capital when they reach adulthood. This two-pronged social investment can break a vicious cycle whereby poverty is transmitted across generations (the "dynastic traps"). This is why some refer to the CCTs "as close as you can come to a magic bullet in development."[3]

Noble objectives of a program do not necessarily imply that the program should be adopted. In this respect, the theoretical considerations for CCTs are similar to those that apply to other social policy programs. They call for answers to questions such as why intervene in the first instance? If there are benefits associated with the intervention, are they compromised by welfare costs arising from conditioning the households to change behavior? Are there better policy alternatives that can achieve more with less? Economic theory provides us answers to these questions, but not without some counterarguments.

## Arguments in Favor of Targeted CCTs

The case for CCTs is strongest when they are targeted to the poor and when the transfer is indeed in cash rather than in kind.

Why "targeted" benefits rather than making the program "universal"? One obvious answer is that universal provision is not fiscally affordable, especially in low-income developing countries. Furthermore, targeting lowers the chance that households will receive transfers for doing something that they would be doing even without the transfer.

The second question is why "cash" transfers rather than using the resources for other free or subsidized social services. One could, for example, use the resources required for the cash transfer for improvements in school quality by buying additional school equipment as well as more books and supplies, or by training teachers better or upgrading school buildings or even constructing rural roads.

One answer is that publicly provided social services often fail to reach the poor. Children not in school do not benefit from improved school quality. Furthermore, the resources for schools often are used disproportionately in wealthier neighborhoods or communities, and so the improvements in school quality may fail to reach the poorest, at least in the short-run.

A second response is that public provision of social services constitutes an in-kind redistribution that creates a deadweight loss unless their quality matches exactly the quality the poor would have chosen to purchase in the market. In this case, and under certain conditions, a cash transfer can reduce the deadweight loss associated with public provision. In addition, it allows the household to use the transfer for purposes that will best satisfy household needs. For example, when PROGRESA was introduced it was seen as a preferred alternative to the electricity and tortilla subsidies that were previously offered to poor households. The cash transfers impose fewer constraints on the household.

An additional argument for the use of the cash transfer is that it is not a permanent commitment to continue public transfers indefinitely. Publicly provided services such as schools or hospitals are difficult to discontinue. Cast in terms of the *Samaritan's Dilemma,* this argument refers to the expectation by citizens that, because the government supports a certain type of policy today, it will continue doing so in the future. This can undermine the household's willingness to take charge of the activity for themselves. A household can depend on the cash transfer only as long as it has school-aged children, after which the household is expected to fend on its own.

Related to the previous argument is the familiar and more generic "second best" argument. In the presence of other government failures, when policies elsewhere generate distortions of their own, the economy is not at the Pareto frontier. In such cases, it is possible that an additional distortion makes things better. For example, in many cases there is an urban bias in the provision of social services that increase the cost of access to these services for the rural poor. Under such conditions, providing some cash that will induce an extra effort by the poor to use whatever services are already available can be socially desirable, given that the expansion of services to rural areas may take considerable time.

All this begs the question of why the government should want to influence the household's decisions of how long a child should remain in school and when the child should enter the labor market. Surely rational and fully informed households who face adequate access to credit will already have been making optimal decisions regarding child schooling and work. However, not all agents are fully informed of the returns to human capital investments. Rural farmers may not know what their children could expect to earn as adults in urban labor markets. Not all agents are rational. They may discount the future to heavily in the sense that they would regret their past actions when the future becomes present. Relatedly, parents may make decisions for their children that emphasize current child earnings at the expense of the children's future earning potential.

While the previous arguments focus on the interplay between what economists would label as privately optimal household decisions and paternalism ("the big brother knows better"), there are additional arguments for targeting benefits. One such argument is that privately optimal decisions of households (e.g., in the case of girls education in some cases) may not be socially optimal. This can be so because of positive externalities or market failures that apply to certain groups of households. For example, the poorest households may face higher interest rates than their wealthier neighbors, causing them to remove their children from school at a younger age. This means that universally offered free social services will not be universally taken up by the poorest groups.

Another argument relates to political considerations of redistributive policies. For example, while many would object giving cash to social outcasts, policies that show their successful rehabilitation and reintegration in the society have generally greater support. Thus conditioning support on "good behavior" can make such programs feasible in the first instance and more generously funded in the future.

## Arguments Against the Targeted CCTs

Not all are in favor of CCTs that have been described by some as "superfluous, pernicious, atrocious and abominable."[4] To start, a condition is a constraint on behavior. What good can come by adding a constraint to a poor households' optimization problem? Why not just make the transfer unconditional?

The concern here is that abiding by the conditions may prove too costly for those the program aims to help, that is, the poorest and neediest households. For example, requiring that a child be in school when child labor is felt to be of greatest need for the household (e.g., during harvest or when the household has experienced an income shock) may cause the household to drop out of the program. Similarly, the CCT may induce the household to engage in behavior that is inappropriate or irrelevant to the household's needs. For example, child time spent in a school of poor quality may not be as valuable as child time spent working on the farm. Neither of these arguments is particularly compelling, as the household cannot be made worse off by being offered an additional option—presumably if the transfer is not sufficient to compensate the household for the lost output of child labor, the household will opt for the more valuable labor and the society saves the value of the unused transfer.

The stronger objection is that the costs of these programs serve as a brake on economic growth that is ultimately the best solution for poverty.

This is particularly true for low income countries that also face severe fiscal and administrative constraints to implement subsectoral programs, CCTs included. If this view is accepted, governments should invest public capital in high payoff areas and avoid targeting that is harder to implement and in any case affects only a minority of citizens.

Finally, there is the concern that CCTs may not target populations appropriately. When households are subject to frequent income shocks, policies aimed at treating groups below income thresholds can exclude deserving households and treat households that are not really poor. In addition, there is the moral hazard problem that parents may try to hide income or may restrict their own labor supply in order to qualify for the transfer. There are solutions to these potential problems. There are significant advantages to using geographic targeting in populations where poverty is nearly universal such as poor rural villages, sidestepping costly identification of the "truly poor." In urban areas, targeting on parental education may be less expensive and will be a better proxy for permanent income than is current income. In addition, parents cannot hide schooling as easily as they can alter their income and so the moral hazard problem is less severe.

## Theory Conclusions

A simplified conceptualization of the debate is presented in table 12.1. Households are classified as rational or irrational depending on how heavily they discount the future. Irrational households discount the future more heavily than the rate at which they could borrow money. Households are further divided into myopic or non-myopic based on their knowledge base. Myopic households do not know the possible returns from schooling in the form of future earnings potential. Each household fits into one of four groups depending on whether they are rational or irrational and myopic or non-myopic. The theoretical case for some form of intervention is relatively clear for all except the group that is labeled rational and non-myopic.

**Table 12.1**  Decision matrix for government intervention in child labor

| | Household Decision Capacity | |
| --- | --- | --- |
| *Household Information* | Rational: *Households discount the future appropriately* | Irrational: *Households discount the future faster than "they should"* |
| *Myopic*: households are unaware of benefits | Intervene | Intervene |
| | (provide information) | (provide more information and encourage behavioral change) |
| *Non-myopic*: Households are fully informed | Don't intervene | Intervene |
| | (unless there are other market failures) | (encourage behavioral change) |

However, even that group could be targeted for the policy if the "second best" arguments apply or if market imperfections such as credit market failures mean that the household's optimum allocation of child time is different from the social optimum.

In practice, all four groups are present in any economy. Moreover, whether CCTs are a cost-effective policy may hinge on the relative size of these groups. To make the point with a simplistic example, if there is only one household that is cash-constrained from pursuing some desired behavior, the CCT is not worthwhile. But the answer would be different in practice, if half of the population is below the poverty line or out of school.

## Characteristics of Targeted CCTs

Thus far, CCTs have varied considerably in behavioral objective, design, targeting, coverage, and compliance criteria. Some representative program characteristics are listed below:

- Some programs are very large such as the 11 million households covered in Brazil's Bolsa Familia. Others are very limited programs such as the few thousand families targeted by the pilot in Nicaragua's Red de Protección Social (chapter 11).
- Some target very broadly, covering almost 40% of the population in Ecuador. In bigger countries (Brazil and Mexico) they only reach around 25% of the population and only about 5% in Chile.
- In terms of budget, they range from 0.6% of GDP for Ecuador's Bono de Dessarolo Humano; around 0.4% for Mexico's Oportunidades; and Brazil's Bolsa Familia; and less than 0.1 in Chile.
- The benefit level ranges from 20% of mean household consumption in Mexico to 4% of mean household consumption in Honduras.
- Some programs use geographic targeting (Brazil's PETI); others have income tests (Brazil's Bolsa Escola); and still others combine the two or supplement them with community assessments (Dominican Republic and Peru).
- Some programs vary the benefit level by household income. Others set the benefit level depending on household structure such as the number, age, or gender of children.
- Benefits can be paid monthly, bimonthly, quarterly, twice a year or even annually. The recipient may be the head of the household, parents, mothers or children. Funding is handled alternatively through government offices, banks, post offices, or schools.
- In some countries (Brazil, Mexico, Jamaica) the programs aim to offer comprehensive social assistance combining maternal and child health, education and nutrition. Others focus on a single narrowly defined outcome such as Peru's Juntos that aims at the nutrition of young children.
- Some programs have evolved from preexisting social assistance programs such as the ones in Brazil and Mexico while others have no precedents (e.g., Honduras and Jamaica).
- Some cover children from birth (or even prenatal) through to their teens. Others may focus only on preschool ages or primary school (Bolivia).

- Programs can be administered directly by existing government institutions or be free-standing agencies.
- Programs in some countries are yet to be evaluated though others (notably in Mexico) provided for evaluations right at the start of the programs.

All these differences, coupled with differences in country economic conditions and policy environment, make it difficult to reach clear conclusions about what works, where and when. For example, under certain conditions a program may perform better in terms of poverty reduction rather human development or child labor outcomes. The effect on schooling will naturally be different in a country where enrolment is 90% (as in Colombia or Mexico) than in another where it is considerably less. Similar considerations apply to comparisons between countries where the incidence of child labor varies significantly.

Thus the relative impact of CCTs on poverty reduction and human development, the two key objectives of such programs, can be different. This necessitates that programs take into account the initial status of human development and poverty levels and then are adjusted as both change over time.

## Evidence and Policy Lessons for Targeted CCTs

The essays in this volume suggest that CCTs can reduce poverty, increase education enrolment and reduce child labor. This is also the finding of a recent global review[5] that argues that transfers have generally been well targeted to poor households, have raised consumption levels, and have reduced poverty—in some countries, by a substantial amount. The review goes further to argue that offsetting adjustments that could have blunted the impact of transfers, such as reductions in the labor market participation of beneficiaries, appear to have been relatively modest. Overall, the CCTs have caused poor households to make *more use* of education and health services.

The evidence on *final outcomes* in health services and education is more mixed. Though CCTs have increased the likelihood that households take their children for preventive health checkups, this has not always led to better child nutritional status. With respect to education, though school enrollment rates have increased substantially among program beneficiaries, the evidence on improvements in learning outcomes is rather thin."[6]

Evidence on education outcomes comes from Mexico's PROGRESSA, using test scores in language and mathematics using in-classroom tests,[7] and from Ecuador's Bono de Desarrollo Humano using test performance among second-grade students.[8] Methodological considerations aside,[9] the results of these two evaluations suggest that neither program had a significant effect on test scores. This is disappointing as it suggests that, despite the transfer, the treated children learned no more than other children who go to school without the transfer. On the other hand, one can argue that the additional children brought into school by the programs appear to do as well as other children. If one accepts the former argument, then the case for CCTs is weakened in favor of more conventional forms of public spending on education. If one accepts the latter argument, the case of CCTs is strengthened as it shows that by relieving low income households from a likely credit constraint enables their children not only to enroll in schools but also become potentially equally productive as non-treated children who can be reasonably assumed to come from wealthier families.

Where the evidence is relatively less clear is in the case of child labor. CCTs can reduce the prevalence and amount of work among children through the conditional nature of the programs, creating greater awareness of the importance of schooling among parents, and through the additional income they provide that reduces the income pressure on households and makes them less dependent on the monetary or in kind income of their children. In addition to the evidence on Brazil's PETI (chapter 9), Mexico (chapter 10), and Nicaragua (chapter 11), the Familias en Acción program in Colombia also significantly reduced the incidence and hours of work among children.[10] Moreover, Ecuador's unconditional transfer program Bono de Desarrollo Humano also resulted in a significant negative impact on the prevalence of child work (Schady and Araujo, 2008). However, there is no evidence of reductions in child labor in the urban Brazil *Bolsa Escola* (chapter 8) or in Honduras (Glewwe et al., 2004). Note that none of the CCTs imposed conditions on child labor but only on school attendance, and so it was possible to meet program criteria and still send children to work.

The rather mixed picture in terms of the longer-run effects of CCTs on child labor is thus to some extent a matter of design: the programs do not explicitly condition benefits on the child not working. The apparent decrease in child labor that occurred in many of these programs must be due solely to the reduced household need to send their children to work as a result of improved household income.

The Brazilian PETI is the only program that directly attacked child labor (chapter 9), although the mechanism was by requiring that the child attend a longer school day. Constraining child time while raising household income can generate both income and substitution effects away from child labor. In contrast, the other Brazilian program, Bolsa Escola, required children be in school only four hours per day and it had no impact on child labor. In that instance, relying only on the income effect to eradicate child labor proved unsuccessful.

Another type of program that transfers resources to the household without altering the value of child time is workfare aimed at increasing the parents' time at work. Workfare programs require work in a publicly provided job or project as a condition for receiving cash (or, at times, food). These programs are like unconditional transfer programs in terms of their impacts on child time. Could workfare programs have an effect on child schooling and child labor while targeting the employment of adults?

Workfare programs do appear to be effective at reducing the incidence of poverty. The Employment Guarantee Scheme in Maharashtra (MEGS) in India provides jobs to unskilled manual workers in rural areas. The program does lower poverty substantially,[11] although it has been argued that an un-targeted transfer could have a greater impact on poverty at the same budget cost.[12] The Argentine workfare program (Trabajar) provides cash conditioned on part-time work on small-scale infrastructure projects in poor areas and has also been shown to raise incomes for the poor.[13] Do the children of these adults spend more time in school? To our knowledge, that question has not been explored.

The question has been explored in the United States following the welfare reforms. Programs that included earnings supplements to participants had been found to have positive effects on elementary school-aged children in terms of higher school achievement, improved social behavior and health (Morris et al., 2001). However, given these children's initial high levels of disadvantage, the documented improvements are considered to be rather modest. This implies that welfare-to-work programs do not eliminate the need for child-focused interventions aiming to raise school enrolment and achievement.

## Future Directions for Targeted CCTs

CCTs are no longer just an idea with a theoretical argument suggesting their potential usefulness. These policies have been subjected to an unprecedented level of sophisticated monitoring across many different countries and varied settings. Although they have not been universally successful, it seems that we have gone beyond the question of whether CCTs should be used but rather where, when and how they should be used. It goes without saying that monitoring should continue to improve our knowledge of the factors that lead to their relative success.

An issue that would require attention in the future is how these programs succeed as they are scaled up from pilot or limited introduction to regional or national adoption. This has already happened in Brazil and Mexico. In Brazil, Bolsa Escola began in Brasilia and the municipality of Campinas. It was gradually adopted by more municipalities. Today, these municipal programs have been eclipsed by the federal Bolsa Familia program which serves 11 million families or 46 million people. PROGRESA started with about 300,000 beneficiary households in 1997 and was confined to very poor rural areas. The successor program Oportunidades covers now 5 million households. The same is happening elsewhere. In Colombia, the program's initial goal of 400,000 beneficiaries has quickly expanded to reach 1.5 million.

One important issue to examine as these programs are expanded is whether the supply of public services changes in response to what are essentially demand-side interventions. It is meaningless to require that households increase their demand for schooling or health services if those services are in such short supply that the household cannot access the services. Undoubtedly, these programs are most effective when there is underutilization of preexisting schools or health clinics. However, it is important to see if these programs motivate households to act more proactively to press for increased public delivery of these services or whether they seek out private sector providers when the public sector is lacking.

A second issue is that as these programs expand, there are general equilibrium issues that may not crop up in isolated pilot settings. A large increase in schooling attainment may depress the wages of better-educated cohorts as they mature, although the supply of these educated workers may spur innovations from entrepreneurs interested in taking advantage of a newly available resource. Increased demand for teachers and clinicians may raise wages more generally, increasing the government's costs of providing those services to all income groups. The emergence of these large effects will no doubt be attracting the attention of doctoral students for the next decade.

A third issue is how these programs are integrated into the broader social programs in the country. Will CCTs coexist with other government programs aimed at providing other public services such as elder care or sanitation; improving economic infrastructure such as transportation or energy transmission; or social protection such as police or emergency assistance? Or will these programs displace some programs and constrain others. Their popularity among the electorate will make them very difficult to reel in once implemented on a broad scale.

A final issue frequently occurs as promising programs are expanded. Governments may face budgetary pressures as these programs grow, and ironically, those pressures are greatest when the programs are successful in altering the behavior that was originally targeted. In Nicaragua, chapter 11 shows that the program successfully increased time in school and reduced child labor. The effects there were as large or larger as any witnessed elsewhere in the world. One problem is that as more children persist in school relative to prior experience, the cost is actually larger than would be projected from past school utilization rates. Similarly, the Colombia voucher system was initially aimed at 90,000 secondary students.[14] The cost proved larger than projected because the voucher recipients were more successful in school and persisted to graduation at rates higher than anticipated. In both of these cases, the government abandoned these programs despite very promising cost-benefit evaluations, presumably in part because the current government only sees the costs while benefits will only be enjoyed by future administrations. Whether these programs survive the political climate is a question every bit as interesting and important as whether they meet economic tests of efficiency and equity.

## Notes

1. Though CCT programs are found in Africa (Kenya), MENA (Yemen), and five are found in Asia considered as a whole (Bangladesh, Pakistan, Cambodia, Indonesia

and Turkey), at least 15 Latin American and Caribbean countries have tried CCT programs in various forms: Argentina, Bolivia, Brazil, Chile, Colombia, Dominican Republic, Ecuador, El Salvador, Honduras, Jamaica, Mexico, Nicaragua, Panama, Paraguay, and Peru. See World Bank (2008).

2. Cardwell (2007). The scheme in New York would provide up to $5,000 a year through payments that range from $25 for exemplary attendance in elementary school to $300 for a high score on an important exam, or for going for a medical checkup or holding down a full-time job.
3. Nancy Birdsall quoted in an article by Dugger (2004).
4. Freeland (2007).
5. World Bank (2008).
6. Ibid., 1–2.
7. Behrman et al. (2005).
8. Ponce (2007).
9. See World Bank (2008).
10. Attanasio et al. (2006).
11. See Dreze and Sen (1991) and Ravallion and Datt (1995).
12. Murgai and Ravallion (2005).
13. See Jalan and Ravallion (2003).
14. See Angrist et al. (2002; 2006) for favorable evaluations of the Colombia voucher program known as PACES.

# Bibliography

Akabayashi, Hideo and George Psacharopoulos. 1999. The Trade-Off between Child Labor and Human Capital Formation: A Tanzanian Case Study. *Journal of Development Studies* 35 (June): 120–140.

Alderman, Harold, Peter F. Orazem, and Elizabeth M. Paterno. 2001. School Quality, School Cost and the Public/Private School Choices of Low-Income Households in Pakistan. *Journal of Human Resources* 36 (Spring): 304–326.

Angrist, Joshua D. and Alan B. Krueger. 1991. Does Compulsory School Attendance Affect Schooling and Earnings? *Quarterly Journal of Economics* 106 (November): 979–1014.

Angrist, Joshua D., Eric Bettinger, and Michael Kremer. 2006. Long-Term Educational Consequences of Secondary School Vouchers: Evidence from Administrative Records in Colombia. *American Economic Review* 96 (June): 847–862.

Angrist, Joshua D., Eric Bettinger, Erik Bloom, Elizabeth King, and Michael Kremer. 2002. Vouchers for Private Schooling in Colombia: Evidence from a Randomized Natural Experiment. *American Economic Review* 92 (December): 1535–1559.

Arcia, Gustavo. 1999. *Proyecto de Red de Protección Social: Focalización de la fase piloto.* Report to Inter-American Development Bank.

Arcia, Gustavo, Hector Mendoza, and Ronaldo Iachan. 1996. *Mapa de pobreza municipal de Nicaragua.* Report to Nicaraguan Social Investment Fund.

Ashagrie, Kebebew. 1993. Statistics on Child Labour: A Brief Report. *Bulletin of Labour Statistics.* International Labour Organization.

———. 1997. *Statistics on Working Children and Hazardous Child Labour in Brief.* International Labour Organization.

Attanasio, Orazio, Emma Fitzsimons, Ana Gómez, David López, Costas Meghir, and Alice Mesnard. 2006. "Child Education and Work Choices in the Presence of a Conditional Cash Transfer Programme in Rural Colombia." University College London, Institute for Fiscal Studies Working Paper, W06/01.

Baland, Jean Marie and James A. Robinson. 2000. Is Child Labor Inefficient? *Journal of Political Economy* 108 (August): 663–679.

Barros, Ricardo Paes de, Rosane Mendonca, and Tatiana Velazco. 1996. A Pobreza é a Principal Causa do Trabalho Infantil no Brasil Urbano? *Economia Brasileira em Perspectiva,* IPEA: 537–563.

Basu, Kaushik. 1999. Child Labor: Cause, Consequence, and Cure, with Remarks on International Labor Standards. *Journal of Economic Literature* 37 (September): 1083–1120.

Basu, Kaushik and Pham Hoang Van. 1998. The Economics of Child Labor. *American Economic Review* 88 (June): 412–427.

Basu, Kaushik and Zafiris Tzannatos. 2003. The Global Child Labor Problem: What Do We Know and What Can We Do? *The World Bank Economic Review* 17 (December): 147–173.

Becker, Gary. 1982. *Treatise on the Family*. Harvard University Press.

Beegle, Kathleen, Rajeev Dehejia, and Roberta Gatti. 2006. Child Labor and Agricultural Shocks. *Journal of Development Economics* 81 (October): 80–96.

———. 2007. The Consequences of Child Labor in Rural Tanzania: Evidence from Longitudinal Data. Mimeo.

Behrman, Jere and John C. Knowles. 1999. Household Income and Child Schooling in Vietnam. *The World Bank Economic Review* 13 (May): 211–256.

Behrman, Jere and Petra Todd. 1999. *Randomness in the Experimental Samples of PROGRESA (Education, Health, and Nutrition Program)*. International Food Policy Research Institute.

Behrman, Jere, Piyuli Sengupta, and Petra Todd. 2000. *Final Report: The Impact of PROGRESA on Achievement Test Scores in the First Year*. International Food Policy Research Institute.

———. 2005. Progressing through PROGRESA: An Impact Assessment of a School Subsidy Experiment in Rural Mexico. *Economic Development and Cultural Change* 54 (October): 237–275.

Bell, Clive and Hans Gersbach. 2001. "Child Labor and the Education of a Society." IZA Discussion Paper 338.

Ben-Porath, Yoram. 1967. The Production of Human Capital and the Life Cycle of Earnings. *Journal of Political Economy* 75 (August): 352–365.

Bourguignon. François and Pierre-Andre Chiapori. 1994. The Collective Approach to Household Behavior. *The Measurement of Household Welfare*. R. W. Blundell, I. Preston, and I. Walker, eds. Cambridge University Press.

Brière, B. and Laura B. Rawlings. 2006. Examining Conditional Cash Transfer Programs: A Role for Increased Social Inclusion? Social Safety Net Primer Series, No. 0603. World Bank.

Cain, Mead and A. B. M. Khorshed Alum Mozumder. 1980. Labor Markets Structure, Child Employment, and Reproductive Behavior in Rural South Asia. Working Paper 89. International Labor Office.

Caldés, Natàlia, David Coady, and John A. Maluccio. 2006. The Cost of Poverty Alleviation Transfer Programs: A Comparative Analysis of Three Programs in Latin America. *World Development* 34 (May): 818–837.

Camargo, José Márcio and Francisco Ferreira. 2001. "*O benefício social único.*" Texto para Discussão No. 443. Rio de Janeiro. PUC.

Card, David and Alan B. Krueger. 1992. Does School Quality Matter? Returns to Education and the Characteristics of Public Schools in the United States. *Journal of Political Economy* 100 (February): 1–40.

Cardoso, Eliana and André Portela F. de Souza. 2003. The Impact of Cash Transfers on Child Labor and School Attendance in Brazil. University of São Paulo (November). Mimeo.

Cardwell, Diane. 2007. "New York City to Reward Poor for Doing Right Thing." *New York Times*, March 30.

Carnoy, Martin. 2007. *Cuba's Academic Advantage: Why Students in Cuba Do Better in School*. Stanford University Press.

Cavalieri, Claudia. 2003. Children's Contribution and Family Income: An Evaluation for Brazilian Rural Areas. PUC. Mimeo.

Cigno, Alessandro, Furio C. Rosati, and Zafiris Tzannatos. 2002. "Handbook of Child Labor." Social Protection Discussion Paper No. 0206. World Bank.

Coady, David and Susan Parker. 2004. A Cost-Effectiveness Analysis of Demand and Supply Side Education Interventions: The Case of Progresa in Mexico. *Review of Development Economics* 8 (August): 440–451.

D'Amico, Ronald. 1984. Does Employment during High School Impair Academic Progress? *Sociology of Education* 3 (July): 152–164.

Deaton, Angus. 1997. *The Analysis of Household Surveys: A Microeconometric Approach to Development Policy.* Johns Hopkins University Press.

Dehejia, Rajeev and Sadek Wahba. 1999. Causal Effects in Non-experimental Studies: Re-evaluating the Evaluation of Training Programs. *Journal of the American Statistical Association* 94 (December): 1053–1062.

Demombynes, Gabriel. 2001. "Incentive Oriented Poverty Programs and Child Time Allocation: The Case of *PROGRESA.*" Paper presented at the Population Association Meetings. Mimeo.

Dreze, Jean and Amartya Sen. 1991. *Hunger and Public Action.* Oxford University Press.

Dugger, Celia W. 2004. "To Help Poor Be Pupils, Not Wage Earners, Brazil Pays Parents." *New York Times* (January 3).

Duryea, Suzanne. 1998. *Children's Advancement through School in Brazil: The Role of Transitory Shocks to Household Income.* Inter-American Development Bank. Mimeo.

Duryea, Suzanne and Andrew Morrison. 2004. "An Evaluation of the Programa de Atencion Immediata in Costa Rica." Research Department Working Paper W-505. Inter-American Development Bank.

Duryea, Suzanne and Mary Arends-Kuenning. 2003. School Attendance, Child Labor and Local Labor Market Fluctuations in Urban Brazil. *World Development* 31 (July): 1165–1178.

Duryea, Suzanne, David Lam, and Deborah Levison. 2007. Effects of Economic Shocks on Children's Employment and Schooling in Brazil. *Journal of Development Economics* 84: (September): 188–214.

Edmonds, Eric. 2002. Is Child Labor Inefficient? Evidence from Large Cash Transfers. Dartmouth. Mimeo.

———. 2008. Child Labor. *Handbook of Development Economics, Volume 4.* T. P. Schultz and J. Strauss, eds. Amsterdam: North-Holland, 3609–3709.

Edmonds, Eric V. and Nina Pavcnik. 2005a. Child Labor in the Global Economy. *Journal of Economic Perspectives* 18 (Winter): 199–220.

———. 2005b. The Effect of Trade Liberalization on Child Labor. *Journal of International Economics* 65 (March): 401–419.

Edmonds, Eric V., Kristin Mammen, and Douglas L. Miller. 2005. Rearranging the Family? Household Composition Responses to Large Pension Receipts. *Journal of Human Resources* 40 (Winter): 186–207.

Ehrenberg, Ronald G. and Daniel R. Sherman. 1987. Employment While in College, Academic Achievement, and Postcollege Outcomes. *Journal of Human Resources* 22 (Winter): 1–23.

Emerson, Patrick M. and André Portela F. de Souza. 2000. Is There a Child Labor Trap: Inter-Generational Persistence of Child Labor in Brazil. Mimeo.

———. 2002. "Bargaining over Sons and Daughters: Child Labor. School Attendance and Intra-Household Gender Bias in Brazil." Vanderbilt University. Department of Economics Working Paper Series 02-w13.

———. 2003. Is There a Child Labor Trap? Inter-generational Persistence of Child Labor in Brazil. *Economic Development and Cultural Change* 51 (January): 375–398.

———. 2008. "Is Child Labor Harmful? The Impact of Starting to Work as a Child on Adult Earnings." Oregon State University. Mimeo.

Fernandes, Reynaldo and André Portela F. de Souza. 2002. *A Redução do Trabalho Infantil e o Aumento da Frequência à Escola: Uma Análise de Decomposição para o Brasil dos Anos 90.* Universidade de São Paulo. Mimeo.

Ferreira, Francisco and Kathy Lindert. 2003. Principles for Integrating and Reforming Social Assistance in Brazil. World Bank. Mimeo.

Flug, Karnit, Antonio Spilimbergo, and Erik Wachtenheim. 1998. Investment in Education: Do Economic Volatility and Credit Constraints Matter? *Journal of Development Economics* 55 (April): 465–481.

Freeland, Nicholas. 2007. Superfluous, Pernicious, Atrocious and Abominable? The Case against Conditional Cash Transfers. *IDS Bulletin* 38 (May): 75–78.

Fundação Instituto Brasileiro de Geografia e Estatística. 1983. *Metodologia da Pesquisa Mensal de Emprego* 1980. Rio de Janeiro, Brazil.

———. 1991. *Para Compreender a PME*. Rio de Janeiro, Brazil.

Galbi, Douglas A. 1997. Child Labor and the Division of Labor in the Early English Cotton Mills. *Journal of Population Economics* 10 (October): 357–375.

Galor, Oded and Joseph Zeira. 1993. Income Distribution and Macroeconomics. *Review of Economic Studies* 60 (January): 35–52.

Glewwe, Paul. 2002. Schools and Skills in Developing Countries: Educational Policies and Socioeconomic Outcomes. *Journal of Economic Literature* 50 (June): 436–482.

Glewwe Paul, Pedro Olinto, Priscila Z. de Souza. 2004. Evaluating the Impact of Conditional Cash Transfers on Schooling in Honduras: An Experimental Approach. Mimeo.

Glomm, Gerhard. 1997. Parental Choice of Human Capital Investment. *Journal of Development Economics* 53 (June): 99–114.

Gomes-Neto, Joao Batista and Eric A. Hanushek. 1994. Causes and Consequences of Grade Repetition: Evidence from Brazil. *Economic Development and Cultural Change* 43 (October): 117–148.

Grootaert, Christiaan and Harry Anthony Patrinos, eds. 1999. *The Policy Analysis of Child Labor: A Comparative Study*. St. Martin's Press.

Grootaert, Christiaan and Ravi Kanbur. 1995. Child Labor: An Economic Perspective. *International Labour Review* 134 (March): 187–203.

Guarcello, Lorenzo, Fabrizia Mealli, and Camillo Rosatti. 2003. "Household Vulnerability and Child Labor: The Effect of Shocks, Credit Rationing and Insurance." Social Protection Discussion Paper No. 322. World Bank.

Gunnarsson, Victoria, Peter F. Orazem, and Mario Sanchez. 2006. Child Labor and School Achievement in Latin America. *World Bank Economic Review* 20 (January): 31–54.

Hanushek, Eric A. 1986. The Economics of Schooling: Production and Efficiency in Public Schools. *Journal of Economic Literature* 24 (September): 1141–1177.

———. 1995. Interpreting Recent Research on Schooling in Developing Countries. *The World Bank Research Observer* 10 (August): 227–246.

Heady, Christopher. 2003a. The Effect of Child Labor on Learning Achievement. *World Development* 31 (February): 385–398.

———. 2003b. What Is the Effect of Child Labour on Learning Achievement? Evidence from Ghana. *World Development* 31 (February): 385–398.

Heckman, James J. 1978. A Partial Survey of Recent Research on the Labor Supply of Women. *American Economic Review* 68 (May): 200–207.

———. 1979. Sample Selection Bias as a Specification Error. *Econometrica* 47 (January): 153–161.

Heckman, James J., Robert La Londe, and Jeffrey Smith. 1999. The Economics and Econometrics of Active Labor Market Programs. *Handbook of Labor Economics, Volume 3A*. O. Ashenfelter and D. Card, eds. North-Holland.

Horrell, Sara and Jane Humphries. 1995. The Exploitation of Little Children: Child Labor and the Family Economy in the Industrial Revolution. *Explorations in Economic History* 32 (October): 485–516.

Howard, Ian. 1998. Does Part-Time Employment Affect A-level Grades Achieved? *PSSI Forum* 26 (October): 10–11.

Instituto Brasileiro de Geografia e Estatística (IBGE). 1982. *Manual do Entrevistador. Pesquisa Mensal de Emprego.* Departamento de Estatísticas de População e Sociais.

International Food Policy Research Institute (IFPRI). 2000. *Second Report: Implementation Proposal for the PRAF/IDB Project—Phase II.*

International Labour Organization, Bureau of Statistics. 2004. *Economically Active Populations: Estimates and Projections, 1950–2010.* International Labour Organization.

Jacoby, Hanan G. and Emmanuel Skoufias. 1997. Risk, Financial Markets, and Human Capital in a Developing Country. *Review of Economic Studies* 64 (July): 311–335.

———. 1998. Testing Theories of Consumption Behavior Using Information on Aggregate Shocks: Income Seasonality and Rainfall in Rural India. *American Journal of Agricultural Economics* 80 (February): 1–14.

Jalan, Jyotsna and Martin Ravallion. 2003. Estimating the Benefit Incidence of an Antipoverty Program by Propensity-Score Matching. *Journal of Business and Economic Statistics* 21 (January): 19–31.

Jensen, Peter and Helena Skyt Neilsen. 1997. Child Labour or School Attendance? Evidence from Zambia. *Journal of Population Economics* 10 (4) (October): 407–424.

Kassouf, Ana Lúcia. 2001. *Lisboa. Marcos and Naércio Aquino Menezes-Filho. Microeconomia e Sociedade no Brasil.* Contracapa.

Kiefer, Nicholas. 1988. Economic Duration Data and Hazard Functions. *Journal of Economic Literature* 26 (June): 646–679.

Killingsworth, Mark R. 1983. *Labor Supply.* Cambridge University Press.

Kim, Jooseop, Harold Alderman, and Peter F. Orazem. 1999. Can Private School Subsidies Increase Enrollment for the Poor? The Quetta Urban Fellowship Experiment. *The World Bank Economic Review* 13 (September): 443–465.

King, Elizabeth M., Berk Ozler, and Laura B. Rawlings. 1999a. Nicaragua's School Autonomy Reform: Fact or Fiction? World Bank. Mimeo.

King, Elizabeth M., Peter F. Orazem, and Elizabeth M. Paterno. 1999b. "Promotion with and without Learning: Effects on Student Dropout." Working Paper Series on Impact Evaluation of Educational Reforms, Paper No. 18. World Bank.

Kremer, Michael R. 1995. Research on Schooling: What We Know and What We Don't: A Comment on Hanushek. *The World Bank Research Observer* 10 (August): 247–254.

Lam, David and Robert F. Schoeni. 1993. Effects of Family Background on Earnings and Returns to Schooling: Evidence from Brazil. *Journal of Political Economy* 101 (August): 710–740.

Levinas, Lena and M. Bittar. 1999. Special Tabulations of the Minimum Income Programs. IPEA. Mimeo.

Levinas, Lena and Maria Lígia Barbosa. 2001. Assessing Local Minimum Income Programs in Brazil. International Labour Organization.

Levison, Deborah. 1991. Children's Labor Force Activity and Schooling in Brazil. University of Michigan. Ph.D. Dissertation.

Levison, Deborah, Jasper Hoek, David Lam, and Suzanne Duryea. 2007. Intermittent Child Employment and Its Implications for Estimates of Child Labor. *International Labour Review* 146 (September–December): 217–251.

Levy, Victor. 1985. Cropping Pattern, Mechanization, Child Labor, and Fertility Behavior in a Farming Economy: Rural Egypt. *Economic Development and Cultural Change* 33 (July): 777–791.

Lillydahl, Jane H. 1990. Academic Achievement and Part-time Employment of High School Students. *Journal of Economic Education* 21 (Summer): 307–316.

Lindert, Kathy, Anja Linder, Jason Hobbs, and Benedicte de la Briere. 2007. "The Nuts and Bolts of Brazil's Bolsa Familia Program: Implementing Conditional Cash

Transfers in a Decentralized Context." Social Protection Discussion Paper 0709. World Bank.

Lleras-Muney, Adriana. 2002. Were Compulsory Attendance and Child Labor Laws Effective? An Analysis from 1915 to 1939. *Journal of Law and Economics* 45 (October): 401–435

Lopez-Calva, Luis-Felipe. 2002. Social Norms, Coordination, and Policy Issues in the Fight against Child Labor. *International Labor Standards: History, Theory, and Policy Options.* K. Basu, H. Horn, L. Román, and J. Shapiro, eds. Blackwell.

Lopez-Calva, Luis-Felipe and Koji Miyamoto. 2004. Filial Obligations, Technology, and Child Labor. *Review of Development Economics* 8 (August): 489–504.

Maluccio, John A. 2008. Household Targeting in Practice: The Nicaraguan *Red de Protección Social. Journal of International Development.* Forthcoming.

Maluccio, John A. and Rafael Flores. 2005. "Impact Evaluation of a Conditional Cash Transfer Program: The Nicaraguan *Red de Protección Social.*" IFPRI Research Report No. 141. International Food Policy Research Institute.

Mello e Souza, Alberto de and Nelson do Valle Silva. 1996. Income and Educational Inequality and Children's Schooling Attainment. *Opportunity Foregone: Education in Brazil.* Nancy Birdsall and Richard Sabot, eds. Inter-American Development Bank.

Mincer, Jacob. 1974. *Schooling, Experience and Earnings.* National Bureau of Economic Research.

Ministry of Education. 2002. *Bolsa Escola Federal. Relatório de Atividades 2002.* Ministério da Educação.

Moehling, Carolyn M. 1999. State Child Labor Laws and the Decline of Child Labor. *Explorations in Economic History* 36 (January): 72–106.

Morris, Pamela A., Aletha Huston, Greg Duncan, Danielle Crosby, and Johannes Bos. 2001. *How Welfare and Work Policies Affect Children: A Synthesis of Research.* Manpower Demonstration Research Corporation.

Murgai, Rinku and Martin Ravallion. 2005. "Is a Guaranteed Living Wage a Good Anti-poverty Policy?" Policy Working Paper No. 3640. World Bank.

Neilsen, Helena S. 1998. "Child Labor and School Attendance: Two Joint Decisions." Centre for Labour Market and Social Research. University of Aarhus and the Aarhus School of Business, Working Paper No. 98–15.

Orazem, Peter F. and Elizabeth M. King. 2008. Schooling in Developing Countries: The Roles of Supply, Demand and Government Policy. *Handbook of Development Economics, Volume 4.* T. P. Schultz and John Strauss, eds. North-Holland.

Parker, Susan W. and Emmanuel Skoufias. 2000. *The Impact of PROGRESA on Work, Leisure, and Time Allocation.* International Food Policy Research Institute.

———. 2006. Labor Market Shocks and Their Impacts on Work and Schooling: Evidence from Urban Mexico. *Journal of Population Economics* 19 (January): 1–19.

Parsons, Donald O. and Claudia Goldin. 1989. Parental Altruism and Self-Interest: Child Labor Among Late Nineteenth-Century American Families. *Economic Inquiry* 28 (October): 637–659.

Patrinos, Harry A. and George Psacharopoulos. 1997. Family Size, Schooling and Child Labor in Peru—An Empirical Analysis. *Journal of Population Economics* 10 (October): 387–405.

Pianto, Donald and Sergei Soares. 2003. Use of Survey Design for the Evaluation of Social Programs: The PNAD and the Program for the Eradication of Child Labor in Brazil. University of Illinois. Mimeo.

Ponce, Juan. 2006. The Impact of (Unconditional) Cash Transfer Programs on Students' Cognitive Achievements: The Case of the *Bono de Desarrollo Humano* of Ecudaor. Institute of Social Statistics, The Hague, Ph.D. Dissertation.

Post, David and Suet-ling Pong. 2000. Employment during Middle School: The Effects on Academic Achievement in the U.S. and Abroad. *Educational Evaluation and Policy Analysis* 22 (Fall): 273–298.

Psacharopoulos, George. 1985. Returns to Education: A Further International Update and Implications. *Journal of Human Resources* 20 (Fall): 583–597.

———. 1997. Child Labor versus Educational Attainment: Some Evidence from Latin America. *Journal of Population Economics* 10 (October): 377–386.

Ranjan, Priya. 2001. Credit Constraints and the Phenomenon of Child Labor. *Journal of Development Economics* 64 (February): 81–102.

Ravallion. Martin. 2001. The Mystery of Vanishing Benefits: An Introduction to Impact Evaluation. *World Bank Economic Review* 15 (February): 115–140.

———. 2008. Evaluating Anti-poverty Programs. *Handbook of Development Economics, Volume 4.* T. P. Schultz and J. Strauss, eds. North-Holland.

Ravallion, Martin and Gaurav Datt. 1995. Is Targeting through a Work Requirement Efficient? *Public Spending and the Poor: Theory and Evidence.* Dominique van de Walle and Kimberly Nead, eds. Johns Hopkins University Press.

Ravallion, Martin and Quentin Wodon. 2000. Does Child Labor Displace Schooling? Evidence on Behavioral Responses to an Enrollment Subsidy. *Economic Journal* 110 (March): C158–175.

Rawlings, Laura B. and Gloria Rubio. 2003. Evaluating the Impact of Conditional Cash Transfer Programs: Lessons from Latin America. *Policy Research Working Paper No. 3119.* World Bank.

Ray, Ranjan. 2000a. Analysis of Child Labour in Peru and Pakistan: A Comparative Study. *Journal of Population Economics* 13 (March): 3–19.

———. 2000b. Child Labor, Child Schooling and Their Interaction with Adult Labour: The Empirical Evidence and Some Analytical Implications. *World Bank Economic Review* 14 (May): 347–367.

Rosati, Furio Camillo and Mariacristina Rossi. 2003. Children's Working Hours and School Enrollment: Evidence From Pakistan and Nicaragua. *The World Bank Economic Review* 17 (December): 283–295.

Rosen, Sherwin. 1977. Human Capital: A Survey of Empirical Research. *Research in Labor Economics Volume 1.* R. Ehrenberg, ed. Stamford, CT: JAI Press.

Rosenbaum, Paul and Donald Rubin. 1983. The Central Role of the Propensity Score in Observational Studies for Causal Effects. *Biometrika* 70 (April): 41–55.

Rosenzweig, Mark R. and Kenneth I. Wolpin. 1994. Are There Increasing Returns to the Intergenerational Production of Human Capital? Maternal Schooling and Child Intellectual Achievement. *Journal of Human Resources* 29 (Spring): 670–693.

Rosenzweig, Mark R. and Robert Evenson. 1977. Fertility, Schooling and the Economic Contribution of Children in Rural India: An Econometric Analysis. *Econometrica* 45 (July): 1065–1079.

Schady, Norbert R. and Maria Caridad Araujo. 2008. Cash Transfers, Conditions, and School Enrollment in Ecuador. *Economía* 8 (Spring): 43–70.

Schultz, T. Paul. 2004. School Subsidies for the Poor: Evaluating the Mexican PROGRESA Poverty Program. *Journal of Development Economics* 74 (June):199–250.

Sedlacek, Guilherme, Ricardo Paes de Barros, and Simone Varandas. 1990. Segmentação e Mobilidade no Mercado de Trabalho: Carteira de Trabalho em São Paulo. *Pesquisa e Planejamento Econômico.* 20 (1): 87–104.

Singh, Kusum. 1998. Part-Time Employment in High School and Its Effect on Academic Achievement. *Journal of Educational Research* 91 (January/February): 131–139.

Skoufias, Emmanuel. 1994. Using Shadow Wages to Estimate Labor Supply of Agricultural Households. *American Journal of Agricultural Economics* 76 (May): 215–227.

Skoufias, Emmanuel. 2005. "*PROGRESA* and Its Impacts on the Human Capital and Welfare of Households in Rural Mexico: A Synthesis of the Results of an Evaluation by IFPRI." IFPRI Research Report No. 139. International Food Policy Research Institute.

Skoufias, Emmanuel, Benjamin Davis, and Sergio de la Vega. 2001. Targeting the Poor in Mexico: Evaluation of the Selection of Beneficiary Households into *PROGRESA*. *World Development* 29 (October): 1769–1784.

Skoufias, Emmanuel and Susan W. Parker. 2001. "Conditional Cash Transfers and Their Impact on Child Work and School Enrollment: Evidence from the PROGRESA Program in Mexico." *Economía* 2 (1) (Fall): 45–96.

StataCorp. 2001. *Stata Statistical Software: Release 7.0.* Stata Corporation.

Strauss, John and Duncan Thomas. 1995. Empirical Modeling of Human Resources. *The Handbook of Development Economics, Volume 3.* J. Behrman and T. N. Srinivasan, eds. North-Holland.

Tabatabai, Hamid. 2007. *Eliminating Child Labour: The Promise of Conditional Cash Transfers.* International Programme for the Elimination of Child Labour, International Labour Office.

Tzannatos, Zafiris. 2003. Child Labor and School Enrollment in Thailand in the 1990s. *Economics of Education Review* 22 (October): 522–536.

UNESCO Institute for Statistics. 2002. *Education Statistics 2001—Regional Report on Latin America.* Welch, Finis. 1966. Measurement of the Quality of Schooling. *The American Economic Review* 56 (March): 379–392.

World Bank. 1995. *Republic of Nicaragua Poverty Assessment.* Report No. 14038-NI.

———. 2001a. *Engendering Development: Through Gender Equality in Rights, Resources, and Voice.* Oxford University Press.

———. 2001b. *Nicaragua Poverty Assessment: Challenges and Opportunities for Poverty Reduction.* Report No. 20488-NI.

———. 2002. *Brazil: An Assessment of the Bolsa Escola Programs.* Report No. 20208-BR.

———. 2008. *Conditional Cash Transfers for Attacking Present and Future Poverty.* World Bank Policy Research Report.

Zelizer, V. A. 1985. *Pricing the Priceless Child: The Changing Social Value of Children.* Basic Books.

# Contributors

**Eliana Cardoso,** a Ph.D. in Economics from MIT, is Professor of Economics at the Fundação Getúlio Vargas in São Paulo. A former William Clayton Professor at the Fletcher School (Tufts University), her most recent book is *Fábulas Econômicas* published by Prentice Hall in 2006. She writes opinion pieces for *Valor Econômico* and *O Estado de São Paulo.*

**Suzanne Duryea** is a Senior Economist at the Inter-American Development Bank in the Department of Social Sectors. She holds a Ph.D. in Economics from the University of Michigan where she is a Research Affiliate at the Population Studies Center.

**Patrick M. Emerson** is Associate Professor of Economics at Oregon State University and Research Fellow at IZA—the Institute for the Study of Labor. Professor Emerson received his Ph.D. in Economics at Cornell University in 2000. He also received a master of arts degree in Public Policy and Administration from the Center for Development at the University of Wisconsin—Madison in 1994.

**Victoria Gunnarsson** is an Economist at the World Bank Independent Evaluation Group involved mainly in impact evaluation work in the human development and capacity building fields. She has previous experience, from the Fiscal Affairs Department of the International Monetary Fund, with public expenditure policy and measurement of the efficiency of health and education expenditure in various country contexts. Her research has focused on the impact of child labor on educational attainment and the effect of school autonomy on schooling outcomes.

**Emily Gustafsson-Wright** has a Ph.D. in Economics from the University of Amsterdam—the Tinbergen Institute. Her doctoral work analyzed the impacts of social capital on vulnerability to poverty and primary education and malnutrition. She currently works for the Amsterdam Institute for International Economics (AIID) and is visiting at Brookings Institution in Washington, DC. Her recent research focuses on health risk and subsidized low-cost private health insurance programs in Africa. Previously she worked as a consultant for the World Bank as well as for Innocenti Research Center—UNICEF, focusing on education and child labor, conditional cash transfer programs, and risk and vulnerability in Latin America.

**Jasper Hoek** completed his Ph.D. in Economics at the University of Michigan in Ann Arbor in 2004. He is currently in the International Affairs division of the U.S. Treasury Department.

**Nadeem Ilahi** is a Senior Economist at the IMF. Work on his chapters in this volume was completed while he was in the Latin America and Caribbean Department of the World Bank. He has also been a visiting faculty member at the Economics Department, McGill University, Canada.

**David Lam** is Professor of Economics at the University of Michigan. He has been a Visiting Researcher at the Instituto de Pesquisa Econômica Aplicada (IPEA) in Rio de Janeiro, Brazil, and in the School of Economics at the University of Cape Town, South Africa.

**Deborah Levison,** an Economist and Demographer, is a professor at the Hubert H. Humphrey Institute of Public Affairs at the University of Minnesota. She has been conducting research on children's work and education in poor countries since the mid-1980s.

**John A. Maluccio** is currently Assistant Professor in the Economics Department at Middlebury College. Prior to arriving at Middlebury, he was a Research Fellow at the International Food Policy Research Institute (IFPRI) in Washington, DC.

**Marcelo Côrtes Neri** is the Chief Economist of the Centre of Social Policies (CPS/IBRE/FGV); and, also Professor at the Post-Graduate School of Economics at Fundação Getulio Vargas. Neri holds a Ph.D. in Economics from Princeton University. His main areas of research are public policy evaluation and microeconometrics. He has published the following books: *Microcrédito, O Mistério Nordestino e o Grameen Brasileiro, Cobertura Previdenciária: Diagnóstico e Propostas, Retratos da Deficiência no Brasil, Ensaios Sociais*, and *Inflação e Consumo.*

**Peter F. Orazem** is University Professor of Economics at Iowa State University where he has been since 1982. He is co-author of chapters in the *Handbook of Development Economics* and the *Handbook of Agricultural Economics.* He served as a member of the core team for the World Bank's 2007 *World Development Report* and he co-authored the challenge paper on education for the 2008 Copenhagen Consensus.

**Susan W. Parker** is Associate Professor at CIDE in Mexico City and partner of Spectron Desarrollo, a new research organization and consulting firm dedicated to social issues and evaluation in Mexico City. She earned her Ph.D. in Economics from Yale University in 1993 and her B.A. in Economics and Mathematics from Franklin and Marshall College in 1987, and has been living and working in Mexico City since 1993. Her research interests include program evaluation, conditional cash transfer programs, and health and education policy.

**Mario A. Sánchez** is currently working at the Inter-American Development Bank as a Social Development Specialist in the Social Protection and Health Division. At the Inter-American Development Bank, he has worked in the areas of education, social protection, and labor markets. He holds a Ph.D. in Economics from the University of Chicago.

**Masaru Sasaki** is an Associate Professor at the Institute of Social and Economic Research, Osaka University, Japan. He obtained a Ph.D. in Economics from Georgetown University. Previously, he served at the World Bank, the Asian Development Bank, and Kansai University.

**Guilherme Sedlacek** is a Lead Human Development Specialist at the Office of Evaluation and Oversight of the Inter-American Development Bank. He worked previously as a Senior Economist at the World Bank, and at the Brazilian Planning Ministry—IPEA. He taught at the Graduate School of Business Administration of the Carnegie-Mellon University and at the Pontific Catholic University of Rio de Janeiro.

**Emmanuel Skoufias** is a Lead Economist at the Poverty Reduction Group of the World Bank. His professional experience includes senior appointments at the Poverty and Gender Group in the Latin American and Caribbean Region of the World Bank, the Research Department of the Inter-American Development Bank, and the IFPRI where he led a project evaluating the Education, Health, and Nutrition Program (PROGRESA) of the Government of Mexico. Emmanuel also held academic positions as Associate Professor at the Economics Institute in Boulder, Colorado, and as an Assistant Professor of Economics at the Pennsylvania State University.

**André Portela F. de Souza** is at the São Paulo School of Economics, Getúlio Vargas Foundation in Brazil. He is a Researcher at the National Research Council of the Ministry of Science and Technology of Brazil (CNPq/MCT) and is currently the Executive Secretary of the Brazilian Econometric Society. He has held Visiting Professor positions at Cornell University and Vanderbilt University. His research focuses on human capital formation, education, child labor, poverty, inequality, and social security in Brazil. He holds a Ph.D. in Economics from Cornell University.

**Zafiris Tzannatos** is Advisor at the World Bank Institute. He was previously Manager for Social Protection for the Middle East and North Africa (MENA) Region and also Leader of the Child Labor Program at the World Bank. He has held a number of senior academic and honorary appointments in Britain and is a former Chair and Professor of the Economics Department at the American University of Beirut. He has advised many governments in the OECD and developing countries as well as in other international organizations.

**Yoon-Tien Yap** received an M.S. degree in Economics from Iowa State University in 2000. His work on this book was conducted while serving as a Research Assistant at the World Bank. He currently works as a Statistician at IXI Corp., a database marketing firm in northern Virginia.